A DIFFERENT ROAD

BOB LATCHFORD

A DIFFERENT ROAD

BOB LATCHFORD
IN COLLABORATION WITH JAMES CORBETT

To Sam

Best wishes

Bob Latchford

deCoubertin
B O O K S

First published as a hardback by deCoubertin Books Ltd in 2015.

deCoubertin Books, Basecamp, Studio N, Baltic Creative Campus, Liverpool, L1 OAH

www.decoubertin.co.uk
First Hardback Edition.

ISBN: 978-1-909245-29-7
Special Edition ISBN: 978-1-909245-33-4

A CIP catalogue record for this book is available from the British Library.
Cover design by Leslie Priestley.
Special Edition Design by Allen Mohr/ Steve Welsh.
Typeset design by Allen Mohr.
Layout by Sabahat Muhammad.

Printed and bound by Standart.

FOR MY FAMILY

As you go through life it's a long, long road
There'll be joys and sorrows too
As we journey on we will sing this song
For the boys in royal blue.
We're often partisan – la la la
We will journey on – la la la
Keep right on to the end of the road
Keep right on to the end
Though the way be long let your heart beat strong
Keep right on to the end
Though you're tired and weary
Still journey on 'til you come to your happy abode
With all our love we'll be dreaming of
We'll be there. Where? At the end of the road.

– *Keep Right On*, Birmingham City club anthem.

CONTENTS

FOREWORD

AS A FORMER FOOTBALLER AND CAPTAIN OF EVERTON, THE TWO questions I get asked the most are: 'Don't you wish you played now, with all the money in the game?' and then, 'Who was your hero growing up on Merseyside?'

The answer to the first question is a simple 'no', as money does not define happiness and we had freedoms back then that players certainly don't have now. Some of my best times were in the pub after Everton had won, celebrating with my teammates as well as supporters.

The answer to the second question is also very simple: 'Can your hero be a player you actually played with?'

As a kid, I loved Jimmy Gabriel, a powerful right-half who would chuck himself into a brick wall in the name of Everton. But as I became a part of the team a new figure emerged: someone who became a close friend – someone who continues to inspire me.

I often wonder how much Bob Latchford would be worth if he was playing today. The object of football is to score goals and he did that on a consistent basis. Year after year, he was Everton's most reliable player.

My enduring image of Bob on the football field is him arriving at the front post and throwing his entire weight behind an attempt to reach a Dave Thomas cross. Instantly, the ball would be in the back of the net and the Gwladys Street would be celebrating.

Bob scored thirty goals during the 1977/78 season and many of them seemed to arrive via the same route. For achieving his remarkable feat, Bob was rewarded with £10,000. Most people probably would have spent that on a luxury holiday but not Bob. Half of the prize money went to the Football League Jubilee Provident Fund and the PFA, and most of the other half was divided equally between his teammates.

The gesture summed Bob up. He was the star of our team but you would never find a more sincere gentleman. Brian Labone was the last of the Corinthians but Bob was our reference point. When all seemed lost, Bob would step forward and dig us out of a hole. He was generous, kind and incredibly considerate.

When he arrived at Everton from Birmingham City, you could see straight away that he had strength and ability. It gives me goose pimples thinking of some of his greatest moments in the years that followed: the equaliser against Aston Villa at Hillsborough in the League Cup final replay; the goal against West Ham at Elland Road in the FA Cup semi-final replay. He helped create an electric atmosphere on those nights. Evertonians were singing 'Bob Latchford can walk on water'. He was our talisman. Yet Bob was so unassuming, which is strange for a hero of the terraces.

Bob was the type of person you gravitated towards. Yet he was private. Travelling home from away games, you'd find him reading a book written by an author you'd never heard of.

That was the man: gentle, quiet and absolutely brilliant.

Bob Latchford was my hero.

Mick Lyons, August 2015

INTRODUCTION

ANDALUCIA

'Life is a series of natural and spontaneous changes. Don't resist them. That only creates sorrow. Let reality be reality. Let things flow naturally forward in whatever way they like.'

Lao Tzu

THIS ROAD BEGINS IN AN UNEXPECTED OUTPOST.

In the modern grandeur of the Hotel Melia Atlantico on Andalucia's Costa de la Luz, I pause and unwind at the end of another football season.

It is May 2001 and I am fifty years old. For probably the only time in my life I've come away on holiday on my own. It's a break after a busy year that I've needed and looked forward to. It's a holiday that will change everything.

When you have time to yourself you have that rare window to reflect on your life that has passed and your life still to come.

Over the course of a decade, from the early 1970s until the early 1980s, no player scored more First Division goals than I did. I lived the dream of a thousand schoolboys. I played and starred for the club I'd supported as a boy – Birmingham City – lining up alongside my own brother, David, on match days. I scored goals, lots of them, and helped elevate Birmingham to their rightful status in the First Division. In Trevor Francis I played alongside the most thrilling prodigy English football had seen in a generation. I was a hero, a local boy made good.

Then I became the most expensive player in the country. My name was in every newspaper, on TV and radio. I was a household name. Joining Everton meant I played for one of the biggest and most prestigious names in English football. I scored even more goals, including a famous thirty-goal haul for which most Evertonians remember me. I played in Europe and represented my country, scoring in front of nearly 100,000 of my countrymen. Although it sat uncomfortably with me, to some I was an idol. People even named their children after me.

I remained playing at the highest level until my mid-thirties, unexpectedly topping the table with Swansea City, playing overseas, and encountering a couple of occasionally difficult nomadic years, before finding another trophy at the very end of my playing career. This had occurred over the course of twenty years, a long innings as a professional footballer by most standards.

I had achieved so much, encountered so many emotions and experiences, but always felt I could have managed more. With Everton I was incredibly unlucky not to win the League Championship on at least one occasion, and only bad luck stood between the club and domestic cup success while I was there. I always felt that with one trophy in our cabinet it would have acted as a catalyst for much more success, in the way that Everton's 1984 FA Cup win was a prelude to the club's dominance of English football. At both Birmingham and Swansea, had some things happened differently we too might have enjoyed major trophies. And yet, at the end of my career, I had just three medals to my name, all from winning the Welsh Cup.

My fortunes could have been contrasting had my career choices been different. I might have joined a Liverpool team on the cusp of European dominance, but I'd already agreed to go to Everton and wouldn't go back on my word. I could have signed for Aston Villa shortly before they won back-to-back league and European titles, but I could never have played for Birmingham's hated rivals. I might even have won the League Cup had I started out – as I could have done – a Wolves player, but I never fancied playing in a gold shirt. I always followed my heart and once my mind was set on something I never regretted it for a moment. As it was, I never won a trophy with an English club.

I was back in the game in 2001, back where I'd started, at St Andrew's, working for Birmingham City's academy. I felt at home, serving the club I'd grown up supporting, imparting to young players the knowledge once taught me by Stan

Cullis and Freddie Goodwin, two very different and distinguished Birmingham City managers.

I had a life away from football too. The game had given me many friends, but my truest ones came from other parts of my life. I was the proud father of two children who had grown up to be well-balanced adults, successful in their careers. And yet, for all this contentment, there was a huge void in my life.

*

SIXTEEN MONTHS EARLIER MY WORLD HAD FALLEN IN. AFTER A four-year fight with cancer, I lost Pat, my wife and soulmate of three decades. I was bereft.

We'd gotten together when we were young and just knew that we were meant to be. By the time we were twenty our children, Isobel and Richard, had come along and we had many, many happy years. Football can be a selfish and unsociable profession, but Pat was like my backbone, looking after me and the children, taking on many of the parental responsibilities when I needed to train or rest or travel, supporting me, being my friend and companion. For all the transitoriness of football we tried to keep a regular place to live for the children and to avoid, as far as possible, the moves that can be so unsettling. In our partnership Pat was an unsung hero. I think it's fair to say that without her, I couldn't have achieved half of the things that I did.

Shortly before I returned to Birmingham City in 1996 she was diagnosed with a rare and aggressive form of cancer of the uterus. Cancer had always been a looming presence over her family and mine, taking both of our mothers. Their deaths were devastating, but when it's somebody you've been with for thirty years or more, it's almost incomprehensibly difficult knowing that that person only has a certain time to live.

From the start, we knew she wasn't going to live long. Some eighteen months after the initial diagnosis the oncologist told us at a check-up that he didn't expect her to live for more than six months. She defied that prognosis by more than two years. In a way we were lucky that we had as long together as we did.

There were tears and talking, but she was always a very positive, strong-willed person, and she wasn't going to give up. And she didn't. Although it might sound like a strange thing to say about being with a dying person, I have to say it's probably four of the best years we ever spent together. It was as if I rediscovered her again.

No man understands women. Not totally. I'd been with Pat for thirty-odd years when she was diagnosed with cancer and I didn't totally understand her. But over those four years, it was like a little window opened up into her world and I started to understand her a little bit more, a little bit better, than the previous decades. It was a very calm period; a calm four years. Even though we knew at some point she was going to die, we were so glad of every single day that we were together. It was another day to live, and another day where I understood a little bit more. I'm not saying I totally understood her at the end of the four years, but she let me into her world.

Pat lost all her hair and had to undergo chemotherapy, but she didn't really suffer in the way that my mother did all those years ago. We travelled, we played golf, we spent a lot of time together and with the children. She had excellent care. I'd lost my mother to cancer in 1970 and saw how she went through a kind of living hell, just wasting away, but Pat, mercifully, was spared that.

She started to fade towards the end of 1999. That Christmas we spent together at home in Redditch in Worcestershire as a family and she walked down the stairs for Christmas lunch, but she couldn't get back up, I had to carry her back to bed. And from that day, Christmas Day, she never got out of bed again. Slowly all her faculties started to go, and it got to a point where she was more or less in a coma.

I lost her at the end of February 2000, early in the morning.

At the time I'm not sure if the enormity of her passing quite sank in. There's so much to do when you have a loved one who's died. The process that you have to go through, arranging the funeral, organising probate and getting their affairs organised, is enormously lengthy. It really shields you from what's happened. I had Richard and Izzy around too; that helped. For two or three weeks after Pat had gone it never hit me. It was only after the funeral, when everybody had gone and I was alone in the house, that the feeling of absolute and utter desolation struck.

*

A DIFFERENT ROAD

BIRMINGHAM CITY COULDN'T HAVE BEEN MORE SUPPORTIVE following Pat's death. Trevor Francis was in charge of the footballing side of things and Karren Brady was chief executive, and they gave me as much time as I needed plus, when I was ready to return to work, a purpose too.

I was working with Brian Eastick at Birmingham's academy. We'd started it from scratch and at the start there was really no infrastructure there. However, we had some good players like Darren Carter and Andy Johnson, who would one day follow in my footsteps in the forward line of Birmingham, Everton and England. I'd passed my UEFA B Coaching Licence and was preparing for my A Licence. Work was good, work was busy.

The 2000/01 season had been an eventful one for Birmingham. The first team had reached the First Division playoffs, but fell in the semi-final, and also the final of the League Cup, which we lost on penalties to Liverpool. We got to the end of the season and Brian said, 'You'd better have a holiday in May.' We had an under-18 tournament in northern France in June and May was the only time we had free.

I was at a bit of a loose end. I intended going on my own to play a bit of golf. I was going to go back to Majorca where I had my first holiday with Pat. Then I thought, 'No, I'll go to where we had our last holiday, Andalucia.' I booked it through a golfing company and was going to go back to the same hotel where we'd stayed. The travel agent started talking about a brand-new hotel just down the coast from there. She told me all about it and I don't know why, because I was all prepared to go back to the hotel I was at with Pat, which was much nearer the golf course, but at the last minute I went with this new hotel. I'm a great believer in fate, but little could I have imagined then that this simple, very basic decision would change my life forever.

I was a week into a ten-day holiday when I met her. She had arrived a few days after me, travelling with a friend from her home in Austria. Her name was Andrea.

It was purely chance that we met. I'd had dinner alone and was sat in the bar afterwards, having a drink while the hotel entertainment was unleashed on the unsuspecting guests. The band were awful and I was getting ready to leave when she came over and introduced herself. She'd been having a drink with her friend at the bar and had seen me on my own. It was one of those random comings together – I would never have approached her or any other woman at that time – but we clicked from the outset.

Of course, I told her that I'd been a footballer, had played for England, and had even played in Germany a few times. It didn't mean much to her, she had little interest in football. Andrea didn't know me from Adam: over time she became more aware of who I was and what I did.

I never expected I would meet anybody else after Pat. I never thought that I would fall in love again. During that little window of my life doing anything other than relaxing and spending some time on my own was the last thing on my mind, because I was so completely focused on the tournament coming up for Birmingham's under-18s. With all these other things on my mind, the last thing I expected was to bump into a young woman who I'd spend the rest of my days with. It seemed inconceivable. It was totally the last thing on my mind.

And yet, over the course of that weekend, I realised that I wanted to be with Andrea more than anything else. I have always been big on emotional connections and through my life and through my career my heart has always ruled my head. And so it was with Andrea. I fell in love with her very easily and very quickly. I suppose, looking back, I was still a bit vulnerable, emotionally anyway; I probably wasn't quite through my grieving over Pat. But there comes a time to move on and start living again. That was that moment.

We both felt the need to be together. We felt the need for clean breaks with our pasts. We decided to both get away from the areas that we lived in and try something new. Neither England nor Germany were in our minds.

For me, this would almost certainly mean turning my back on football, a game I'd served virtually continuously as a professional since the age of seventeen.

Professionally, I was in a good place in 2001. I was working for Birmingham, my boyhood club, then under the management of my friend and former teammate Trevor Francis. I liked and respected my colleagues. The head of the academy, Brian Eastick, who I worked with most closely, was technically the most accomplished coach I'd encountered in football. In David Sullivan and David Gold we had ambitious owners who were targeting the Premier League at a time when money was flooding through the game.

I knew that if I remained at Birmingham I would be well looked after. Maybe I'd share in some of the reflected glory of being at a club in the most powerful and watched league in world football. Maybe I could be part of turning Birmingham into a force in English football. As a boy on the St Andrew's terraces I'd watched them play in front of 50,000 crowds, taking on the likes of Barcelona and Inter Milan, and appearing in European and domestic finals. Maybe I could be part of reclaiming these days, part of a resurrection?

Or maybe not.

I loved football. The game gave me some great experiences and moments I will never forget. For my entire life it had been a good living. It was – and remains – a passion, but it was never all-consuming. It was a job, whereas life is life and there for living, not serving an employer.

So, at the age of 50, I turned my back on the game. I chose to go with Andrea. I left my job, my club, my home city, my country, my profession. I chose a different road.

*

THIS IS THE STORY OF MY LIFE UP UNTIL NOW. I'VE WAITED MANY years to sit down and work on it, in part because I view my life as a journey – not a string of happenings and anecdotes – and it goes on, deviating, surprising and delighting.

When I consider my life I always think of the nursery rhyme 'Monday's Child', which tells us, 'Thursday's child has far to go'. Well, I was that Thursday child. I'm still going; I don't know where, and I've never really been in total control of my destiny. I've always gone down these different junctions and avenues before resuming my course. But while the road continues – and will continue for some years yet, I hope – I realise that now, in my 65th year, the time is as right as it ever has been to provide a testimony so that future generations of football fans and my family can look back at and understand the times I lived and played in. I hope this will show my true character and provide an understanding of my person and the decisions that I made on my life's journey. I've waited many years to share it; I hope you enjoy reading just how I came to be.

1

KINGS NORTON

'Having somewhere to go is home, having someone to love is family,
having both is a blessing.'
Unknown

THE JOURNEY BEGINS IN JANUARY 1951 IN LOVEDAY STREET IN THE middle of Birmingham, home of the city's maternity hospital. I was a baby-boomer, the third of four boys born to Reg and Ada Latchford, in a happy and busy working-class family in Kings Norton, south of Birmingham. John, my oldest brother, is a decade older. He was followed by David in 1949, then myself and, two years later, Peter. I don't think either of my parents could have imagined in their wildest dreams that within a generation their boys would make up one of the most prominent families in English football.

These were difficult years of reconstruction and recovery for the whole country. I was born into an era of austerity and rationing. Birmingham was still very much Britain's second city, and while the heartbeat of Britain's age of Victorian reform had suffered terribly from German bombing raids, the harsh post-war reconstruction of brutalist architecture and city-centre motorways from which its reputation suffered in the latter years of the twentieth century was still to be fully imposed. It was a pleasant place to live, to grow up.

Dad worked at Moneyhul Hall Road Mental Hospital, where he was Assistant

Chief Male Nurse. With 1950s standards of mental health care, it was probably a bit like a *One Flew over the Cuckoo's Nest*-type place. But as boys we used to go in there and roam around, because they had a big playing area and a field on which we used to play football as well as cricket. When you consider institutions of the era that had dubious reputations, the facilities were fantastic. Seeing some of the patients was certainly a bit of an education.

My father could be quite strait-laced at times. He was probably the most honest man that I ever knew. He simply wouldn't utter a dishonest word; he was incapable of doing so. If something happened a certain way he wouldn't try and hedge the truth or put his angle on it, he'd tell it the way that it was. One of the things he always said was, 'You make your bed, you lie in it.' It was his famous quote and I always associate it with him. Get on with things, whatever happens. It wasn't a bad philosophy to have.

Physically he was quite an imposing man; he was lean, muscular, six-foot-three tall at a time when there probably weren't too many people of that stature. You wouldn't want to argue with my dad. He had a very easy temperament about him, although – a little like me – he could snap or explode. I remember John, my eldest brother, saying something he didn't like when he was seventeen or eighteen and my dad pinning him up against the wall – John would have been six-foot-two himself – and very quietly telling him the way things were in his house. You didn't cross my father; you didn't do anything out of turn, otherwise he'd lay down the law. We came from a generation where corporal punishment was the norm.

We all loved and respected him, irrespective of whether we got the odd clip around the backside. I would say that his values – being respectful, honest, true to yourself – were engrained in all of us. He had lots of interest in sport – which rubbed off on all of us – and loved fishing, which held less interest for me. He'd fish local rivers in Worcestershire, Warwickshire and sometimes faraway places, like East Anglia or Wales.

Mum was of Irish stock and her own mother had immigrated to the Small Heath area of Birmingham at the start of the century. I know very little about my mother's side of the family. She had four uncles, and my middle name, Dennis, is after one of them. Uncle Dennis was a bit of a tearaway by all accounts and apparently liked to drink, and fight. Every Friday and Saturday night he'd be out with his mates, having a pint, and then invariably ended up in a scrap. One night it went too far and somebody was killed. He and his mates were hauled up in front of the judge and slung into prison. The year happened to be 1914, the outbreak of the Great War, and they gave him the choice of fighting or staying in jail. He decided to fight for the British Army, which was not a good decision. One day he put his head above the trench and had it blown off. I'm not really sure why I was named after him; I hope it wasn't a prophetic choice!

Ours wasn't a religious household. We are all baptised in the Church of England but we weren't church-goers and not particularly religious. It was a normal working-class background, but we never wanted for anything. Dad had a good job, but he was definitely working class, a proud Labour supporter. Brian Viner described me in his book about Everton in the 1970s as being a middle-class boy, but I don't know why he thought that; I must have given him the wrong impression.

Mum had her hands full with my brothers and me. She'd always wanted a girl; that was the big thing in her life. Before she died in 1970 from cancer I fathered a daughter, Isobel – known as Izzy – and she was absolutely thrilled at finally having a girl in the family. When we were growing up she cleaned other people's houses for a bit of pocket money, and worked as a school dinner lady. I think she had enough on her plate with us boys. She struggled at times with four kids and even when John left home she probably struggled with three of us. We could be wild and there were times when we made her life hell. Dinner time was fight time, scrapping to protect your food, otherwise it would be gone. But she never gave up; she was of that era where you didn't. She and my dad had to be like that. They'd gone through the war, rationing and austerity. To baby-boomers like my brothers and myself those experiences still seemed fresh to everyone.

I think becoming a father for the second time over the past decade or so has made me realise just how hard it was for her back then. When my eldest two children, Izzy and Richard, were young in the early 1970s I was away a lot and preoccupied with my career, and my wife Pat took on a lot of the parenting responsibilities. Second time around I'm at home a lot more and would almost consider myself a 'full-time dad'. You can't imagine how hard a job it is unless you do it 24/7. One child is hard enough; two children is difficult; three or four, or more, I don't know how you'd do it and, looking back, I'm not quite sure how Mum coped. I wouldn't want to do it. You really can't rest because every waking minute is occupied. No government can pay families enough money to do the job properly. Parenting really is the hardest job and it's now, later in my life, when I fully recognise just how hard my Mum had it with the four of us.

Family life had its rhythms and routines in the 1950s and the Latchford home was probably not dissimilar to millions of households across the country. I think the only time we had meat was on a Sunday; we always had a Sunday roast, with a dessert afterwards. We had tea later on, with jelly and blancmange; that was always the big thing – Sunday roast and the Sunday tea. There'd be spam fritters and beans on toast during the week, or we'd be given money to visit the fish and chip shop up the road.

There was an extended family network in and around Birmingham. Three of my grandparents were still alive when I was growing up and my dad's sister, my Auntie Mary, who worked at the same hospital as him, lived locally and was often around. She would give us pocket money and sweets; although she remained a spinster, she was a very active woman and left a big impression on me. She would go off on holidays all over Europe during the 1950s, which was practically unheard of at the time, and come back and wow us with photographs of the Alps or France.

Dad and Auntie Mary grew up in the shadow of St Andrew's, so Birmingham City was in the blood and the family heritage. My father always said that his own father used to go and drink with the owners of Birmingham City Football Club, the Morris's, and knew them well. Harry Morris had captained the club before going on to become chairman and develop St Andrew's; his sons Harry and Len served the club for decades as chairman and director. They were of the people.

Although my dad took a great interest in sport and fishing, my parents had no real sporting background in terms of participation. My father had played football in the army, but that was the only time he did. He was in the Eighth Army out in the North African desert, in the Medical Corps, and faced Rommel's forces before ending up in Palestine. He used to tell a story of how he played against Bertie Mee, the great Arsenal manager of the 60s and 70s, who was on the other team during a game in the desert. My brother Peter was on a tour of Australia with West Brom in 1977 and he met Mee, who corroborated the story, although Mee revealed that his side won the game something like 25–0. Dad never told us that bit! We played cricket together as a family – Dad, David, Peter and myself; John would have left home at that stage – for the local cricket side attached to the hospital when we were teenagers. But despite this apparent lack of pedigree my parents happened to produce between them three professional footballers, and my oldest brother, John, who never made it professionally, was probably the best of us all. He had trials with Aston Villa and they were really keen to sign him. Unfortunately these were the post-war years and football wasn't really viewed as a steady profession. If you were fortunate, you'd have a ten-year career, probably on low money, and after that would have to find something else to do to bring money into the house. My mum and dad advised against signing for Villa and he became a tool-maker instead. In terms of football, John remained influential and some of my earliest memories are of going to watch him play for an amateur side called Harlequins.

People now think of Birmingham as some kind of concrete jungle, with the ubiquitous Spaghetti Junction and the M6 snaking through its centre. But it wasn't really like that at all in the 1950s. We had a semi-rural existence. We lived in a pre-fab, one of three houses on the edge of the countryside, and behind us were just fields for miles. We had a little terrier dog, a Jack Russell terrier, who was a very good rat-catcher. There was a Scottish family and an Irish family on either side and we all got to know each other quite well. Eventually the Irish family, who also had someone working at the hospital, moved down the road into accommodation in the hospital grounds. They had three blocks of houses down by the hospital and we eventually moved into one of those too. My brothers and I were part of a gang of kids that just roamed around.

I don't remember much about Birmingham being this great metropolis or really think of it at the time as Britain's second city. We never went into the city centre much as children; it was always on the outskirts to visit family. It was a quiet, peaceful childhood. We lived on a main road but there wasn't much traffic around. Sometimes we used to go and play chicken on the road. There were some local shops, including a fish and chip shop, as well as a school two or three hundred yards away. They built a big estate in the late 1950s not far away; that was the start of all the building in the area and over time the area became more and more built up and the fields behind us disappeared, and by the time we moved down to the other house nearer the hospital other houses were built. When we moved there we had a big garden with a chicken run in it. I'll always remember Auntie Mary coming around at Christmas time and killing the chickens and hanging them up. My father could never bring himself to do it.

I was pretty tame as a child and rarely got into trouble. The only pranks we carried out were on Bonfire Night and we used to cause a bit of trouble up and down the road and upset the residents of the mental hospital by setting off bangers.

The only other major prank I organised was a robbery! I have to admit to this, to finally get it off my chest after all these years. It was the great 1959 Jammie Dodger heist from my local junior school. I was eight years old. We were taught in a pre-fabricated class standing by itself away from the main school. I was a monitor, and it was my job to make sure that the French windows were locked at the end of the day. Anyway, I decided to leave them open one afternoon, and crept back later that evening, shortly after it turned dark and before the caretaker did his rounds. In the store cupboard was kept a tin of Jammie Dodger biscuits and I raided it and slipped out again before anyone could catch me. I ate them, of course. I'm not sure what the statute of limitations is on biscuit thefts, but I hope it's not longer than 56 years. Anyway, I confess here for the first time the only theft I ever carried out. It was probably the worst thing I have done in my entire life.

They were happy years and it was a happy childhood. We always went on a holiday. Usually we went down to the south coast, or to the Norfolk Broads. We had some relations who had a hotel in Margate and sometimes went there. I'll always remember my first journey in a car; it was on a holiday to the Norfolk Broads. My father couldn't drive, so he hired someone to drive us all the way over to East Anglia. As a young child I thought it was fabulous; I couldn't believe it.

Christmas mornings were always chaotic in the Latchford house, at least until we discovered that Father Christmas wasn't real and that Santa was really our old man. From that point on, it was a little bit of a letdown –but we still got nice presents. Dad always provided; that's what he did, no matter what. He was a working-class man; he considered himself a working-class man, and us to be a working-class family, and it was his inherent duty to provide the basics of what we needed. We always got clothes on our back, food on the table, presents at Christmas and birthdays, and a holiday every year.

I couldn't tell you when I first kicked a football, but certainly by the time I was seven or eight I was playing, kicking away with my two brothers, either in the hospital grounds or at a local park not far away, almost every single day. My brothers can recall playing in the front lounge even earlier with a ball made of rolled-up newspapers and Sellotape. Apparently those escapades came to an abrupt end when one of us broke a window. For that, we all got walloped and a lesson was learned.

There was a gang of kids, eight to ten of us, and we did other things as well as football. Bear in mind it wasn't long after the war and culturally it was fresh in many people's minds, so we'd play soldiers, and make our own weapons, dividing ourselves up among the Allies and the Germans.

Sport, however, played a big part in all of our childhoods, although my ability as a sportsman was slow to dawn on me. I never saw myself as special or different or better, and I'm sure David and Peter would have said the same thing. I never thought at that age that they, or I, would get where we did in professional sport. The very idea of being a professional footballer didn't occur to me until I was fourteen.

As brothers we were close, although I wouldn't say intimately so. We always got on well together. There's quite a gap between John and the rest of us. I'm probably closer to Peter than to David; and David is probably closer to John. We don't see each other very often these days. David's retired to Spain, Peter's up in Scotland, John is down in the south-west, and I'm now in Germany. I can't remember the last time we all saw each other; perhaps it was at a wedding for one of John's sons, but it must have been well over ten years ago. We keep in touch with the odd telephone call.

I was a shy child, very close to my mother. When I started school she used to have to drag me up the road to the school gates because I was so terrified of entering. I simply did not want to go. I was quiet and diffident, as was David, although Peter is – and always has been – very outgoing and could rabbit on forever. It took me years to overcome my shyness, perhaps the whole of my time at junior school.

By secondary school I had started to come out of my shell a little. I enjoyed school and kept out of trouble – I was never caned in an era notorious for corporal punishment – but was never very good at exams. I was never particularly strong at maths or English, but better at history and geography. Sciences I could never connect with; art, I liked. But I think I always had at the back of my mind that I was going to flunk exams, which, in the end, I did.

The 1960s were a time where the conservative social norms of previous decades were fading and there was a growth of counter-culture. Even in suburban Birmingham we were becoming aware of the changing times. So although I was at a school where the headmaster wielded a cane, we had others more attuned to these societal shifts. One teacher who left a deep impression was our English teacher, Harry Dutton.

I'd say that we learned about everything else bar English from Harry. In his lessons we'd listen to Bob Dylan and Joan Baez, while Harry spouted on about Ban the Bomb, love-ins, and sit-ins. Harry's stock with the children was high; all the kids loved him because he was a rebel. One day, very early on, when I was in second year, the headmaster at assembly was about to lead prayers when he solemnly announced, 'There is one person in this room who's not bowing his head; bow your head.' We all bowed heads further, but the prayers did not commence. 'This person is still not bowing his head,' announced the headmaster. 'Please bow your head.' We strained our necks further, awaiting the onset of prayers. Then the headmaster announced, 'Mr Dutton, would you please leave the room.' All the kids' heads whipped around; he'd sent a teacher out for not praying hard enough! Harry's stock from that day rose even higher. In fact, he probably assumed legendary status among us.

Although I was a fairly placid kid, there were certain times when I stepped out of character, as if I put on another persona. I started visiting Birmingham's pubs and clubs at the age of fourteen. It was just one of those things that me and one or two mates could get away with. I was big enough to pass as an adult and we knew where they didn't bother to check your ID. We'd order gin and tonics – these were the 'in drinks' in 1965 – and sit back and make a couple of them last the evening, before sneaking home. That was probably the height of my teenage rebellion.

I was, of course, very conscious of professional sport. We were one of the few homes that possessed a television set in the 1950s and we'd watch the FA Cup final every year. I remember seeing Alfredo di Stefano in a friendly against Wolves, and marvelling at his hypnotic skill as well as the iconic all-white Real Madrid kit. There was a little bit of hero-worship following that.

And then there were the trips to St Andrew's. My father was a supporter, as his own father had been too, and he took us. The match days had a routine that remain imprinted on my mind half a century later. To get there from Kings Heath we'd have to catch at least two buses. Get dropped off by the ground, buy a programme, get something to eat outside the ground, get in there, get our spec, and wait in anticipation. We would stand on the terraces as a family – Dad, David, Peter and I – and watch the Blues. We stood in the main big long block in the Spion Kop, opposite the main stand. In my mind's eye, I can picture my brother David now, standing there with his blue and white hat, his matching scarf and wooden rattle. In that time, you could position yourself anywhere inside the stadium, which was normally packed. As a kid if you were found at the back of the terrace, the men would lift you up and pass you over the heads of the crowd and get a position right at the front, closer to the action. In football terms, it was the last age of innocence.

It was a really good era for Birmingham. In 1960 they became the first British club to reach a European final when they were beaten 4–1 over two legs by Barcelona in the Inter-Cities Fairs Cup (the precursor to the UEFA Cup), a feat they repeated twelve months later when Roma won on aggregate. I wasn't at the Barcelona game, but was at St Andrew's in May 1961 on arguably the ground's greatest night when we beat Helenio Herrera's Inter Milan to reach the final against Roma. Jimmy Harris, a former Everton centre-forward, scored a couple of goals to take us there. When I was twelve, in 1963, we beat our neighbours and rivals Aston Villa to win the League Cup. Throughout this era, Birmingham were a First Division club, a top-flight outfit.

Our team had several internationals. The stand-out players for me were Mike Hellawell, an England outside right, Barry Bridges, a former Chelsea and

England forward I'd later play alongside in the reserves, and Bertie Auld, a crazy Scottish outside left, who'd go on to win the European Cup at Celtic. There were a lot of very good players in a Birmingham shirt while I was growing up.

Aston Villa would definitely be seen as the enemy for us and other Birmingham fans. They've always had the greater success and have always been a bigger club throughout their history; so it's always been a thorn in Birmingham's flesh really, because Birmingham carries the city's name. This would remain imprinted on my mind – and have consequences – much later as a professional player.

Although I made my name as a centre-forward and David and Peter theirs as goalkeepers, as kids our destinies were not mapped out. Indeed it may well have been that I became a goalkeeper too. My father had been a goalkeeper briefly and I played in goal to a reasonable standard too. It was a physically challenging era to be a goalie. Back then, they were not furnished with gloves, only occasionally wearing mittens, which were not ideal for handling. The balls were also a lot heavier. You needed to have the tough hands of a labourer to deal with the leather and the lace, which stung the palms.

I enjoyed the position and even played as a goalkeeper at county level for Warwickshire Boys, later reverting to the left wing. Later in my Blues career I got 57 minutes' worth of league experience between the posts for Birmingham against Wolves after deputising for the injured Gary Sprake. I think goalkeeping was in the genes anyway. It just so happened that, like John, I could perform at the other end of the pitch.

My education as a young footballer was completely different to the experience young players have today, but probably not untypical of my era. Now children will be selected from the age of five or six to begin associations with club academies or else play for junior teams, while school, district and county football is virtually dead. I, on the other hand, never played for anyone other than my school until I was selected for my district and county. It was exactly the same route for Peter and David.

There's very little of that nowadays. All the best players go to club academies and the government won't pay for teachers to work outside their hours and oversee school football. It's killed it. I sometimes wonder whether it's a good thing: the academy system and clubs recruiting players from such a young age. You have to think, has it worked? Are our young footballers better now than they were in the 1960s or 1970s? The evidence, if you look at the national team, would suggest not.

I started out at the back in junior school, at centre-half. It probably wasn't until I got to late junior school, early senior school, that I went up front. I was probably physically bigger than most lads. Teachers always put the more developed boys at the back because they could stop things happening; then later on they think, 'Oh yeah, we need to score goals, so put the big lad up front, I suppose.'

My natural qualities as a footballer were almost intangible. Fortunately, my main one was that I could always score goals. Partly it was because I was bigger and stronger than most, but I just had a natural instinct to score. It's a talent that I find difficult to explain. A lot of it is down to being in the right place at the right time, but how do you explain instinct? You couldn't necessarily put it down to strength or speed or aerial ability or shot power and accuracy or any one thing; it was just something that I could do and was good at. I could defend too; if you put me in a defensive situation I would be able to work out a solution. It's a bit like my old Everton teammate, Mick Lyons, in reverse. Lyons started out up front, then he moved back; and the same sort of qualities are needed in both areas, because if you know one you know the other. He was naturally suited in the end to being a defender, but I could defend very well too. The bravery bit comes in too; you need that as a defender as well as a forward; although bravery is something I equate to stupidity. Intelligent people would never put their feet where brave players put their heads. It defies rational behaviour, putting yourself in such a position. The bravest and stupidest of all footballers are, of course, goalkeepers.

I played to a good standard at school level, but, as I've said, never really considered myself better than my contemporaries or destined for life at the top. And yet of all those that I encountered in my youth in Birmingham, I think it was only myself and my brothers who became professional.

I think whatever level you play at, you give your all mentally and physically, and certainly that was the case as a schoolboy player. There was one county game for South Birmingham, when I was thirteen, which stands out for me fifty years on, probably because it is really the only time I've cried at a football match. This particular year we were considered one of the favourites to win the Inter-County

Cup; we had a very strong team. And we went and played at Ilkeston in Derby, and I think we lost 2–1, or 3–2. But right at the death I got through and should have scored to equalise. And I missed. That was the first shattering incident of my life; a really devastating moment. It was the first and only time I've ever really cried tears over football. We had been hot favourites to go on and win the Cup and not to do it and knowing I could have scored to get a replay was such a huge blow for my teenage self.

By then the notion had still not clicked in my unassuming mind that I could be doing this on a more regular basis. I played at a high standard of schoolboy football and my brother David had signed schoolboy forms with Birmingham City, having impressed scouts when playing for South Birmingham Boys in the age group above me. But the idea that I was somehow special or could make it just never entered my head. It wasn't something that I sought or aspired to. A Wolves scout was meant to be watching me but I could never have imagined playing in a gold shirt and so I never took this notion seriously. It sounds trivial, but that's how I thought. All I was interested in was achieving as much as possible for whichever team I was playing for. Nowadays I have the impression that many people do things, including playing football and other sports, because they seek fame. I never set out to become famous. Fame is transitory. You can lose it as quickly as you gain it. It's what you achieve; it's that achievement that goes down in history, whether it was my school's history or my country's. That was always the motivation on my part, achieving something that somebody else could not achieve.

One evening, when I was aged fourteen, I was up in my bedroom and my father knocked on the door and told me there was somebody to see me. To see me? I wasn't sure what he meant, but I followed Dad downstairs and there, in our living room, was Don Dorman, Birmingham City's chief scout. What on earth did he want?

'He wants to sign you on schoolboy forms,' my dad told me.

Not until that moment, not even when David had been signed by Birmingham, did I think or consider I could play football professionally. Not in my wildest dreams. The meeting was the most straightforward of my life. In appearance, Don looked like a typical scout. You wouldn't notice him in a crowd. He was a small, squat man who wore a long waterproof coat and often carried around an umbrella to protect himself from the elements. Not all terraces at every stadium possessed a roof, remember. Don had worked tirelessly for Birmingham over a number of years and knew his job well. In my mum and dad's living room, he presented me with a couple of forms and I signed them straight away.

From then on I started training with Birmingham two nights a week. Having played as a defender, goalkeeper and winger as a schoolboy, Birmingham originally took me on as a wide man. If you remember the Burnley and Wolves flanker Stevie Kindon – big, powerful and direct – I was a bit like that. But within a month or two of being there they moved me inside and turned me into a centre-forward.

The real transformation had been the one in my head. From the moment that Don Dorman told me Birmingham wanted to sign me it was like a light being switched on. Instead of being unassuming and not considering the future, I suddenly thought, 'Yeah, I can do this. I can be a professional footballer.'

2

ST ANDREW'S

'The only true wisdom is knowing that you know nothing.'

Socrates

UNTIL THE EVENING DON DORMAN CAME THROUGH OUR FRONT door I entertained no thoughts whatsoever of becoming a professional footballer. Even when my brother David had been taken on by Birmingham a year or so before, the notion that I'd also be able to take that step up never occurred to me. Maybe it was on account of being so unassuming, of possessing a natural diffidence that had followed me through childhood. Life inside a professional dressing room seemed so remote as to be inconceivable. And yet from the moment I was presented with schoolboy terms there was no other thought in my head. It was all that I thought of: *They want me, so I'm going to be a professional football player.*

Life didn't change very much at first as an affiliated schoolboy. I was fourteen years old and still played football at schoolboy level, but travelled to the training ground out towards the old Elmdon Airport twice a week to train with Birmingham. Academically I probably suffered because of the overwhelming focus on football. I always liked school life and enjoyed most of the work, although I was pretty average if I'm honest. When it came to exams, as I've already mentioned, I was no good and flunked most of them. I came out at sixteen with five or six CSEs. But it didn't matter too much to me. Waiting at St Andrew's was an apprenticeship with Birmingham and as soon as I started getting into the routine of training and playing for the club's youth team I knew there was only one thing I was going to do.

I had never been discouraged either by teachers or parents from following the route of professional football, which was in contrast to my brother John a decade earlier. My school had a reputation for sporting excellence and as well as my brothers and me, there was another pair of brothers, the Stewarts, who were very good track athletes and competed nationally. My father wanted me to go down the football route because David had done so and I think he was pleased and proud of me – as he was all of us – for progressing to a standard where making a living out of the game became a distinct possibility. If there was ever any advice against abandoning my studies I ignored it.

That said, I don't think the certainty that I would make it came until that first professional contract. I knew in the back of my mind I was going to do it but until they gave me a contract it could have gone either way. One of the reasons underlying that instinct was that Stan Cullis, Birmingham's manager, paid close attention to my development from when I was a fourteen-year-old. He watched, guided and gave his time; a level of devotion that was in stark contrast to his main duties as manager.

I would find that as first-team manager Stan seemed completely uninterested. His assistant was Joe Mallett, a Geordie who had played at wing-half for South-ampton and Queens Park Rangers either side of the war before going into coach-ing. He had previously been manager of Birmingham, but was sacked after his disastrous reign brought relegation in 1965. Surprisingly, perhaps, Cullis retained Mallett as a coach when he succeeded him as Birmingham boss in December 1965. Sometimes you'd wonder who was in charge. Joe used to do most of the coaching and Stan would walk around half the time looking in the ditches on the edge of the training ground. He had a strange way about him. I think it was because he struggled with communication. For example, my brother David tells a story of how he used to walk twenty yards to ask one of his staff to tell him he wanted to speak to David, even though David initially was standing only five yards away.

Stan, nevertheless, had a natural authority and presence at Birmingham. He was a mountain of a man; he was impressive. England centre-half; Wolverhampton Wanderers centre-half; an absolute legend. He'd had a distinguished but war-interrupted playing career with Wolves and England and at the age of just 31 became manager at Molineux, presiding over the most successful period in the club's history. Three times they were crowned league champions, twice winning the FA Cup, the last time in 1960. But Wolves struggled to replicate that success in the early 1960s and in 1964 Stan was surprisingly sacked. He said he was walking away from football, purportedly turning down the Juventus manager's job, but he returned a year later at St Andrew's. Maybe it was a year too soon. He seemed distracted and had never, perhaps, got over the disappointment of being moved out by Wolves – a club he loved. In his autobiography, Bill Shankly, who idolised Stan, speculated whether he was heartbroken. Shankly spoke of someone who was 100 per cent Wolves – someone, indeed, whose blood must have been made of old gold.

You wouldn't want to argue with Stan. He was big; an imposing person. He never swore either, and was one of the very few people in football I encountered who did not utter profanities. Instead of using the F-word he'd shout 'Flipping this' and 'Flopping that'! Yet for all that he was the type of person you just wouldn't argue with.

At that stage of his career Cullis was a bit like the Bill Shankly I got to know in the late 1970s, after he had left Liverpool. Shankly had retired from Liverpool at too early an age, but had been excluded from the club by his successor, Bob Paisley, who felt he was a distracting influence. Shankly had long lived in a modest house on Bellefield Avenue, overlooking Everton's training ground. In the absence of anything else to do he'd squeeze through the fence and take his dogs for a walk across the pitches, chatting to the players and sometimes getting involved in the training – all this despite his links with Liverpool. Shankly was a lost soul. Similarly, Stan had been pushed out by Wolves, the club he'd been synonymous with, when he expected a place on the board. He'd wound up at Birmingham, but I felt his heart was never really in it. He seemed constantly on the periphery of things.

When he was coaching youngsters, however, Stan was a different person. I don't know whether that's because we were more impressionable, but he took a great interest in our development as players. When I was fifteen and going in to train during the summer holidays for a week or two, he'd take me aside and do some one-on-one work with me. I think he must have seen something that he hadn't seen in other players. Because he took that personal interest I can honestly say he had an impact on me. But whether he had such an impact all the way through the club, I'm doubtful.

Like all the young hopefuls, my apprenticeship contained menial tasks in and around St Andrew's. We were organised by the kit and boot man, Ray Devey, a former centre-half at the club, who on match days served as physio, wielding the ubiquitous magic sponge. He kept us in line and when we weren't on the training pitch, he was in charge of us. We were essentially a pool of free labour. We did all the jobs, from cleaning boots to sweeping down the terraces. We used to paint like mad during the summer down at the training ground and St Andrew's.

There was a hierarchy with the apprentices and pros at Birmingham that I don't remember there being at other clubs later on in my career. You always knocked on the door to the dressing room to be allowed to go in, and never addressed the first-team players by their first names. It was 'Mr Hennessy' or 'Mr Bridges'; 'What do you want?' 'How may I help?' And they'd tell you what they wanted doing. They treated us fairly well, unless we did something stupid, at which point they'd come down hard and deliver a clip. Nobody ever gave me a clip, but others weren't so fortunate. The senior players would not stand any backchat.

It's just the way the culture of football was back then, but it was something I never liked or agreed with. I don't think making boys do menial tasks was any-thing other than exploiting a source of cheap or free labour. I don't go along with this idea that it provided them 'grounding' in the real world. When I made the grade I like to think I treated my apprentices well. I was very friendly with them because I appreciated what they were doing and I used to sling them a bit of money. I don't remember who cleaned my boots at Birmingham or Everton, but at Swansea it was Colin Pascoe, who went on to play for Wales and, until the summer of 2015, was Brendan Rodgers' assistant at Liverpool. By the time I was youth coach at Birmingham in the 1990s, the apprentices looked after their own equipment, tidied up their own areas and their own equipment, but all the other menial tasks had been scrapped.

Birmingham was old-school in the mid-1960s. Things were very sparse and the club at the time was very frugal. I think we may have had two lots of kit, but they tended to dump a muddy pile in the middle of the dressing room and everyone helped themselves. You got one pair of boots for the season and that was it. The first pair of boots I had was like a throwback to the early 1950s; they were big leather things, and you had to put grease inside them and on your feet to break them in because they were so tough and uncomfortable. If you didn't, you'd just get blisters. For about two weeks or more you kept shoving this grease all over your feet and the boots just to get them a little bit softer. Nowadays boots are like velvet slippers.

SHORTLY BEFORE BEGINNING MY APPRENTICESHIP, AND STILL DURING my last days at school, I had a brush with glory. Being within touching distance of silverware is, as you'll read, a recurring theme in this book.

When I was aged fifteen I started playing for Birmingham City's youth team. The highlight of the year was the FA Youth Cup, in which all league clubs entered a team. A bonus for aspiring players was that you got to play at the club's actual stadium and these affairs were normally well attended. I recall playing in front of crowds of 12,000 or more, which as a fifteen-year-old was quite a thrill.

Despite a level of professionalism, things were still quite basic. There were certainly none of the comforts or accruements today's young players have. The club relied on a local schoolteacher to run the youth team. I suppose it was appropriate, as we were still mostly just schoolboys.

In 1967 we put together a run. We had a good team. There was David and myself and Garry Pendrey, who was already on the fringes of the first team and would himself go on to enjoy a stellar City career. As we progressed in the competition the crowds got bigger and our opponents better. I found myself coming up alongside players I'd be facing (or in some cases playing alongside) in the First Division and for England in the following decade. I was part of the team that knocked out the West Ham of Trevor Brooking and Frank Lampard Snr in the fifth round at Upton Park. We beat Mick Channon's Southampton in the two-legged semi, and then in the final we were up against Sunderland. They were an excellent young side and their best player, Colin Todd, the future Footballer of the Year I'd play alongside at Everton, wasn't even in the youth team as he'd already made the step up to the senior side.

By now Birmingham's Youth Cup run was quite a big issue. The press became interested and I remember a photographer turning up at school to do some posed photographs with me. Birmingham's success-starved public had taken us to their hearts. For me, I think I was a bit young to really take it in. I just went from game to game and round to round. The fact that we found ourselves in the final was, I think, quite incredible. But it was always going to be tough against Sunderland; they had a very good side. We lost 1–0 in both legs, but it was a tight affair; it wasn't a runaway victory by them. We were all disappointed that we didn't quite pull it off, but our focus as players remained on making the grade.

I SETTLED IN QUICKLY TO THE ROUTINE OF LIFE AS A FOOTBALL apprentice. It was useful having an older brother at the same club and I was helped too by my physique. At sixteen I wasn't quite fully grown, but I was a man. I could hold my own. At the same time there were some rude awakenings.

I learned some very important lessons in my first pre-season as an apprentice professional at Birmingham in 1967. Stan Cullis put me straight into a reserve team game, a pre-season match at the training ground against Coventry. Coventry had a centre-half, George Curtis, a big guy with a face like Herman Munster, who was at Highfield Road for nearly all of his career. He was in his late twenties –I don't know why he played in that game, he was probably just coming back from injury. I remember that during the game I came off him to receive the ball, laid it off, and went to spin to go in behind. As I span he blocked me – he simply stood there with his size and might – and I literally hit him and went up in the air. As I landed back on my arse about three feet away I looked up at him and he stood there with his fists on his hips, smiling at me. I thought, 'Oh fuck, what am I going to do?'

Coaches always said back then, 'Go and win the physical battle.' I was used to being big for my age and winning that battle, but I realised that day that there are some physical battles you're never going to win, ever. It made me play in a different way. I played the rest of that game trying to avoid George – coming short, going deep, going wide, getting in between. It was a lesson that you've got to sometimes play in a different way; that I wasn't going to win every physical battle; that because of my size perhaps I'd had it a little too easy at youth level.

Later that first pre-season there was another incident that remains imprinted on my mind. It involved the inside-forward Bobby Thomson. There were two Bobby Thomsons at Birmingham around that time. There was a left-back who came from Wolves two years later and had played for England. Then there was this Bobby Thomson: a Glaswegian inside-forward who had previously played for Aston Villa and Wolves. Bobby was a good player, skilful but nasty. He had just turned thirty then, coming towards the end of his career.

During this game, the ball came in to me, and Bobby was coming towards me so I laid it off to him first time. It wasn't the best pass – I'd overhit it – but it wasn't the worst one either. It was literally just half a yard past him. He could have turned around and got it but he stopped, looked at me, and his finger came up.

'You little fucking cunt; if you ever do that to me again I'll break your fucking legs.'

He said that in a ferocious Glaswegian accent and he absolutely meant it. It wasn't said for effect. That's the difference between players back then and players now, because he meant absolutely everything – his words and his sentiments. He would have done me if I'd misplaced a ball again, no question about it. It was a hard lesson, but one that I had to learn quickly. I was sixteen years of age, nobody had sworn at me, ever, before that. And then he said it to me; my own teammate!

I practically shit myself. I really thought, 'Fuck, I don't know what to do.'

It was a sink or swim moment, and I swam. What it did for me was to teach me a lesson I've never forgotten in how to concentrate. Whatever I did from then on, my level of concentration, with him or anyone else, was at a different level.

These were mere bumps along my early journey and I progressed quickly as a player. The Central League, the competition for reserve teams in those days, was of a good standard and my game improved. I came to terms with the physical side of professional football – or at least adapted to it – and I scored goals. I had to find a different way to play against certain people, but I think that's true throughout your professional career. You're always running up against different types of players and it's never a case of one size fits all. Some you can intimidate and frighten, and others you've got to be a little bit more careful and sneaky with. Back then you learned those lessons early in life. We learned important lessons in the Central League, playing with and against men. There were so many good young players and first-team pros playing reserve team football that it drove up your standards. You soon learned the ins and outs of what it was like to play football at a professional level.

I'm by no means a precocious person and have never taken anything for granted, but preying on my mind by Christmas 1967, as I neared my seventeenth birthday in January, were thoughts of a professional contract. Some were already talking me up as being ready for the first team. I was a regular in the reserves. It seemed to me the logical next step. Shortly before I turned seventeen I bumped into Don Dorman, the Birmingham chief scout who had 'discovered' me for Birmingham.

I was quite straightforward in my question: 'So, am I going to be getting a professional contract when I turn seventeen?'

Most players didn't; even the lucky ones usually had to wait until they were eighteen. Don just gave me a knowing look and a smile. It told me what I needed to know.

A few weeks later I was called into the Birmingham secretary's office and given the first professional contract of a career that would last twenty years. It was January 1968, I'd just turned seventeen. My wages jumped from £8 per week to £30, which was more or less the average national salary. For me it was massive. It was enough for me to move out of my parents' place and into my own home with my girlfriend Pat, who'd later become my wife and mother to my two eldest children. I was also able to buy my first car, a white Ford Popular.

*

AFTER SIGNING THAT FIRST PRO CONTRACT AND ENTERING THE

Birmingham squad as a professional and equal, I was fortunate to be in the position of being alongside a couple of former England forwards. Fred Pickering had once been a British record domestic signing when he crossed from Blackburn to Everton in 1964. He'd possessed a phenomenal scoring record in his first two seasons, but fell out of favour with Harry Catterick and was infamously left out of the 1966 FA Cup final. I've always said he's probably one of the most underrated Everton centre-forwards there has ever been; he was certainly one of the most prolific. Barry Bridges, once of Chelsea, was more of a winger, but he – and particularly Fred – would help me with my positional play and were generous in their praise.

It was also a help having a brother in the dressing room with me. Because David was a couple of years older, he was a conduit between me and some of the senior pros. Obviously, having been there longer, he knew them better than I did, so it was always useful to have him around; I could sort of go through him and be part of his set-up. Because you always have a little clique of three or four players that you're always around, it was easier getting into his group and being part of it.

Being part of a family with two professional footballers and a third in Peter well on his way, you might have thought there was talk about nothing other than football. But it wasn't quite like that. We'd talk about our days, our lives, and what we'd been doing, but it wasn't just football, football, football. Eventually, because my dad was a fan, the conversation would at some stage turn to Birmingham and what was happening at St Andrew's, but it wasn't the dominant topic.

The Birmingham City first team at this time were hovering around mid-table in the Second Division. We finished tenth in 1966/67, fourth a year later, then seventh, but rarely troubled the top of the table at a time when only the top two were promoted. There were cup runs – a League Cup semi-final in 1967 and one in the FA Cup a year later – and these invariably lifted spirits at the club. But there was a sense that while we didn't belong in the Second Division, under Stan Cullis's management that was where we were staying.

My professional debut came on 21 March 1969, a Friday night under flood-lights at St Andrew's. Stan Cullis had talked about playing me before Christmas and I'm not sure why he never did. I thought I was going to get my chance then, but Stan must have changed his mind, and I had to wait.

I was eighteen years and two months old when I was selected to lead the Birmingham front line. Our season was going nowhere. Stan had told me a week before the game that he was going to play me. Too far off the top to make a meaningful promotion challenge, we were also well clear of those teams threatened by relegation. There were nine games remaining when I pulled on that number nine shirt for the first time so, I suppose, given that we hadn't won in two months, there was still a vague danger that we could get pulled into a relegation battle.

That night Fred Pickering, who had become something of a mentor to me, was selected as centre-half. Fred was the loveliest man you could ever wish to meet; he was just wonderful. He must have known I was some sort of threat to his long-term future at Birmingham, but you would never have known it from his attitude to me. That night against Preston I gave notice of my potential. It was something of a dream debut, I suppose. We won 3–1 and I scored twice, both headers. When I scored Fred was the first person to come up to me and shake my hand. 'Great, Bob, well done,' he said. He was very sincere; there was nothing false about it.

Despite my brace I was left out of the following Tuesday's game, a 5–0 home win over Bolton Wanderers. I was recalled for the next match, a trip to Huddersfield, where I partnered Fred Pickering up front. But despite past and future Everton number nines lining up in attack, the game ended goalless.

I returned to the Central League for a few weeks, during which time Dave made his first-team debut – I actually beat him to that milestone, although it must be said there are always more opportunities for outfield players than goalkeepers. In the penultimate game of the 1968/69 season, against Hull City we were teammates. We won 2–1 before rounding our season off with a 3–1 victory over Middlesbrough at St Andrew's.

✱

ALTHOUGH I ATTENDED TRIALS AT SCUNTHORPE ONE YEAR, I HAD missed out on representing England at schoolboy level. But at youth level, for the first time I got the call to represent my country. Obviously the players were of a higher quality and it was run very professionally. The FA, at every level, had all the top people on the coaching staff, particularly at a time when England were reigning world champions. It was of a very good professional standard; Wilf McGuinness, who soon after became Manchester United manager, was one of our coaches.

So at the end of the 1968/69 season I was called up for the England Youth squad that was competing in that summer's European Youth Championship. Guess where it was? East Germany. Of all the places you could have gone to, East Germany. In West Germany it would have been terrific, but East Germany, locked as it was behind the Iron Curtain, was grim.

It's an experience that very few people had at the time, going into the territory of what was notionally a Cold War enemy. I always remember passing the Berlin Wall at Checkpoint Charlie. It took us absolutely ages to get through. Once the border guards had returned our documents and sent us on our way it was like going into a ghost town. East Berlin was just dilapidated, there was nothing there. We had a female interpreter on the bus, and two other guys, but when we tried to engage her in conversation, there was just nothing she would talk about. Instead she sat impassively and kept looking out the front. We realised later that the two East German officials were probably Stasi and positioned at the front of the bus to keep their eyes on her, and us.

We were based in Dresden, which had suffered heavy Allied bombing during the Second World War. The squad included Steve Kindon, the Burnley winger; Aston Villa's Neil Rioch, whose brother Bruce would be a teammate of mine at Everton; and the midfielder Stuart Metcalfe, who had a long career with Blackburn Rovers. The stand-out player, though, was the young Burnley winger Dave Thomas, with whom I'd become much better acquainted a decade later. For a group of young men, easily bored, it wasn't the best place to go. We couldn't find a bar anywhere. There was nothing that offered any excitement whatsoever. It was hard to comprehend that it could be like that. Some of us had heard stories or seen films about what it was possibly like behind the Iron Curtain, but until we went there and saw how people were living it was hard to imagine. We just trained, ate, slept; trained, ate, slept – and played.

The full England team were, of course, world champions and we were hotly tipped for this junior tournament. There was an expectation at that time that England would succeed at whatever level they were playing. We were in a group with Malta, Czechoslovakia and East Germany. Just one country would progress from the group to reach the semi-finals and, after ourselves and East Germany won our opening games against Malta – I scored four in a 6–0 thrashing of the Maltese – and Czechoslovakia, it set up a winner-takes-all conclusion to the group, when we met the East Germans in Magdeburg. East Germany turned us over, winning 4–0, and would go on to reach the final against Bulgaria. This they lost on a coin toss after drawing 1–1 after extra time.

WHEN YOU'RE TWELVE YEARS OLD, YOU THINK THAT BEING A professional footballer is the ultimate accomplishment. But within a few years I had that hallowed Birmingham shirt on my back and I never really looked back at my twelve-year-old self and thought, 'You know, there's ten thousand kids my age out there who'd want to do this.' I don't think you have that sense of self-awareness as a young professional footballer. You just get on with what you're being paid to do, a job that you love doing. Having an awareness of what you've done and what you're doing doesn't come until later in life when you've stopped; you become really conscious of all these things that have happened, which you didn't take for granted but you took for being normal. It was like going and watching Birmingham against Inter. As a kid I thought, 'It's Inter Milan, great.' But now, when I consider who they were up against, I realise what a mega event that was in the context of Birmingham's history. And I'd been there, and witnessed it.

Life as a professional footballer always was insulated from supporters. I think you are aware of them but you perhaps don't grasp or appreciate the vast hopes and expectations that are vested in you. As a player you're not aware at times that you might only get the one chance in your career to affect a certain game that will go down in club lore. You're not aware of that until your career is finished and you think, 'Wow, if that had turned out that way instead of that way, we could have changed history.' You don't really consider the effect that you have – or could have had – on a club's destiny and, by default, people's lives.

I've had scores of people, many of whom I've never even met, who have named their children after me. To have made such an impression on a stranger that they'd name a child after you is a huge honour, but also slightly disconcerting. At the same time, it's amusing to see these progeny appear from time to time. I've even had a boyband popstar – Lee Latchford Evans from Steps – carry my name. I think I got off lightly. Some of my teammates weren't so fortunate. Duncan McKenzie and Gordon Lee have Jamie Lee Duncan Carragher bearing their names!

*

AT THE START OF THE 1969/70 SEASON I WAS BIRMINGHAM'S FIRST-choice centre-forward. I don't think my opportunity to impress arrived out of necessity, more that Stan Cullis thought he'd give me a run. He played me in Birmingham's first three games, but I didn't score and we won just a single point. Then he decided to change the team and I got dumped out.

The 1969/70 season was a difficult time at St Andrew's. I don't think Stan was totally committed. I think his mind and his heart were elsewhere. Joe Mallett took more and more responsibility for the day-to-day running of the team and what was going on, and as a team and a club we never really progressed.

Birmingham were still spending big money for a side in the Second Division. We bought players like Bobby Thomson, a very stylish former England left-back from Wolves, and the former Liverpool centre-forward Tony Hateley from Coventry. We had some good players already in place, but the team didn't crack on. If the structure is right at the top and the passion is there, players feel it, and they'll get behind it. But if there's a lack of understanding and willingness and passion, and the structure and tactics and strategy aren't right, it just becomes a mish-mash and you go from one game to the next not really understanding what should be going on and what you should be doing. Nothing gelled that year. It was like being stuck in a pot of glue, trying to get your feet out but realising you were trapped.

As a young footballer, trying to break into a struggling team is a double-edged sword. It's an opportunity, but coming into a failing team can damage a young-ster's progress if he is not fully prepared for it. As a senior player I witnessed this towards the end of my time at Swansea, when John Toshack started throwing in young players to try and turn things around and shift momentum. They might have been good enough but it's the wrong time to introduce newcomers when the side is struggling. It's not easy as a senior pro, because you're dependent on all components, everybody in the team, performing so as to pave the way for in-experienced players. You can do so much but you rely on everybody else around you, and if five, six, seven of them are having nightmares or not performing, it's hard work.

There was a sad, slow inevitability about Stan's eventual departure. To be honest, he'd become so peripheral that I don't even remember him leaving. I just remember that Joe Mallett, who was already running most things anyway, became interim first-team manager in March 1970.

There was a danger at that stage that Birmingham might go down to the Third Division. If things hadn't changed, if they had continued the way they were going, we might have been relegated. In a struggling dressing room, relega-tion is not something that's discussed. I think it's a little bit taboo – you don't want to talk about it just in case. It's like speaking of the Devil and the Devil appears. You don't want to speak about it because you don't want it to happen. At Swansea in the early 1980s we never talked about relegation. It was always positive: 'How can we win the next game, what can we do to win a game and turn things around.' It was the same at Birmingham. I don't think relegation was in anybody's mind.

On the final day of the 1969/70 season our Second Division status was con-firmed and Villa went down to the third tier instead. It would have been a bit much for the city for both clubs to have been relegated in the same season. So for us to have stayed up, I think we probably did celebrate that and gave thanks that it was our arch enemy and not us. But as a team we had little to cheer. We'd rounded off an utterly miserable campaign with a 6–0 defeat at Norwich City.

Villa's relegation to the Third Division meant that I would never experience a Birmingham derby as a player; I'd been left out of the two derby matches that season. I'd like to have tasted a derby game before I had to experience the Merseyside derby, because I didn't know what to expect then. Besides those first years at St Andrew's, Villa simply weren't on the horizon when I was at Birmingham.

Things progressed at St Andrew's in the summer of 1970 when there were two significant arrivals. Birmingham brought in a sixteen-year-old from the West Country, blessed with genius. It's something that happens perhaps once every generation in English football, when a kid comes in and just wows everybody, and I was fortunate to be there when this happened. When this young lad, who had only just turned sixteen, stepped onto the pitch for his first appearance in training, you looked at him and thought, 'Wow'. You knew you were in the presence of somebody who was going to be really outstanding. His name was Trevor Francis.

People talk about Wayne Rooney, but Trevor would leave Wayne standing in terms of overall ability and technique. Wayne's only advantage over Trevor would be that at sixteen Wayne was a man, Trevor wasn't; Trevor was still a boy. But in terms of everything else Trevor was well ahead. Despite his tender years, Trevor came straight into the Birmingham first team. He was absolutely phenomenal. People ask me, 'Who's the greatest player you've ever played with?' On pure natural talent Trevor stands head and shoulders above everybody, absolutely everybody. If you add other criteria into the mix, Kevin Keegan comes into the picture. But as a footballer Trevor was simply the best.

He had it all: pace, skill, ability, a thought process that was faster than anything I ever encountered in a footballer. He was thinking so much further ahead than everybody else. He put balls into areas where people should be, but we weren't always there – he was so far ahead. Fortunately, when I got in and around the box, I knew he would deliver. That was the easy part; the hard part was in general play. But you quickly learned to get into the correct positions. That's the secret of being able to play with footballers that can do things other players can't, to stay one step ahead.

The other man who would make a difference at St Andrew's and have a profound effect on my career came from Brighton via the United States, where he'd had a successful spell as a manager. His name was Freddie Goodwin. His arrival as manager would be the making of me as a professional footballer.

3

ORIENT

'Don't practise until you get it right. Practise until you can't get it wrong.'
Unknown

FREDDIE GOODWIN WAS ONE OF THE LAST OF THE ERA OF footballer-cricketers, a now almost forgotten breed of sportsman who played professional football during the winter months and first-class cricket during the summer. One of Manchester United's Busby Babes, he was a member of the squad that won League Championships in 1956 and 1957. Fortunately, he was not selected in the travelling party when United played Red Star Belgrade in February 1958 and was one of the men who helped the club make a comeback following the horrors of the Munich air disaster. In the mid-1950s he also made eleven first-class appearances for Lancashire Country Cricket Club as a right-arm fast-medium bowler. Later he became part of Don Revie's resurgent Leeds team. In Revie and Busby, Freddie came under the charge of two of the most influential managers of the post-war era. This wide array of experience would influence his later career as a manager.

When his career was effectively ended by a triple fracture of the leg following a collision with his former Leeds teammate John Charles in an FA Cup tie against Cardiff in 1964 he turned to management, first with Scunthorpe, then New York

Generals. He returned to England in 1968 with Brighton & Hove Albion, where two years of progressive stewardship brought him to the attention of the Birmingham board. Following the conclusion to the bitterly disappointing 1969/70 season, Freddie was named Stan Cullis's successor as Birmingham manager.

I immediately found Freddie was not just a charming, lovely man, but to be one of football's great thinkers. He was very well versed in the game, but also in other areas. His experience in the United States – which in many aspects was and remains years in advance of the UK – made him a decade or two in front of most managers at the time. He would explore and express new ideas about how to go about his work, not only on the pitch but off it too. He introduced dance and yoga into our training routines as well as a specific weight training programme that was practically unheard of in the late-1960s and early-1970s. We were educated and advised on our diet too.

Freddie was a big man and seemed to have the presence to go along with the acumen and intelligence to put across what he wanted. He was very much more approachable than someone like Stan Cullis. But despite his friendliness he still wanted things done correctly and properly. He wouldn't be sloppy about anything and wanted you to conduct yourself in the right way. He was far-sighted for his day and it was refreshing. He came with all these new ideas, and was quite lively and bubbly too. If he was in today's game with the qualities that he possessed he'd be a star, a major football manager.

I was grateful for the hours Stan Cullis had put in with me as a teenager, but it was Freddie who put me on the road to becoming the professional footballer I developed into. In the first pre-season ahead of the 1970/71 campaign he spent a lot of time with me working on my game. It was just the two of us, one-to-one: trying to show me which areas to run into; when to come off, when to go in behind; how to get into certain areas; what to do when I'd collected the ball. Then we'd be having heading practice, shooting practice, essentially everything that a centre-forward needs to do.

I played four games for Birmingham in 1968/69, then ten the following season when we had struggled. But at no point did I really feel as if I was a member of the first-team squad. It's very difficult to feel part of something when you're a bit player. I think you only feel involved a group when you're there permanently and playing week in, week out.

Everything was to change for me in the 1970/71 season. I was nineteen years old and my days on the periphery of the first team were at an end. Only a year earlier Cullis had spent a lot of money bringing in Tony Hateley from Coventry, but when the new season opened at home to Queens Park Rangers on 15 August, he was nowhere to be seen. Instead, wearing the number nine shirt was me.

I knew I had to repay Freddie's faith. He had spent a lot of time working on me and now he was giving me this big chance. Whether he couldn't offload Tony or whether he couldn't buy another centre-forward I'm not sure, but I was his choice to lead the Birmingham line. I like to think I repaid that faith and, although a goal was elusive that summer afternoon, we won 2-1 with goals from Phil Summerill and Geoff Vowden. A week later we travelled to Carlisle and I scored a brace; they were the first two goals in an eventual tally for the season of thirteen.

My own establishment into the first team would be eclipsed by the emergence of Trevor Francis as a regular as a 16-year-old. When Trevor was first introduced into the team, his impact was huge and he scored a lot of goals very quickly, including four in a league win over Bolton Wanderers in February 1971. Suddenly there was a national focus on Birmingham City because of this wonder kid, the very future – some said, but we all knew – of the England team. Our profile certainly went up. I would think anybody who was due to play Birmingham City was suddenly very much aware of who they were playing against. Trevor's presence lifted the club, media-wise, to a new level. There was now a focus on us every week. His was a rare, raw talent that you had to see to believe. His 16 goals in 21 appearances outstripped my own total in what was a breakthrough season for both of us.

We finished the 1970/71 season mid-table in the Second Division. It was a time of transition as Freddie imposed his ideas and personnel on the Birmingham team. The attendances for a club in such a position were magnificent, often over 30,000, and peaking at 49,025 for a game against Cardiff in March. There was a real sense, perhaps swelled by Trevor, that Freddie was building something at St Andrew's. Certainly my fellow Brummies picked up on it. For me, I loved playing in front of my own people; knowing that you were playing in front of people you knew, maybe somebody you'd grown up with. I look back on those days with such pride: I was achieving something within my own city that a lot of other people could only dream of.

Trevor was the star and could have played for any club, anywhere, even at that age. But his progress and mine were helped by a backbone of rock-solid players, whose experience and hard work allowed us to flourish.

At the back we had Roger Hynd, probably one of the toughest, strongest centre-halves you're ever likely to run up against. He was just so solid. In training, and when I later played against him, he was one of those rare players that you could not out-muscle or out-fight, because he was so physically hard. He was built like the proverbial brick shithouse and although he had his limitations as a footballer, in terms of what he could do – stopping opponents – he did very well. Partnering him was Garry Pendrey, who was just a couple of years older than me, but had been in first team for longer and had established himself as a regular during the 1969/70 season. Garry was a very dependable centre back and an intelligent lad. There was nothing really fancy about him, he was just a good, solid pro who knew his job, got on with it, and really made the most of the talent he had. Similarly, his fellow defender Malcolm Page was someone you knew inherently was going to give the same performance week in, week out. Reliability was the hallmark of these sort of players.

In midfield was our captain, the Yorkshire-born Welsh international, Trevor Hockey. In an era when capacity for hard work and the ability to get stuck in became important qualities, a combative player like Trevor was well suited to the game. He picked up suspensions and fines and was targeted by opposition fans, but seemed to revel in his notoriety. Off the pitch, he had a rare celebrity for the time and his own fan club, which supposedly had more than a thousand members. He played the guitar and was said to own a bright pink piano. He even produced a single, 'Happy Cos I'm Blue'. He was known by some as 'The Beatle of Brum', but in the dressing room he had a reputation – perhaps unfairly – as a loner and a bit of an oddball. He left for Sheffield United halfway through the 1970/71 season.

Birmingham, through my time there, tended to be better attacking than they were at defending and, even discounting Trevor Francis, we had gifted forwards and attacking midfielders throughout my time at St Andrew's. Johnny Vincent was a great talent with a fearsome shot and formidable scoring record from his position in midfield, but one of those players who probably couldn't sustain his talent for long enough. He had all the ability in the world; he could be, and often was, terrific. Phil Summerill was a talented winger-cum-inside-forward, who often partnered me in the forward line in my first seasons at the club. There was a general solidity and reliability about him that was mirrored in many of our teammates. Geoff Vowden, who signed from Nottingham Forest, was another in that mould. In today's game these sort of players would be considered really good footballers, but back then they were just viewed as good solid pros, who gave a performance week in, week out.

Aside from Trevor, the players I felt really pushed Birmingham on and, in the process, advanced my own career, emerged during the 1971/72 campaign. Gordon Taylor had been signed from Bolton Wanderers the previous season, but injuries kept him out of the team and it was only from August 1971 that St Andrew's saw him as a regular. He was the first really good winger I played with. He could deliver a cross, had good speed and all-round ability. There was a natural intelligence to him on and off the field, which you still see now in his capacity as head of the Professional Footballers' Association, the PFA. He used to moan a bit, but even as a nineteen-year-old you took no notice of him!

The other player of note was Bob Hatton, who Freddie signed for a club record £80,000 fee from Carlisle United in October 1971. Bob had had a bit of a nomadic career until then and Birmingham was his fifth club in a little over four years, but it was as if he found his place at St Andrew's. He was a terrific player and a great foil for me: hard-working, energetic and technically accomplished. I would have loved, later in my career, for Billy Bingham or Gordon Lee to have signed him as my partner at Everton. If you leave Trevor aside, he's probably the next best forward I played with.

*

BY CHRISTMAS 1971 BIRMINGHAM WERE UNBEATEN AT HOME BUT had drawn a lot of games. Yet there was solidity and balance to our team, which, combined with the unpredictable and effervescent Trevor, gave us all real optimism as a group of players. We lost against Bristol City on New Year's Day, but after that would remain unbeaten until the end of the season.

Our main rivals for the Second Division title were Norwich City and Millwall. We played Norwich at St Andrew's on 4 March. I was in a good run of form, having scored seven in my previous seven league and cup appearances. We'd previously drawn 2–2 at Carrow Road in November, when I also scored in a hard-fought game. This time we emphatically showed our credentials as a top-flight team in waiting, winning 4–0.

Five unbeaten weeks later we faced Millwall at St Andrew's; 43,483 people filled the old stadium. On a tense, tight afternoon I scored the only goal of the game to put us within touching distance of the summit. At full time the ground was engulfed in a crescendo of noise. Birmingham's fans knew we were destined for the top flight.

We still, however, had to edge over that line and our failure to convert draws into wins in the first half of the season ultimately proved costly. Norwich had too much momentum from that period and were guaranteed the title. It left one promotion place remaining when we travelled to Orient on Tuesday 2 May. Millwall had completed their fixtures and had 55 points. We were third, on 54 points, but with a superior goal average. A win or a draw would see us promoted – lose and Millwall were up.

It was a crazy night. Fifteen thousand Blues fans had made the journey to East London and more than 33,000 people – not far off its record attendance – crammed inside Orient's tiny stadium, Brisbane Road. Hundreds of Millwall fans poured into the ground too, trying to disrupt the game and cause trouble. It was a tense, raucous atmosphere and although Orient – who had nothing to play for – rarely threatened and a draw would have been enough for promotion, you could never be sure how these games would play out. In the 57th minute my moment arrived when I met Gordon Taylor's corner with my head and planted it into the net for the only goal of the game.

The remaining half-hour was played out to a cacophony of cheers from our fans and insults and vitriol from Millwall's. At the final whistle we raced to the dressing room as thousands of Blues filled the pitch in celebration. It was a scene of madness: elation from the players and our fans and something more sinister from those Millwall supporters who weren't quite so willing to accept another year in the Second Division. As chaos unfolded between rival fans – quite what Orient's supporters did during this game is unclear – crates of beer and champagne were opened in the dressing room as we toasted our victory.

Breaking through the disorder came the urgent voice of the Tannoy announcer. 'For God's sake, clear the main stand. Get out now. This is urgent.'

There was a bomb threat – a hoax, it turned out, probably originating from a Millwall supporter. But on a powder-keg night, the explosions had already happened. There were champagne corks flying from the moment we got back to the sanctity of the dressing room, through fighting and bomb threats, all the way to our arrival back in Birmingham. It was a blur then and, more than forty years on, remains a blur now.

*

I'D ENDED THE 1971/72 SEASON WITH 23 LEAGUE GOALS AND PLAYED virtually every minute of every game. Between Trevor, Bob Hatton and myself we scored fifty league goals. I was more or less the figurehead of the attack. Bobby used to operate either side of me; he would say he did all my running, which was probably true. We had Gordon Taylor on the left and Trevor just floated, either out wide right or inside.

Our partnership worked naturally. Freddie did not have to work very hard at improving our appreciation of one another. At times there was a sense that the attack was taken care of and we just had to make sure our defence was firm. We were never overly secure defensively, that was our big problem, which was ironic because Freddie was a defender when he was a player.

Because we had such a strong influence going forward, there were times when we were unstoppable, particularly at home. St Andrew's became a fortress. A player I've not previously mentioned is the Scottish midfielder Alan Campbell, who loved getting forward, driving on with or without the ball. Because we had so many players like that, who naturally could get forward, it created a momentum that allowed us to overpower teams at home.

St Andrew's traditionally, certainly from mid-October onwards, would be like a ploughed field through the middle; it was just a bog. It was not much better than Derby County's notorious Baseball Ground. We had to play on it every couple of weeks. Those were the standards of the pitches in the 1970s. Of course, you would rather play on a pitch without too much mud on it, but many teams played in conditions like that. There were very few pitches that didn't turn into a bog at some stage of the season that I can recall. But certainly St Andrew's was boggier than most, and while we got used to it, it was a hindrance to visiting teams and something that worked to our advantage.

During the 1971/72 season we were blessed with home draws in the FA Cup in four straight matches. Starting with a third-round tie against Port Vale, which we won 3–0, we went on to face First Division opposition in Bobby Robson's Ipswich in the fourth round. One goal separated us and it came from me.

By the time we faced Portsmouth on 26 February there was huge momentum behind us. We were flying in the league and had put six goals past Pompey only six weeks earlier, when we'd played them in the league. I'd scored two that day and would add another brace in a 3–1 cup win.

That set up a quarter-final tie with Huddersfield Town, then enjoying a rare foray in the top flight. A crowd of 52,470 crammed into St Andrew's, the Blues' biggest attendance in thirteen years, going back to a time when I'd have watched on from the terraces with my father and brothers. By then Dave and I were lining up in the same starting XI. Although two of my brothers were goalkeepers, I never felt any obligation to be nice to keepers I came up against – including the two of them, when I faced them as an opponent – and the first thing I did that game was whack the Huddersfield keeper, David Lawson (who would later be a teammate at Goodison). The first cross came in and I hit him, just to make my mark. It was a psychological tactic more than anything else, but it worked. I felt it gave me the upper hand and the result bore that out. We won 3–1 and I scored along with Malcolm Page and Bob Hatton.

We could have gone all the way that year, except we played the wrong team in the semi-final. We drew the one team that we did not want, Leeds United. Stoke and Arsenal, who played in the other semi-final, we could have dealt with. But Don Revie's Leeds were a different proposition. Psychologically we felt that too. There was a sense that whatever we did, we'd never be good enough to beat them. For one of the few times in my career the game had been lost before we played it. When we met at Hillsborough it was like men against boys. I don't think we saw the ball, they were that good. They were a cut above everybody else, and they just strolled around, while we ran around like headless chickens trying to get the possession off them. The majority of the time we were nowhere near. They won 3–0, but it could – and should – have been much more.

There is a brief epilogue to that FA Cup run. During the early 1970s the FA experimented with a third-place playoff in the FA Cup. It was a short-lived and ill-conceived plan and barely 5,000 people had watched the previous year's match between Everton and Stoke. Our venture into this obscure corner of football history was slightly better attended – a respectable crowd of 25,841 came to St Andrew's to see us take on Stoke on the eve of the 1972/73 season. They were rewarded with no goals, but the first penalty shootout in the competition's history. Birmingham won 4–3 and I was given my first piece of silverware as a professional footballer, one that was very much in keeping with the era: a silver tankard.

THERE WAS, OF COURSE, EXCITEMENT AT ENTERING THE FIRST Division for the first time, but the gulf between the top flight in business terms wasn't anything near the same magnitude that it is today. Now a place in the Premier League is worth a guaranteed £130 million in prize money, TV revenues and parachute payments. Then it was just a step up the sporting ladder, on to a better level, a new challenge. As Birmingham players we got a new bonus structure for being in the First Division, but I don't remember a new contract with more money. Bonuses were better, and obviously the end of season tour was an incentive as well. That was it; we were told to get on with it.

Life, initially, was difficult in the top flight, even though I think the gap between divisions was probably narrower than it is now. There were a lot of good-quality sides even then still below us and the quality in depth of all the sides was that much closer. Yet we found converting draws into wins particularly hard and encountered separate two- and three-month winless streaks.

My younger brother Peter had by then graduated to the West Bromwich Albion first team. There have been a few football dynasties over the years and several during my playing time. There were the five Clarke brothers (Frank, Allan, Derek, Kelvin and Wayne), the four Wilkins brothers (Ray, Dean, Stephen and Graham) and, in the 1980s, the Wallaces (Danny, Ray and Rod). Aside from the Wallaces, who played on the same team, very rarely would more than a couple of brothers be called into action in the same match. Yet although Birmingham met West Brom twice that season, and I played in both games, David was not in the Birmingham team for the first match and Peter had lost his place in the Baggies' side by the time of the second game, when of course David was playing alongside me. Fate worked against us and the only time I played with both my brothers was a testimonial later in the decade.

Whenever we came up against each other as players we were all very conscious of the fact that a game was coming up. It was talked about within the family and a few comments were passed about what I was going to do – or not do – to Peter. Dave, of course, joined in the winding-up. There was nothing malicious, it was simply to get him going. And when we actually played the game, one of the first things I did was to clatter Peter. How did he react to that? Professionally, of course.

Like all brothers we used to have one or two scraps when we were younger, playing football among ourselves. It was just a normal thing to do to clatter them. I always gave David a bump or a shove in later years … but I had to – I couldn't be seen not clattering my brothers while I clattered everybody else. I suppose I had to give it that little bit more against those two because they were family. Did they clatter me back? I think they were more concerned where the ball was, because if the goalkeeper doesn't keep his eye on the ball, it is lost. Goalkeepers always talk about bravery, but to me bravery is being stupid. It means putting yourself at risk. Goalkeepers have got to be brave and stupid to succeed and my brothers were both very brave and very stupid.

Over the years I'd have a pretty good scoring record against the two of them – David in particular – and that late-August afternoon I opened my account against my family by scoring in a 2–2 draw. Naturally I gave Peter plenty of stick about that, and when we get together I still remind him of the goals I scored against him, as I do David. It was always (and still is) a brotherly thing; but it was always good-natured and never boiled over, ever.

Despite Birmingham's transition into the top flight having a few challenges on the way, there was never any real threat of relegation. We won eight of the last ten games that season but I think we just got it together, rather than it being a great escape. The team started to perform better, and we put the sort of results together that we were capable of. We got caught out at times in the first part of the season and we didn't really learn until the second part how to cope against better opponents. I think Freddie sorted things out in his own mind of how we wanted to play and who he could play to get the right results. I think it was a learning curve for everybody. I think we adapted in the end, adjusted our game and got out of trouble.

In the end we finished the campaign tenth, above clubs like Manchester City, Chelsea, Manchester United and Everton. If that happened today to a club like Birmingham City it would be celebrated almost like winning a trophy.

For me it was a season of personal success. I'd played every minute in every game and scored nineteen league goals, the fourth highest tally in the league. At the time I didn't recognise the achievement. I was just pleased with the number of goals I'd scored in the First Division. But, like for a lot of footballers, it was always a question of what to do next and could I do better? Bettering an achievement was what really drove me throughout my career.

The one frustration I did have at Birmingham was being overlooked for the England team. Looking back, I reckon I was in the best shape of my career both there and – although this will surprise some people – at Swansea at the end. Physically I felt unstoppable in these periods. I was playing for England under-23s around this time but felt that Sir Alf Ramsey should have selected me for the full squad. Mick Channon was there, Allan Clarke was there, and so was big Martin Chivers. But I was scoring as many goals as, if not more than, most of them.

Alf was a conservative character and I can understand him being afraid of selecting fresh blood because he had a lot of seasoned pros from England's glory days still around. But later, in October 1973, when I witnessed the now notorious World Cup qualifier against Poland that saw the end of his managerial career while sat at home watching the game on the television, I could imagine myself on that bench being called on late by Alf and saving the day for my country. Instead, I was in my lounge, and could only watch as he brought Derby County's Kevin Hector on too late to make an impression. My frustration was probably shared by every centre-forward in the country; my disappointment by every Englishman.

*

AT BIRMINGHAM, AS WITH ALL DRESSING ROOMS I WAS PART OF, I wouldn't say I had close personal friends. This wasn't through any sense of diffidence, or because I was a loner; in fact wherever I was I got on with just about everybody. I would take everybody as I found them and as a rule, when you do that, people will do the same to you.

The 1970s and 80s were an era where players garnered reputations as great socialisers. It was before sports science took hold and footballers started adopting the ascetic lifestyles we know many of them to have today, but a time when play-ers – for the first time – were relatively well paid and had lots of spare time. I was never part of the notorious all-day boozing sessions many consider synonymous with the era. If we'd been on an away trip and got back, then a gang of us may have gone out for a drink or to a club or something after the game.

Because of my size as a teenager, I'd been able to go to pubs since the age of 14 and have no problem getting served. I suppose like most people I went through different stages of drinking. After starting out as a fourteen-year-old drinking gin and tonic, it was on to Bacardi and Coke and later pints of beer and lager. I developed a taste for wine too, but that was later. I had a bad experience with red wine while a teenager at Birmingham, which put me off for years. We'd been invited to the opening of an Italian restaurant and all sorts of people were there, like Jeff Lynne from the Electric Light Orchestra. Later we went to a nightclub where Dave Allen, the Irish comedian, was performing and I could hardly see him through the haze of red wine. The wine had gone straight to my head, my eyes went and my mind closed under a fug of booze. I was spotted at the end of the night swigging straight from this infernal two-litre flagon of Chianti and I woke with the hangover from hell. But that was rare; it wasn't like that all the time. For me, big drinking sessions were never a regular thing.

Most often, I was at home with my family. I settled down very early with Pat, a schoolteacher, and by the time I was twenty I was father to two great kids, Izzy and Richard. Ostensibly I had the glamorous life of a footballer, but the reality was more prosaic: I was living a fairly quiet, suburban life, devoting a lot of time and energy to being a father.

We lived in a Victorian semi-detached house in Kings Heath, south of Birmingham, before moving to Knowle, a little village outside Solihull, where we bought a newish house on an estate. I think we paid about £14,000 for it, which back then was a lot of money. We splashed out a bit and it was a nice four-bedroomed house, but by the standards of today's footballer mansion-pads it was humble.

I still had my pretty basic car, the white Ford Popular. I've driven two Fords in my life and had accidents with both of them, so my mantra is: 'Never buy a Ford!' I had to change the Popular after smashing it up while reversing out of a pub car park: my brother David was reversing out at the same time and we smashed into each other. Maybe my belief about Fords should be: 'Never drive a Ford after going out for your Christmas lunch!'

As footballers the regular socialising came either at the end of the season or pre-season when you had some downtime and you'd go out together and have a drink. Freddie Goodwin loved a trip. In 1973 we went to America first, played in Baltimore, New York and Toronto, stayed in LA for 48 hours, then we went over to Tahiti, then Australia. We even spent 24 hours in New Zealand because of an air-crew strike. We basically circumnavigated the entire planet. It was a hell of a trip.

These were bonding trips as much as anything else. The beer would be flowing from the minute we took off until the minute we landed. We'd be into everything. It was downtime, a big thank you for a good season. We played a bit of football, but I don't remember doing much training beforehand. The games went well, though; we won them all. It was really one of the best trips I've ever been on.

*

HAVING ENDED THE 1972/73 SEASON SO STRONGLY, WE BEGAN THE following campaign with something of a hangover. From the opening ten league games we took just three points, failing to win any of those matches. Dave fell out of favour with the manager and the Leeds goalkeeper, Gary Sprake, was brought in and replaced him almost immediately.

It was an injury to Sprake that proved a turning point in our season. In the eleventh league game of the campaign we faced Wolves at St Andrew's when Gary broke his little finger. These were the days of a single substitute and on the bench that particular day was Roger Hynd. Big Roger was a formidable defender, but he was no goalkeeper. I, on the other hand, had represented Warwickshire Schoolboys in that position. So I inherited the green jersey and donned a pair of gloves with those ping-pong-bat style grips. It was the first time I'd been in goal for eight or nine years at any level, but I did everything you could expect from a keeper and did not concede a goal. Now, many years later, I can still recall the moment I tipped a Derek Dougan header over the crossbar. We won the game 2–1.

For all the flippancy about goalkeepers being daft, I can see the qualities you need to succeed in that position. You do have to be a certain type of person to be able to perform week in, week out between the sticks. There's the bravery/ stupidity quota, of course. You also have to have a bloody thick skin because any mistake and you're going to get slaughtered; you are the last line of defence. I can appreciate the quality of goalkeepers like Peter Shilton and Neville Southall who performed at such a level consistently for years. I spent fifty-odd minutes and that was enough for me; that gave me a reminder of what it was like.

Although there was no upswing in form for the team after beating Wolves, I kept on scoring even as we struggled. Freddie needed to change something around and bring in new players and there was a sense that I was the most likely to be sold to fund the new acquisitions. For me, I don't think I had itchy feet, but I recognised that as I was about to turn 23 I needed to move on to progress my career and enhance my chances of playing for England.

As autumn turned to winter I think it became obvious – yet without anything being said either by me or anybody else – that Freddie was approaching a position where he needed to make some big decisions. At the same time I was reaching a point where I felt I wasn't going to get much further with Birmingham. I never expressed those views in so many words to Freddie, and he never expressed any views to me either. It was just something that evolved over a period of time, and it came to that junction where he was forced to do something to alter his team and he knew in his heart that I was ready to move and I knew too. It was like a coming-together of these unspoken assumptions.

And then, one February morning, the call came.

4

EVERTON

'If you don't change direction, you may end up where you are heading.'
Lao Tzu

IT'S HARD TO DEFINE THE FEELING OF WANTING TO LEAVE THE PLACE where you've grown up and been part of for as long as you can remember.

Birmingham City was a good club, my home-town club. I'm a Birmingham boy born and bred, and had stood on the St Andrew's terraces with my father and my brothers, one of whom now played alongside me. In a way the football club was like an extension of my family. But, like growing up in a family, you get to a certain point where you know you're going to have to leave and go your own way. You can't stay around them forever. I think I got to that stage with Birmingham by the time I was 23. I'd outgrown the club; I needed to go somewhere else.

The transfer to Everton happened very suddenly, almost out of the blue. There had been a little bit of newspaper talk about my future, with one report linking me to Derby County and Liverpool, but I never paid any attention to the press. I'd learned the lesson from an early age not to read newspapers. Most of it was bullshit – either overly negative or too positive – and I knew for my own sake I had to treat both with equal contempt.

It was February 1974 and Britain was in a state of crisis. Civil unrest in Northern Ireland had spread to the mainland and the Provisional IRA were engaged in an increasingly deadly bombing campaign (later that year they'd hit Birmingham with their deadliest attack yet). The country was also riven by industrial disputes. Miners were striking and, in an effort to conserve energy, the government placed severe restrictions on the usage of electricity, particularly for commercial users. One of the consequences of this was a three-day working week, which had enormous repercussions, not just for football, but the whole country.

This was the backdrop to an unexpected phone call from Freddie Goodwin early one morning. 'Everton are interested in talking with you,' he announced. 'I'm coming to collect you.' Within a few hours he had collected me and we travelled up the M6, where we met the delegation from Everton at a hotel midway between Liverpool and Birmingham.

Only when we were in the car did Freddie explain the deal. It was going to be complicated as it involved the exchange of two other players: Howard Kendall, Everton's talismanic midfielder and captain, and the young defender Archie Styles. Howard was valued at £180,000, Archie £90,000, while £80,000 cash was making up the difference. Only later, when we sat down to negotiate the finer points of the transfer, was I told that it was a British record deal. It fulfilled Freddie's desire to bring in defensive reinforcements that would assist Birmingham's attempts to remain in the First Division.

I'm as surprised now as I was then that Birmingham got Howard. Archie was Archie – he was another body, another player – but Howard was a big capture. He was the Everton captain, part of the acclaimed 'Holy Trinity' midfield that had brought Everton the 1970 League Championship, and many considered him the finest English player never to have been capped by his country. Birmingham's problems were defensive and they were always leaking goals. While Howard may not have offered ready answers to those issues he had leadership and experience and was a terrific player. I'm sure Freddie saw him as someone to knit a side around.

Considering it was a record transfer, everything was very low key. I wish I could regale you with stories of subterfuge, grandstanding, aggressive negotiating, media blitzes, super-agents and months of speculation, but there was none of that. I went in and talked to the Everton boss Billy Bingham and the club's secretary, Chris Hassell. Billy said that they had had me watched six times, which seemed a lot back then and made me think they'd put in the hours. By the standards of today's meticulous video and data analysis it's probably nothing at all.

There was no agent, no lawyer, no intermediary. It was basic stuff and didn't take that long for me to agree to move. Everton had a reputation for doing background checks on players, to make sure they weren't signing party animals or players that led excessive lives, but as far as I know that never happened with me. I didn't even get a pay rise and my basic weekly wage stayed at £200 (around three times the national average salary). The win bonuses were decent – up to £150 and you got £50 for a draw – but it was also an era when the highest rate of taxation was 83 per cent. The only difference from Birmingham was the addition of a pension. I tried to negotiate on my basic salary, but Billy wouldn't budge. I admit I was naive, totally and utterly naive, but I wanted the move. Everton were a big club and I grabbed at it.

The main thing I remember was that it was the first time I ever met Howard Kendall off the pitch. I recall passing him as I went into one room and he went into another; we nodded at each other and smiled. When I came out, Howard was on his way back from his talks with Freddie.

'Everything OK?' I asked.

'Yeah, and you?'

'Yeah, thanks.'

And that was it. A brief, inconsequential, perfunctory chat marked the end of my association with my boyhood club and Howard's with an institution with which he was synonymous. We never got the chance to play together, nor did I play under him when he turned to management, but our paths would cross many times in the years afterwards.

When I got back home that evening, I told Pat I'd done the deal and we were going to be moving up to Merseyside. To her it was presented as a *fait accompli*. That was simply the lot of the footballer's wife in the 1970s.

To me, I suppose it was too. If I'd have said no to the move I'm not quite sure what Freddie would have done. I suppose looking back he might have tried to offer me some cash. Maybe I should have said no! But such a thought never occurred to me, because the time seemed right to leave St Andrew's. I was at a point where I wanted to move so it never occurred to me to reject it. Everton were a bigger club and it was an opportunity.

That evening Pat and I sat up talking late into the night. I had just turned 23 and it would be my first time living away from my home city. Moving at any time creates a lot of upheaval, but more so mid-season. There were the logistics of the move, finding a place to live, a new school for Izzy and so on. It must have been eleven o'clock that night when there was a knock at the door.

I went to the door and my teammate Roger Hynd was standing there. Big Roger was a huge, hard-as-nails centre-half, with a broad Scottish accent. He was also the nephew of one of the most prominent men in football at the time, Liverpool manager Bill Shankly.

'Have you signed? Have you signed?' he growled. 'Shanks wants you; Shanks wants you.'

I told him it was too late, that I'd already signed for Everton and done the deal. Seven years earlier Billy Bingham's predecessor, Harry Catterick, had foiled Shankly in his pursuit (ironically) of Howard Kendall, by moving quickly and discreetly to seal the deal. Now, history had repeated itself.

After a few more words we were wishing each other best wishes for the future and shaking hands.

'Who was that?' Pat asked when I went back inside the house.

I told her that Roger had come to sound me out about a move to Liverpool on behalf of his uncle.

'How do you feel about that?' she asked.

'I don't feel anything,' I told her. 'I made my decision to go to Everton, and it's the right decision.'

I think what I said to Pat that night in our old home in the village of Knowle near Solihull is as true now as it was forty-odd years ago. I've never been one to dwell on hypotheticals. Whatever might have been going on in life, I could only make a decision on the facts available at the time.

Of course, I'm aware that things might have transpired differently had I joined Liverpool. I could have partnered Kevin Keegan at club level, I might have enjoyed a multitude of domestic and European success at Anfield, my England career might have extended beyond a dozen appearances. But it's ultimately meaningless to dwell. Anyone that comes and says you could have done this or done that, it doesn't mean anything to me. I made an honest decision to commit myself to Everton. I'm very thankful for that, to have played for such a great club; and I enjoyed every single minute of playing for them. It's totally irrelevant that Roger Hynd happened to turn up at eleven o'clock on the night I joined them asking, 'Have you signed?' because Shanks wanted me. To be honest, if Bill Shankly had wanted me that badly, he should have come in earlier.

Looking back at the transfer, there was a slight sense of destiny about it. Not long before Everton came in for me, Pat had been to visit a clairvoyant in a little village near Solihull. She had been bullied into it by a friend and was really very reluctant and sceptical. 'I feel as if I'm going to the dentist,' she complained beforehand.

Anyway, very reluctantly, she went to this old lady's house where she was given a watch to hold. The clairvoyant started talking about all sorts. One of the things she said to Pat – which stood out – was that she saw 'water and woods' in her life. This meant nothing to her at the time, but at the end, she walked Pat to the door and the lady said to her, 'Well, my love, it's not as bad as going to the dentist after all, is it?' Pat was absolutely gobsmacked. Soon afterwards, we moved to Merseyside and made our home in Formby, with the Pinewoods in between our home and the Irish Sea.

*

LEAVING A CLUB WITH WHICH I HAD SUCH CLOSE BONDS WAS never going to be easy. I was not only leaving behind teammates, but my own brother. Being a professional player, David was not surprised; he knew how I felt and my desire for change. Generally footballers are not surprised when other players come and go because it happens so often throughout your career.

While we sorted out a house on Merseyside, Pat and the children stayed in Birmingham. I stayed in a hotel in Liverpool (and then Southport) for a few nights a week and travelled up and down to see the family when I could. The journey on the M6 wasn't any better than it is today. Because of fuel restrictions you could only drive fifty miles per hour on the motorways so it wasn't an ideal time to be an inter-city commuter. It wasn't a great situation and once training was over it was, frankly, quite boring without my family there. For those few months as the 1973/74 season reached its conclusion, I essentially saw Bellefield, my hotel room and the motorway.

It wasn't a glamorous life, but then football rarely was. You travel a lot, you see lots of hotels and transit points, but very little of the towns and countries that you visit. If I'm honest, the only glamorous thing about being a professional footballer is actually playing the game. The rest of it is very mundane, and hard work, because you've got to keep yourself at a certain level of fitness. I suppose it's the same for rock stars, or film stars; most of their work is probably very dull. Have you ever been on a film set? They just repeat everything and go through the same scene again and again until they get it right. The glamour bit comes after, when they're doing a show, or on the red carpet, or on celluloid when the picture's finished and it's been released. But everything else around the life is probably tedious and businesslike. Football is just like that. It's a huge privilege to pull on the shirt of your club or country, but it can be boring too.

Aside from the set-routine of my day-to-day life, how did it feel to be the most expensive player in Britain? It was a little bit terrifying when it finally dawned upon me.

At Birmingham I'd never ever thought about how valuable I was to the club or would be to anybody else. Even as I signed the transfer papers, the realisation that I'd cost my new club £350,000 never struck home. That was later, when I met up with my new teammates ahead of my debut against West Ham. Then it suddenly dawned on me: 'Oh, bloody hell, I'm a British record transfer, and they're going to be expecting…'

It is daunting. It can be a burden; I can imagine how heavy it would be if a player doesn't start to perform as people expect. There's enough case histories of players who have gone for large sums of money and not produced the goods. I don't know how some of these players cope now, like Cristiano Ronaldo or Gareth Bale, who have cost £80 million. But they perform. Ronaldo certainly does. And that's what you have to do. Once I scored my first goal in the blue of Everton, it was just like riding a bicycle. You get on it and you start riding it and you start performing, and all thoughts of any pressure that I felt about the fee or the size of it dissipated.

As well as all the pressure that came with the price tag, I had to contend with the fact that my arrival precipitated Howard's departure. Howard really was one of Everton's key players. With Alan Ball and Colin Harvey he had formed the centrepiece of Everton's 1970 League Championship-winning side. Even today Evertonians speak of that 'Holy Trinity' in hushed, slightly awed tones. A large section of Evertonians were upset and not happy at all with the fact he'd left. It only added to the pressure until I scored. Until that first goal hit the net I felt it was something hanging over me, waiting to be used against me.

My Everton debut came against West Ham at Upton Park on 16 February 1974. It was a strange sort of match, very up and down, and we ended up losing 4–3. George Telfer scored twice as did Colin Harvey. I don't remember much about the game, other than I didn't score and we lost.

The following week we played Coventry City at Goodison and that's when the pressure started to take hold. I had the weight of my price tag hanging over me, but I also hadn't had a lot of time to develop much of an understanding with the other players; I felt a bit like a spare part at times. Everton won 1–0, with John Hurst scoring, but I wasn't over-comfortable throughout the match.

Because of Howard's departure, I'm not sure if the excitement of having a British transfer record-breaking centre-forward was as potent for Evertonians as it might have been had it happened in a different way at a different time. The 1973/74 season was petering out for the club in a disappointing way. Everton were fifth in the First Division and, although still in contention for a UEFA Cup place, far off the title battle being played out between Leeds and Liverpool. They had been knocked out of the FA Cup in the fourth round too.

We travelled to Leicester at the start of March. I'd been an Everton player for little over a fortnight, but there was a mounting unease within me because I was without that precious goal to my name. I thought I had one in the first half when I headed past Peter Shilton, but Roger Kenyon was penalised for being offside.

We fell behind to goals by Steve Earle and Frank Worthington and were drifting towards a defeat. Then, in the 72nd minute, Colin Harvey tried his luck with a shot from outside the area. The ball ricocheted to Mick Lyons, who passed to me. I held off a defender, found space and curled a shot past Shilton. All that pressure, all that anxiety dissipated in that moment. Although we lost the match, I started riding that bike as calmly and as smoothly as I'd ever done.

A week later Birmingham City, now captained by Howard, came to Goodison. David was in goal, but there was no sentiment shown whatsoever. Roger Hynd gave me a kick early on and together with my new teammates we went to war. We won 4–1; I scored twice. I still remember the second one – I was put through in the inside-right channel, past Big Roger, and knocked it under David. I had arrived as an Everton player.

MY NEW MANAGER BILLY BINGHAM WAS AN INTELLIGENT MAN. HE was shrewd. Charming. Irish charming, was Billy. I probably didn't over-think about Billy at the time. It was just the fact that I was joining Everton Football Club; that was the main thing. But Billy was charming in that Irish way of his.

Born in the midst of the great depression, Billy had been raised in the shadow of Belfast's great shipyards, where he served as an apprentice in a manufacturing shop. As a footballer – having turned professional with Glentoran aged seventeen – he made his name with Sunderland as a goalscoring winger, and played for Northern Ireland at the 1958 World Cup finals in Sweden. He joined Everton, then managed by Johnny Carey, in 1960 and as a veteran was part of Harry Catterick's team that lifted the League Championship three years later. He turned to management with Southport in the mid-1960s and there were spells in charge of the Northern Ireland and Greece national teams. In 1973, after negotiations with front-runner Don Revie broke down, Bingham was the Everton board's surprise choice to succeed Catterick as manager.

Yet for all that easy charisma, he was also a disciplinarian and could be distant and stand-offish. When I scored my first goal for Everton at Leicester and I turned and celebrated, I looked at Billy as I went towards the dugout, but he showed no reaction whatsoever. I just felt that was a little odd. I always look at managers and their reaction to people who score goals for them; I think it can tell you a lot about a club and the mood there. Freddie and, later, Gordon Lee were very excitable. Billy, on the other hand, seemed more in control of his emotions.

It was almost as if feelings didn't come into it for him, and yet football is an emotional sport.

Billy also liked things done in a certain way. He tried to instil a certain structure and discipline with the players and kept us on a very tight, short leash. With players it's very difficult if you restrict them. Off the field it can build up resentment. You have to find that balance where there's discipline but you have to give players a little bit of leeway. And I don't think Billy quite got that balance right.

Billy's coaching team were second to him. It included Stewart Imlach, Eric Harrison and Ray Henderson, but he was the main man. I would say they did what he wanted; I would imagine they said, 'Yes, Billy, no, Billy'. That was the set-up. He ruled the roost.

But in those first days at Goodison, his desire and expectation pushed me on and made me a better player. He probably wanted a lot more out of me, in terms of what and where I should be at any given time, with or without the ball. So he was expecting a lot more from me. He was structured in his attitude, in the way he presented things and wanted things done. He was less flexible than Freddie, more rigid in terms of his tactics and what he expected out of players.

Everton were presided over by John Moores, the Littlewoods Pools magnate, a self-made millionaire and giant of the city of Liverpool. Physically he was small, but this belied his power. He was a little, powerful man; extremely powerful. He made you aware of the club, of what was expected as an Everton player. Very early on – it could have been my first home game – I met him. He told me what he expected and what the club was all about. Then he went off on a tangent, like a Victorian patriarch. 'You have to live within your means, Bob,' he said and started on about money, about not overspending and living frugally. I couldn't help but wonder what he was on about. But then, who was I to question? He was one of the wealthiest men in Britain and entirely self-made.

Our training base was Bellefield and it was certainly a big step up from what I was used to at Birmingham. I always thought Birmingham was OK; it was out by the airport and a nice little complex. But Bellefield was a big progression. The Brazilian national team realised this and trained there during the 1966 World Cup. It had an indoor gym, we got a meal at lunchtime and again after training if it went on into the afternoon. When you're not used to those things you just get changed and go home, or go to the pub and have something to eat. Bellefield was different and certainly a good complex by the standards of the 1970s.

Despite coming in with such a hefty price tag there was no hostility or lingering suspicion from my new teammates. It was a nice set-up at Everton, maybe some would say too nice. There were not the same rivalries and animosities witnessed in dressing rooms at other clubs, such as Liverpool where Tommy Smith and Emlyn Hughes were at war with each other. I was probably helped because I never tried to come across as something I wasn't. I've always tried to be just me, which was essentially the same as most people I played with throughout my career: a working-class lad who had made good playing football.

Billy was still imposing his own vision of Everton's future upon the team. Everton had been league champions just four years earlier, but had fallen into steep decline afterwards as Bingham's predecessor, Harry Catterick, suffered from ill health. While Alan Ball and Howard Kendall were controversially sold and Brian Labone and Tommy Wright had retired, there was still a core group from that team, including Colin Harvey, John Hurst, Joe Royle and Gordon West.

Although he'd suffered from injuries, Colin was probably the best player at the club when I arrived. He was so technically gifted and one of those players who was always demanding more out of everybody. Hursty was a decent player and a very steady pro. He was someone you could rely upon; you knew what you were going to get from him every single week.

Gordon West was in a odd situation. He was still under contract and used to come in and train, but I don't think he actually played a game under Billy Bingham. This was perhaps strange, as goalkeeper was Everton's problem position throughout the Bingham and Lee eras; if we'd have had a top-class keeper I'm sure a barren decade would have been one filled with success. Gordon had a very dry sense of humour and would make some caustic comment now and again. On the two men who stood between him and the green jersey – David Lawson and Dai Davies – he was not shy in making his feelings felt. He would make coarse comments about them, which you could take either way. But that was Gordon. He was larger than life, one of those characters that have probably long died out in the game. I don't quite know what the situation was between him and Billy. If he had the potential to cause the manager problems with his outspokenness we never saw it, although it may have occurred privately.

And then there was Big Joe, who partnered me for about eight games. Evertonians love their number nines and I'm privileged enough to have worn that shirt of legends for seven years. What was nice was that for three decades there was a symmetry and overlap between the careers of some of those players that made the shirt famous: Alex Young played alongside Fred Pickering and Joe Royle, who both played alongside me (although it was at Birmingham with Fred); later I'd partner – for one game anyway – Graeme Sharp, who filled the shirt with such distinction through the 1980s.

Joe was terrific. He probably wasn't as mobile as he had once been because of his back, but we did OK together. I think, looking back, Joe is perhaps a little peeved we never played more together. I'm not sure whether he acknowledged it, but he must have known in his own mind that I was going to be the first centre-forward on the team sheet. Maybe he was hoping he could have had a longer spell with me. I think he felt capable of playing with me, but Billy ultimately decided against it.

I've always been very fortunate with the teams and players that I've played with. I think 99.9 per cent of them have been good stand-up pros. You always get on better with some than others but there was never any animosity and I never had that in a club, ever. It was always the case, whether at Everton or Swansea or, later, NAC Breda or even Lincoln, where I would spend the first two or three games just getting to know the players. I think once I started scoring goals they quickly saw the value of what I could bring.

Wherever I went I developed relationships with players. That's always an ongoing thing, because players come and go; in and out of teams. At the same time I've never developed a close friendship with any player. I don't know whether it has anything to do with what Stan Cullis said to me on the day that he signed me when I was sixteen. 'Believe me, son, you'll have no friends in football.' That always stuck with me, and because of it I retained a certain distance with whomever I played alongside. Friends, yes, but friends-*friends*, no.

Part of that aloofness, for want of a better word, was bred from being a young father and having a family to go home to. The only time we socialised as a team was probably after games, briefly in the players' lounge, and on away trips. It was the same at Birmingham and at most of the clubs I played for, apart from NAC Breda, where they used to socialise win, draw or lose.

Being famous then – even being the most expensive footballer in Britain! – never brought the sort of intrusions from the general public you'd expect today. It was a completely different world, pre-internet, pre-social media, pre-celebrity culture, pre-camera-phone. More often than not I was able to go out, for instance with Pat for dinner or out to a pub, without being bothered.

I can honestly say the only time I ever got any bother whatsoever was when we went out with a lot of players to a nightclub in Formby called Shorrock's Hill. We went there one night and got some abuse from some lads who were going out of the door. Mickey Bernard, the Everton right back, went up to them and said, 'If you fuckers don't move off I'm going to bounce you off every tree out there. So fuck off.' Mickey was not someone you messed with. But that's the only abuse I can ever remember receiving anywhere in the world.

And yet if I'm making the world of 1970s professional football sound tame that's not intentional. There was a very hard drinking culture all the way through my career. I always thought, starting out in Birmingham, it couldn't get any worse. But when I got to Everton it was even heavier. Later in my time at the club there'd be the notorious F-Mob, a drinking and partying clique that included George Wood and Andy King (though never me!) that would go out and raise hell. By the time I got down to Swansea, I couldn't believe the Welsh boys' drinking. When we went on a trip to Magaluf we drank beer on the coach to the airport, there was drinking on the plane and then it was straight out on the town. I can honestly say some boys stayed out for four days and nights on the trot. I did two, then I flaked out; but some of them remained a lot longer.

For me, unlike some others, there was never a stage where I couldn't get away with it. I was probably drinking more in my thirties than in my twenties, because I was with the Swansea boys by then. They were massive drinkers, absolutely massive drinkers, some of them; but everywhere I played that was part of the culture.

*

EVERTON FINISHED THE 1973/74 SEASON SEVENTH IN DIVISION ONE. Despite playing just thirteen games, I ended the campaign second highest scorer with seven goals. We were four points off a UEFA Cup place, but only eight from relegation, which my former Birmingham teammates evaded by a single position. Indeed just twelve points separated eighteen clubs, spanning European qualification and the drop zone.

Rather than being some sort of symbol of mediocrity I think it was emblematic of how competitive the First Division was back then. Every team had a core of six or seven or eight really good-quality players, many home grown, with a few added in from the other Home Nations. Every game was competitive because of the quality each club possessed. Although the title race was much more of an open field, to actually win that championship took some doing because of that level of competition. It was, I think, more difficult through that late 1960s, 1970s era, because every single team had quality players. There was a spread of talent.

As my Everton teammates and I went our separate ways for the summer of 1974, title hopes seemed a distant prospect. We had a decent team, but we were all conscious that this was a work in progress. I think from Billy's point of view he still wanted to reshape and remodel the team to his vision. It was very much an ongoing project. But football is nothing if not a game full of the unexpected, and we were about to surprise a few people, including ourselves.

5

CARLISLE

'Success consists of going from failure to failure without loss of enthusiasm.'

Winston Churchill

SOMETIMES A NEW SIGNING CAN SET THE TONE OF A CLUB AND ITS ambitions for the future. The new player will bring momentum, a change of direction, herald a new start. There will be a freshness to the team and renewed hope for the supporters. Rivals will look on with fear and longing.

In late August 1974 Billy Bingham followed up his British record acquisition of myself by paying a record cash fee of £300,000 for Burnley's England international midfielder Martin Dobson. It was a real statement of intent.

'The players are a club's wealth, not cash in the bank,' said Billy at the time. 'I think we have an excellent player in Dobson. He is a classy man in midfield, can score goals, is intelligent, and has an excellent character.'

Billy was completely right on all counts. Martin was a terrific boy, a very good player, highly talented. He could do so many things. If you needed somebody to calm the situation down, Dobbo was the man; he'd just keep the ball and play to his own rhythm. He was the one cog in the team that could dictate the tempo of how we all played. If he wanted to slow it down he'd slow it down, and if he wanted to quicken it up he could do that too. He was a big lad; as big as me, if not bigger, and he could get forward and score goals too.

The man I felt Billy should also have gone for was my old Birmingham team-mate, Bob Hatton. Bobby was such a very good, all-round player. He'd give you everything you wanted from a forward: he had the pace, he had the strength, he could score goals, he was intelligent in his play. Like I said before, at Birmingham, Bob claimed he did all of my running – and he probably did because he was such a workhorse, but he was a clever workhorse. He was just the sort of player who would have gone down really well at Everton with me.

The other player Everton should have broken the bank for was Peter Shilton. Between the end of Gordon West's career and the ascent of Neville Southall in the early 1980s, this was always the club's problem position. Shilts was attainable: if you look at his career path – Leicester, Stoke, Forest, Southampton, Derby – it's not as if he ever played for a truly big club. At the time there were few bigger than Everton and he would have jumped at the opportunity.

Funnily enough, Billy had told me after signing me, 'I'm going to be signing Peter Shilton; I'm going after him and will get him.'

Whether he was just telling me a story I don't know, even to this day. But for whatever reason neither Billy nor Gordon Lee ever went for him, or at least signed him. Instead, in November 1974, he joined Stoke from Leicester. Had it been Goodison rather than the Victoria Ground, what happened later on that season might have been very different.

Pre-seasons were always hard. I've never known a pre-season not to be tough. They differed from manager to manager, but in essence they were a slog. In those days players did not retain their fitness during the summer like they do now. You just tried to give your body as much of a break as possible. It was as much of a mental break as it was physical. You needed to get away from going in every day, going through the same routine; getting changed, going out, doing whatever you had to do, and playing the game either midweek or on a Saturday.

After summers spent completely relaxing, it was tough getting back to fitness. At Birmingham we went on long cross-country runs. But at Everton, under Billy at least, it was a notorious club tradition: down on the sand dunes at Southport. For a whole week we'd do nothing but run. I'm sure there were one or two that found it easier than others, but I always found it hard. You lose your footing constantly, running up and down those dunes. For a whole week you're just slip-ping and sliding. All the time you knew that Bob Paisley would be saying things to our rivals at Liverpool like, 'We train on grass where football is played.' Which is a fair point; why do you need to run on sand?'

Later, when I was under John Toshack at Swansea, we saw the ball from day one. We never ran further than 1,800 metres in pre-season, otherwise it was all ball. Everything with the ball, and short, sharp routines too. Tosh did as a manager what Liverpool did in the 1970s. So while we were slogging at Everton, doing miles and miles of running, they had the ball out from practically day one.

Quite a lot was made at the time about Billy Bingham's 'scientific training techniques', but I think that was really just a lot of spin. Billy was essentially an old-school manager, albeit that he could talk a good game. Freddie Goodwin, versed as he was in his experiences in America, was far more innovative and tried to introduce ideas from other disciplines – such as yoga and dance – into our routines, which were practically unheard-of ideas in the early 1970s. He had more lasting influence too and was a great mentor for the fledgling managerial career of Howard Kendall.

Summer 1974 was a time of change in English football. Don Revie had left Leeds United to become England manager, while Bill Shankly shocked the game by retiring as Liverpool manager at the age of just 61. Two great footballing dynasties were seemingly at an end.

When we heard about Shankly at Everton we couldn't really believe it. Why he retired when he did remains to this day a complete mystery, as 61 is no age. He could have gone on for a few more years; it was far too early for him to retire.

Shankly's house backed on to Bellefield and after being barred by Bob Paisley from Melwood, for want of anything better to do he would appear at the Everton training ground. It was ironic really, not just the fact that the former Liverpool manager was turning up to see us, but also that his 1960s Everton rival Harry Catterick had been given an 'upstairs' job at Goodison, but we never *ever* saw him.

You knew by Shankly's actions that he wasn't a happy man. He spent a lot of time with the Everton physio, Jim McGregor, and he'd be taking Liverpool to task, slagging them off. He was a bitter man. With us players he was a bit more circumspect. I suppose he opened up more with Jim because they were fellow

Scots. Occasionally he would pop in, put his head into the treatment room to say hello and exchange a few words with the players. It was just general football talk with Shanks; nothing really in-depth. He wouldn't talk out of place in front of players and Jim was always reluctant to repeat what Shanks said. But you just knew that he wasn't happy about the way his relationship with Liverpool had ended.

Martin Dobson's arrival signalled the end for Colin Harvey, who joined Sheffield Wednesday early in the 1974/75 season. A few months later Joe Royle was sold to Manchester City, despite starting the first nine games of the season as my forward partner. Under Billy, Gordon West had become an outcast within the club and never played again. It left John Hurst as the only remnant of the 1970 title-winning team, although Roger Kenyon had played a cameo role.

I think there was maybe an element of getting rid of these players a little too soon. Joe, for example, earned an England recall at Maine Road. But I think at that stage Billy wanted to clear the decks of players who were associated with the championship-winning side; he wanted his own players in there, which is understandable. A lot of managers are like that.

In my view it would have been better to have had them around for a year or two more. Although he is only twenty months older than me, Joe had an awful lot of playing experience that could have been very useful. He knew what it took to win things – and how it felt to lose them too. In a title race you can't put a price on that and, John Hurst aside, we had nobody with comparable experiences. I understand the reason why Billy got rid of them, but I think it would have been better for the squad and the team to have had that experience around for longer. I think it was short-sighted: short-sighted to sell him, but also not to replace him properly at the time.

I'M NOT QUITE SURE HOW YOU'D DESCRIBE THE START OF THE 1974/75 season. We lost just one of the first fifteen games, but won just four. 'League Championships are won as much by luck as by skill,' the *Liverpool Daily Post* wrote after one of those victories, at home to Stoke, where they outplayed us for long stretches, but we won by virtue of two Joe Royle goals.

The draws, however, were problematic. Why did we draw so many games? Was it because we weren't quite the finished article, or was it due to the competitive nature of the First Division? In my view it was definitely a bit of both. We obviously weren't the finished article, and we were certainly lacking one or two players in certain areas, as I've already discussed. It was also a very competitive league. There were probably seven or eight teams capable of challenging for the league title. We're not talking what we'd consider, by today's standards, big clubs either. Manchester United were in the Second Division, Chelsea would end up relegated and Spurs nearly went down. Instead, the top of the table was dominated by the likes of Derby, Ipswich, Stoke, Sheffield United and Middlesbrough. How many provincial clubs could you imagine challenging for the title today? It's almost inconceivable.

Billy was like a later Everton manager, David Moyes. Moyes worked to percentages and hedged his bets a little, and so it was with Billy. He was one of those who tried to work out how to get the advantage in any way that he could, and if he couldn't get the advantage he might go the other way and be negative.

The London-based press used to call us the 'clockwork orange' (a reference to our amber away kits) and 'robotic', which was probably over the top. But some of the criticism wasn't totally unfair. We were certainly a very difficult side to beat. Billy wanted everybody working 100 per cent up and down the pitch. It probably took away a little bit from the positive play; hence the reason we ended up drawing quite a lot of matches. It was instilled into us to defend a situation rather than to exploit it. Not losing was always the first priority. Billy put more emphasis on what we did when we *didn't* have the ball than when we had it. That sometimes manifested itself in very defensive tactics. Our thought pattern as players was always dictated by being told, 'Do this, do that, go here, when you haven't got the ball; get back here.' Such a tactical outlook does ultimately detract from what you do when you actually have possession.

This Everton squad may ultimately have been one or two players short, but make no mistake, it was full of quality and full of character.

At right-back we had Mickey Bernard, a very old-fashioned full-back, a hard man on and off the pitch. If you were ever in trouble you'd want Mickey there with you. He'd stand up and be counted if there was anything going on, both on and – as I mentioned in the previous chapter – off the pitch too. When I came into football in the 1960s, full-backs were full-backs and defended first and foremost. I'm not saying that they didn't go forward and join in, but most were in the mould of good, solid, hard-tackling players. Mickey was one; another, at left-back, was Steve Seargeant. He was an OK player, probably never going to become a regular, but one of those who would come in and do a decent job for a period.

Partnering John Hurst at centre-half was big Roger Kenyon, a man you didn't mess with. He was hard and would give it as well as take it, but this belied the fact that he was technically a very good player and made it to the brink of the England team. He had character and guts and led from the front, and was crucial to Everton.

Dave Clements, our captain that season, was by that stage of his career probably a better talker than he was a player. He had a good left foot on him and read the game well. He was an intelligent man, but he was probably right at the end of his playing days then and wasn't capable of doing the things he had done maybe five years earlier when he was in his prime at Coventry City. He certainly had bags of experience and by the end of the 1974/75 season was not only captain of Everton, but had progressed from being Northern Ireland's captain to their player-manager.

Alongside him and Martin Dobson in midfield was the late Mick Buckley. He was a good little player, technically very accomplished, but there were question marks over his consistency and whether he could sustain spells of good form over a longer period.

On the flanks I had a number of men supplying me with crosses. The Scot John Connolly was a slippery player who could go in and out and deliver crosses, although perhaps not as regularly as you'd like. Gary Jones, a local boy, was even more enigmatic. Barring Trevor Francis, he was technically as gifted as anyone I played with. He could be absolutely brilliant and fly down the Everton flank, but he simply couldn't sustain it week in, week out, or at least that's how I viewed him. George Telfer and Ronnie Goodlass were also both good players, but not comparable to my old Birmingham teammates, Gordon Taylor and Trevor Francis, and the man who would succeed both George and Ronnie later at Goodison, Dave Thomas.

I'd played my first Merseyside derby soon after joining Everton. In fact it was my first ever derby experience – at Birmingham, Aston Villa had nearly always been in a different division to us, so I never encountered that special intensity you get in derby fixtures. (Ironically I played for the first time against Villa early in the 1974/75 season in a League Cup tie; I scored a second-half equaliser to prevent an inglorious exit, but we fell 3–0 in the replay). It was something else, unlike any game I'd ever played in, a blur; an absolute blur. That was the template for all Merseyside derby matches I played in.

We were very aware of the expectations placed upon us in the build-up to a derby. You couldn't get away from it. The whole city would be obsessed with it and at Bellefield Billy took it to extremes. He made sure you knew you were playing Liverpool and upped our already exhausting training regime. I'm sure that's one of the reasons we had such a long winless streak against our great rivals: we were paralysed by fear of losing, but too tired to have the momentum to win. There were a lot of goalless Mersey derby draws in my time at Everton and I never scored in a Mersey derby, despite having a really good record against Liverpool at my other clubs. Under Billy we were never going to get the better of them; mentally and physically we just couldn't give any more because we had left it all on the training ground.

During October and November I was out with a nagging thigh injury, but when I returned on the last day of November we were close to the top and unbeaten in the league in almost three months. Our football was good, attracting critical notices too. 'Everton, at times, looked close to the magnificent side of the mid-1960s,' recorded the *Sunday Times*'s Chris Lightbown after a goalless draw in the Goodison derby, which I watched from the stands.

Our opponents on the day of my return were Birmingham City. It was ten months after my transfer; I'd spent all my life before that as a Birmingham fan and then a player, but that gap was long enough not to feel too much disappointment for them if they lost. And they lost resoundingly that day – 4–1, just as they had done in March. It was a really physical encounter with 39 fouls, but, as was the way those days, no sendings-off. Dave was in goal and I enjoyed beating them. In fact, my only regret was not seeing my name on the scoresheet. Howard Kendall, returning to Goodison, probably summed up both our feelings after the match: 'It's great when you are here, but not so good when you come back to it.'

*

BESIDES LIVERPOOL, WHO WERE OUR BIGGEST RIVALS? LEEDS WERE always a bogey team; we hardly ever got anything out of them. Arsenal were another one. We rarely beat Arsenal; it was always a tough game and we never got much at Highbury. I don't know what it was, but I never liked Highbury. It wasn't purely because I didn't score, it just didn't seem to have a good atmosphere. Maine Road was a bit like that as well; I never enjoyed playing there, although unlike Highbury I did score goals. Although Liverpool were a bogey team, Anfield was always good to play at. I always enjoyed Old Trafford too. And Loftus Road was one of my favourite away stadiums. It was small, compact, and you felt more alive, more connected. Middlesbrough and Sunderland had that feel too. Similarly Derby County had that atmosphere, even though the Baseball Ground was always a complete quagmire. It was a football place.

We met Derby County at the Baseball Ground a fortnight after the Birmingham match on the usual mudbath of a pitch. There was simply no other word for it: it was always just a layer of mud that varied in levels of thickness and stickiness between August and May. I'm not sure if there was ever any grass on it, even during the summer months.

Under the management of Dave Mackay, Derby were a very good team with lots and lots of very good experience. But that afternoon we were too good for them. It's a strange thing looking back over your career. Some players can remember every single goal they scored; others, like me, just certain moments, certain goals. The winner that afternoon – the only goal of the game – came on 65 minutes. I still recall Gary Jones sending in a cross that seemed to hang in the air ready for me to attack. I saw a space in the goal and looped a header beyond the grasp of Colin Boulton. That win took us top.

'Not only are Everton leading Division One, the sixth club to have leap-frogged up there in recent weeks,' reported the *Daily Post*, 'but for the first time since Liverpool's grip was loosened they suggest more ability to stay there than any of the pretenders.'

The following week, a few days before Christmas, Carlisle United came to Goodison for what remains their only league visit. They were rock bottom of the First Division and remained there nearly all season long. They were a team you would expect to beat, both home and away. With just over half the game gone, everything was going according to plan. I'd scored twice and we were cruising, cementing our place at the top of the league.

Yet what happened in the fourteen minutes after my second goal, on 51 minutes, still gives me nightmares more than forty years later.

'Perhaps they thought it was too easy,' reported Michael Charters in the *Liverpool Echo*. 'Perhaps they thought they could score when they liked against a side apparently doomed to return to the Second Division. If so, they were given the shock of their lives.'

We imploded. Joe Laidlaw scored twice in five minutes to bring the game level. Then Les O'Neill, who'd worked his way up from non-league Blyth Spartans to the top flight in a long career, scored an improbable winner.

What on earth happened? Was it inexperience? Complacency? Very possibly both. Because of what happened at the season's conclusion, it's still a bugbear now, something that I still ponder. What was the reason? Why? I keep asking myself, rolling over the increasingly fleeting memories of that afternoon in my mind, and I still can't come up with any answers.

Defeat to Carlisle at Goodison certainly knocked our confidence in the short term. We lost at Wolves on Boxing Day, then could only draw at home to a decent Middlesbrough side 48 hours later.

'Christmas 1974 may well be remembered by Everton as the festive period when the First Division Championship began slipping through their grasp,' reported the *Daily Post*, which just weeks earlier had talked up our staying power. All these years later their words seem wearily prescient.

Matters nearly got much worse. In the FA Cup we drew non-league Altrincham in the third round, enduring a torrid afternoon at Goodison. We fell behind to a first-half goal and were finding it very hard. It was a tough, nasty game. I was having a running battle with the centre-half; we were elbowing, pushing, abusing each other. This was going on all over the pitch. Shortly before half-time Gary Jones lost his temper, got into a scrap with one of their players and was sent off for punching him. Then there was a sickening challenge on John Connolly that broke his leg and pretty much wrecked his Everton career.

I very rarely descended to that level of play, but that afternoon I found myself sucked into it. I was giving the centre-half all sorts of stick – 'Who are you playing for? How much are you earning?' all that business. That sort of thing can rebound on you if they go on and win, but it was part of the mind games, trying to put them in their place. In the end we were saved by a very dodgy penalty that Dave Clements converted, but it wasn't a good afternoon.

We beat Altrincham 2–0 in a replay played at Old Trafford and it provided a turning point of sorts in our season. We won our next three league games and by the time we played Liverpool at Anfield on 22 February, we were second and they were fifth. Top spot and a clear break was in touching distance for us. Everybody said the derby would be fast and furious and you wouldn't be able to take too many touches; and it was just that, another blur. I don't think I touched the ball for the first fifteen minutes; it was flying around like a ping-pong. Mersey derbies were like that though, unlike any game I ever played in: not much football played, but plenty of tackles going in; everybody running around like madmen. It ended 0–0. It wasn't a great experience.

I'd always had played well against Liverpool with Birmingham and they'd always been good games, good footballing games; but with Everton it was a battle, a constant siege, hammering at each other. Nobody could get their foot on the ball and play. If you tried to play football you'd get battered. Nobody wanted to lose, and that was always the big negative about these games, because both teams tended to set out their stall to prevent defeat. Even today I think it's probably the same; they don't want to lose against each other so it provides a very negative games. Some turn out to be OK but most of the time you can forget about them.

Three days later, on a Tuesday evening, we played Luton Town at Goodison. Although we struggled, I scored in a 3–1 win, hooking home a Mick Lyons cross on 52 minutes to send us top. The following Saturday we travelled to Highbury, where we rarely did well, and won comprehensively, the 2–0 scoreline not reflecting our true dominance. 'More than ever on Saturday I was convinced I was seeing the new league champions,' wrote Horace Yates in the *Liverpool Echo*. 'Londoners who labelled them "dull defensive robots" ate their words in the face of an exhibition of quality, composure and confidence.' A third straight win at home, this time to Queens Park Rangers, cemented our position at the summit of the First Division.

Confidence was swelling in our ranks. We travelled to Elland Road, where Everton hadn't won in a quarter of a century (and wouldn't win again for another 25 years), and drew 0–0 with the reigning champions. That was a good result on a day when our nearest rivals, Derby and Burnley, had both been beaten. Afterwards in the players' lounge all the Leeds boys thought we were going to win it. They were six points behind us – so not completely out of reach themselves– but they'd been there and done it before, and saw the signs in us. 'Just keep going,' Johnny Giles was telling us. 'You'll win this.'

There were now just nine league games remaining. We'd played most of our title rivals and were three points clear at the top. But things were about to go badly wrong.

The following Tuesday we travelled to Middlesbrough. Jack Charlton had built a hard and direct team, much in the style that would bring him global notoriety as Ireland boss in the 1980s and 1990s. We should have been too good for them, but gave them an easy start when Steve Seargeant's casual back-pass was intercepted by David Mills, who fired Middlesbrough in front. We tried to fight back, but they were difficult opponents and we couldn't quite find our tempo. Five minutes after the interval David Armstrong cut inside from the left and chipped Dai Davies for Middlesbrough's second. There was no way back after that.

Ipswich were the next visitors to Goodison and they were in with a chance of the title themselves. We were missing Martin Dobson, who was ill with a high temperature. More than 46,000 crammed into Goodison and I think there were a few nerves in the crowd and perhaps among us too. In 1970 Roger Kenyon had come in as an almost untried youngster for Everton's title run-in, but besides him and John Hurst, nobody else had ever experienced anything like this before. Just 74 seconds had passed when Trevor Whymark headed Ipswich in front. Ipswich packed men behind the ball, while we hurried and harried, but we were perhaps too anxious to make our mark. On the hour mark the pressure paid off when I crossed to Mick Lyons, who headed home for an equaliser. We continued to push for a winning goal but it proved elusive.

If that hard-fought draw against a very good Ipswich side gave our rivals a glimmer of hope, what happened next, on Easter Saturday, suggested we weren't viable title contenders at all.

We travelled north to Carlisle, who were rock bottom and all but assured of relegation. Memories still lingered of what had happened at Goodison in December. This was a strange game. For the first hour nothing much seemed to happen. We seemed content to keep it tight, but we weren't creating many chances. But then we capitulated, again. Peter Scott, the young right-back who was deputising for Mickey Bernard, gave away a penalty, which was converted. Steve Seargeant then handled just outside the box and Carlisle grabbed a second. Three minutes from the end, Frank Clarke confirmed a hammering. It was a terrible, terrible result and, worse still, meant Liverpool briefly replaced us at the top of the table.

I don't think you start to process such a poor result until the day after the game. Immediately it can be quite raw, But the soul-searching and questioning usually starts the following morning: why did we lose? What went wrong? We were more than capable of getting a result at Carlisle, just as we were against Middlesbrough and Ipswich. Even now I still ponder those two Carlisle games.

At the time there wasn't much time for reflection. On Easter Monday we played Coventry at a packed and very nervy Goodison. Dobbo scored a brilliant 25-yard volley in first-half injury-time for the winner. It was an edgy and unconvincing performance, but sent us back to the top.

The following Friday evening, we faced Burnley at Goodison; the match was moved to accommodate the Grand National the next day. Burnley had slipped away in the title race, having lost four of their last six games. It was another scrappy affair, but just before the hour mark I calmed some nerves by sending a looping header into the back of the net following a Mick Buckley cross. We seemed to relax and for the first time in weeks started to play as we could do. We could – and should – have had two or three more goals, and maybe things would have turned out very differently if we'd found the back of the net again. But with eleven minutes to go Peter Noble, on a rare foray upfield, headed an equaliser. We were still top, but it was another point dropped.

Next up, on 9 April, were Luton, who had replaced Carlisle at the bottom of the division, at Kenilworth Road. Had we learned our lesson from our nightmare at Brunton Park? We were never knowingly complacent going into any match, and on this occasion we did our utmost to kill the game early. After twenty minutes I had put us in front and could have had another; John Hurst had also hit a post and Gary Jones missed when it seemed easier to score. 'Their first-half display was as good as anything I've seen from them this season,' reported Michael Charters in the *Liverpool Echo*. 'They showed skill, application, technique and, frankly, should have gone in at half-time with at least a three-goal lead.'

But we let ourselves down yet again. Luton scored twice in two minutes shortly before the break and although we rallied in the second half, after we failed to get an equaliser they finished the strongest. This was a rearranged game after the original encounter had been postponed in November when we were in one of our long unbeaten runs. Who knows what the outcome might have been had we played then?

'We only have ourselves to blame,' Billy lamented after the match. 'The defeat has not done us any good, of course. But it's not all over yet. There are still games to go and we shall keep on fighting to the very end.'

From being in first position we had suddenly dropped down to fourth with three games remaining. We ground out a win at Newcastle to keep the pressure on Derby, who were now top. Then we faced Sheffield United at Goodison and probably played some of our best football of the season. We were 2–0 up at half-time after goals by Gary Jones and the young Welsh forward David Smallman, but then – just as we had on several occasions that season – we surrendered. Early in the second half Keith Eddy headed home a corner to give Sheffield a chance. On 73 minutes Dai Davies dropped a cross and it was tapped home by Billy Dearden.

At this point the crowd really turned against us. It was nothing more than frustration, but it did have an impact. I think you try very hard for it not to, but subconsciously it eats away at you. I think it can have an effect on your performance. Sometimes you can be totally oblivious to it but under certain circumstances you become aware that the crowd's a bit edgy. They have an impact and they did that afternoon.

The winner – which probably, at that stage, seemed inevitable to the home crowd – came with five minutes to go from Tony Currie.

'Second-half disaster shatters the dream of Goodison,' recorded one newspaper headline. 'The seat cushions and crumpled programmes which rained from the Goodison stands provided a crude monument to Everton's league title aspirations.'

It was a complete and utter capitulation. More than forty years later Everton still haven't since surrendered a two-goal half time lead at Goodison and been defeated. We did it while on the verge of the League Championship.

Our defeat meant that Derby were three points clear at the top with a game to go; their second League Championship in three years had been confirmed.

I still look back upon that season with such great regret. We weren't the finished article, but rarely will you get so many chances of winning a league title. My mind has always fixed on the two games against a doomed Carlisle team – two matches that had we won would have seen us lift the title – but there were other missed chances too: Ipswich, Luton, Burnley. While writing this book it was pointed out that had we beaten Sheffield United and won our final game against relegated Chelsea (we drew 1–1), even after all those wasted opportunities we would have edged the title on goal average.

Where did we go wrong? As I've said, we were still probably a work in progress, and if anyone had said at the season's outset that we'd finish three points behind the Champions, we'd have probably taken that. But we failed, because we should have won it; there's no question about that. We were good enough to lift the title. Derby won it with the joint-lowest points tally in post-war history and man for man we were every bit as good as Dave Mackay's team. They deserve credit for coming through and winning it, of course, but they had more than a little help from us along the way. It was a little like Rory McIlroy's collapse at the 2011 Masters, where he led until the last nine holes of the final round and blew up.

The lack of a top-class goalkeeper was undoubtedly costly and although Dai Davies and David Lawson were reasonable keepers, they were not the sort of players to win you games. Individual mistakes – and both made them more frequently than they should have done – proved costly and also failed to build the trust of their defenders. This wasn't an irreconcilable problem. Remember: Peter Shilton left Leicester mid-season for Stoke. He would have been the difference between Everton being a team of nearly men and one of winners, not just for that season but throughout the 1970s.

Without question we drew far too many games too – eighteen in total, including nine at Goodison. Part of that was a lack of firepower, which might seem a strange thing to say from the club's top scorer. I'd managed 17 in 36 games, but played within myself on occasion because of a thigh injury I'd suffered earlier in the campaign. I scored around a third of our goals and you can possibly point to other individuals for not contributing more, but I think the real problem was that we suffered from fatigue, particularly in those final crucial six weeks.

Billy gave an extraordinary interview at the end of the season in which he professed a lack of belief in us. 'I felt we were just not quite good enough, even when we were leading the league. I could not convey that opinion to the players as they faced the run-in. It was my job to stimulate them and this I did to the best of my ability. That is my honest answer to what in the end was a disappointing failure.'

Yet we *were* good enough. If the fault lies anywhere it was with Billy, who really failed to find the right balance on the training pitch. The last month or so of the campaign we trained like it was pre-season. I remember doing a session of 'doggies' and Terry Darracott was my training partner. As we were doing sprint after sprint, he turned to me and said, 'Latch, this isn't right, is it?' I could only agree with him.

But that's how it was with Billy. He exhausted us. It was the same sort of anxiety from the manager that drove us then as it did before derby matches. I felt that at some stages of the season rest becomes more important than training, given the amount of games we had to play. Looking back, Billy did not get that balance right.

Failing to win a trophy at Everton is the biggest regret of my career. There would be further opportunities in later years, but the 1974/75 League Championship was the one we should have won and had we done so it would have set the tone for the rest of the decade. I'm sure we would have won more, possibly much more. Instead, it marked us out as a 'nearly' team: we nearly won the FA Cup, we nearly won the League Cup. It set the tone for the rest of the 1970s where we came close but not close enough. We had great times and I wouldn't swap them. I would just have liked to have come out of it with a winner's medal.

6

LOFTUS ROAD

'A fool thinks himself to be wise, but a wise man knows himself to
be a fool.'
William Shakespeare

WE HAD COME WITHIN TOUCHING DISTANCE OF GLORY IN THAT
1974/75 season. It was such a close-run thing that it's agonising contemplating it
even today. We were so close, so very, very close.

Sometimes in football, as in life, it's not what you encounter, but how you
respond to it that matters most. After coming to the brink of success, I would
have expected Everton, if they were serious about trying to push on and be in
contention to win things, to have strengthened the squad. You have to look back
now and think if Billy Bingham had brought in two or three quality players we
could have had a crack at the League Championship the following season. But he
didn't and we, as a team, didn't progress during the 1975/76 campaign.

I don't know why this strange inertia hung over our transfer dealings. We were
still known as the 'Mersey Millionaires' – a hark-back to the early 1960s when
Everton had used serious financial muscle in the transfer market – and the club
had twice broken the transfer record just a year earlier to sign Martin Dobson
and myself. But now? Maybe there was no money left. Or perhaps John Moores
didn't want to give Billy any money. I don't know; as players we were never told.

But there were no new signings in the summer of 1975.

You've got to ask the question: was it purely Billy's decision not to buy players or was it because the club wouldn't finance them? It would be remiss of me to point the finger solely at Billy, if in fact the club had turned around to him and told him, 'You can't buy these players' or 'You can't have him'. However, the failure to improve the squad left us in limbo. We were drifting. I suppose you look back at it and think, where was the ambition of Everton? It didn't manifest itself in new signings. When that happens, subconsciously you start to question what's happening at the club and it ultimately affects performance on the pitch. It was like a snowball effect during the course of the 1975/76 season and carried over into the following campaign.

Whatever happened behind the scenes, Billy never helped himself in other areas. The rot had set in and unhappiness started to bubble away with the players. We had a very tough pre-season where Billy kept a tight rein on us and would not let us out at all. There was the burden of our abortive title challenge hanging over us, a tension that still permeated from that failure. Usually in pre-seasons you get a bit of downtime, but I think Billy cut all that out and we didn't have any time to relax and bond. Some players were getting very itchy about that.

When we started the 1975/76 season at home to Coventry, this unhappiness and tension spilled over. Coventry beat us 4–1 and the hangover continued.

Despite the ultimate disappointment of the previous season, Everton had qualified for European competition for the first time in five years. However, the UEFA Cup draw could hardly have been more challenging: AC Milan, with the second leg away at the San Siro Stadium. Milan were then a club riven by internal disputes and talk of takeover bids. Some newspapers even suggested that factions within the club wanted to see them lose in order to speed up the takeover process – although that would prove fanciful. Despite the apparent unrest at Milan it was a little bit cruel to be up against them first time around, but the experience was terrific.

Between us we didn't have much experience of European football: John Hurst and Roger Kenyon had played in Everton's previous European campaign, but that was about it, whereas Milan were perennial campaigners. Yet we performed well in the first leg at Goodison. We kept the Milan attack at bay, preventing them from getting the all-important away goal, but were equally unable to crack their defence. They massed ranks behind the ball and were guilty of time-wasting and gamesmanship. Two minutes from the end Mike Bernard was sent off for a foul on Romeo Benetti, the Italian captain. Milan's manager Gustavo Giagnoni bragged after the game, 'This is just what we came for. Now we can have them on our ground.'

We were under no illusions of the size of the task facing us in Milan a fortnight later, but a single away goal wasn't unfeasible and would have tipped the balance – perhaps overwhelmingly so – in our favour. It was a terrific atmosphere that night, not just because of the size of the crowd – at 66,000 it was the largest I'd played in front of at that time – but because a significant contingent of Evertonians made the journey. It was at a time when travelling abroad was less convenient and far more expensive than today and they were magnificent.

Unfortunately we were also facing a twelfth man in the East German referee, Rudi Glockner. Five years earlier in Mexico he had become the first German to referee a World Cup final, when Brazil beat Italy 4–1. We saw little evidence to justify a reputation as a giant of his profession and he was certainly not on our side that evening.

Decisions went against us all night. We played really well against a team of genuine quality. We had two clear penalty appeals turned down, firstly when Gary Jones was fouled – according to one report – 'ten yards inside the penalty box', only for a free kick to be awarded outside the area, then later when Jim Pearson was knocked over. It was ridiculous. To compound things, he awarded a penalty against us on 67 minutes for handball, which Milan converted. A brilliant save from Albertosi to deny Martin Dobson a headed equaliser (which would have seen us through on away goals) three minutes from full-time secured the Italians a narrow victory.

Billy, who was usually so cool and collected, let rip when he spoke to the press after the game. He accused Glockner of 'chickening out' of his responsibilities. 'It was absolutely unbelievable. I am bitterly disappointed because I thought we were going to have a quality referee.'

To have lost as narrowly as we did showed that we could compete on the European stage. We had given a good account of ourselves over two legs and it was always difficult to play against Italian teams because they are so naturally defensive, but also have so many highly talented players. Had we faced a different opponent other than AC Milan we could have built up some momentum and gone a bit further in the competition, but we were up against a major European club and it was always going to be difficult – with or without Herr Glockner.

*

OUR LEAGUE FORM HAD SETTLED DOWN SINCE THE SHOCK ON THE first day of the season, but the hangover of 1974/75 still lingered. There was an unease among the players that permeated the fans, while we felt their unhappiness. When supporters start throwing cushions onto the pitch you can tell people are unhappy. The natives were definitely restless. Even at that stage attendances were down significantly and over the course of the season would be down 13,000 per match on the previous average of 40,000.

Billy had what some supporters referred to as 'London Luck' and since the start of the 1974/75 season Everton were undefeated in the capital, winning four and drawing four. We travelled to one of my favourite grounds, Loftus Road, on 11 October 1975, a week after another London victory at West Ham elevated us to seventh. QPR were a good team, in the way that smaller clubs often were in those days, with players like the England captain Gerry Francis, the mercurial forward Stan Bowles and the north-east winger Dave Thomas, whom I'd admired from afar for so long. They would finish the season unbeaten at home and narrowly miss out on the league title to Liverpool.

Even so, it doesn't fully account for what happened that autumn afternoon. Rangers battered us, there's no other word for it. We came away with a 5–0 defeat: Rangers went top, we ended the day eleventh.

It was a poor, poor result. People talk about turning points in a manager's career and in Billy's case they often point to this game. I'm not sure it was a turning point, but it certainly never helped him. When things are going against you results like that are nails in the proverbial coffin.

Although we won the following two matches, against Aston Villa and Wolves, they were two of just four wins over a miserable four-month period. It wasn't

With my brothers David (left) and Peter (centre),
who would also become professional footballers.
(Personal collection)

Back to my schoolwork after scoring Birmingham City's first goal in the FA Youth cup match
against West Bromwich Albion in December
1966. I was a month short of my sixteenth
birthday. *(Mirrorpix)*

With David (left) and Peter (right, cleaning his football boots) as aspirant footballers in December
1967. David was already a young goalkeeper on the books at Birmingham City and Peter had been
capped for England schools basketball team. A month later I would sign as professional with Birmingham. *(Mirrorpix)*

With teammate Alan Childs during a training session at St Andrews in May 1967. *(Mirrorpix)*

In action for Birmingham City. *(Mirrorpix)*

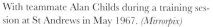

In action for Birmingham City against Millwall during a crucial League Division Two match at St Andrews in April 1972. I scored in a 1-0 victory that set us on the way to promotion. *(Mirrorpix)*

Wearing one of my England under-23 caps with Dad, David and Peter looking on. *(Personal collection)*

With Bob Hatton, Birmingham's new signing from Carlisle, and the prodigious Trevor Francis in October 1971. We were a formidable forward line. *(Mirrorpix)*

Heading the winning goal past Leyton Orient goalkeeper Ray Goddard to secure promotion to the top flight for Birmingham. Birmingham needed just a point to go up and won the game thanks to my solitary strike. *(Mirrorpix)*

A bomb threat greeted or promotion, but on a powder-keg night, the explosions had already happened. There were champagne corks flying from the moment we got back to the sanctity of the dressing room. *(Colorsport)*

Merseyside bound. With Pat, Izzy and Richard on the day that I signed for Everton in a British transfer record deal. *(Personal collection)*

With Billy Bingham and Everton's legendary patriarch owner, John Moores. He told me what he expected and what the club was all about. Then he went off on a tangent, telling me not to not overspend and live frugally. Who was I to question? He was one of the wealthiest men in Britain and entirely self-made. *(Mirrorpix)*

After scoring my first Goodison goals young Everton fans applaud me off the pitch. I scored two and made the other two against my former club Birmingham in a 4-1 win. *(Mirrorpix)*

Meeting Everton fans who drove to Milan in a mini-bus for our UEFA Cup game in September 1975. *(Mirrorpix)*

Touching distance: We came so very close to League Championship success in 1974/75. Here I am celebrating after scoring the opening goal during the League Division One match against Middlesbrough at Goodison Park in December 1974. The match ended in a 1-1 draw. *(Mirrorpix)*

With my eldest two children, Richard (aged 5) and Isobel (aged 7), in August 1976. *(Mirrorpix)*

With Mick Lyons at the end of the League Cup Final match at Wembley against Aston Villa in March 1977. *(Mirrorpix)*

With Stoke goalkeeper Peter Shilton at the Victoria Ground in February 1977. Everton should have broken the bank to sign him. He would have been the difference between Everton being a team of nearly men and one of winners. *(Mirrorpix)*

With the immortal Dixie Dean, who taught me what it meant to be an Everton number nine. In that sense he was one of the most important people I encountered in my Everton career. *(Personal collection)*

On my way to 30 league goals. In action during the League Division One match against Manchester United at Old Trafford in March 1978, in which I scored both Everton goals in a 2-1 away win. *(Mirrorpix)*

I always knew I would score the two necessary goals in Everton's fateful match against Chelsea at the end of the 1977/78 season to reach my tally of 30 league goals. When Everton were awarded a late penalty there were no nerves. At the referee's whistle, I blasted the ball with my right foot. The roar of the Gwladys Street signalled that I'd fulfilled my task. I ran to the fans and sank to my knees. Fans and players raced towards me. I'd done it. *(Everton FC)*

I didn't get much of a look in when I came up against Claudio Gentile on my England debut against Italy at Wembley Stadium in November 1977. *(Mirrorpix)*

Reunited with Trevor Francis and with the brilliant Kevin Keegan ahead of England duty in April 1978. They were the two best players I ever played alongside. *(Mirrorpix)*

In the snow at Goodison in February 1979. We were at the top of the table then, but backroom disharmony meant we were never going to be serious title contenders that season. *(Mirrorpix)*

A final Everton salvo. After scoring a hat trick against Crystal Palace in September 1980 I'm congratulated by Steve McMahon. Soon after injury practically brought an end to my Everton career. *(Mirrorpix)*

Signing on for Swansea City under the watchful eye of John Toshack in July 1981. *(Mirrorpix)*

A debut hat-trick in front of the Match of the Day cameras. *(Mark Leech/ Offside)*

Holding court over cornflakes in Breda. *(Press Association)*

Less enjoyable were spells at Coventry City and Lincoln. *(Mirrorpix)*

Scoring against FC Twente in March 1984 *(Press Association)*

I was aware of Newport's severe financial problems before I arrived, but perhaps hadn't appreciated the sheer scale of them. The whole place looked like it was on its knees, on its last legs. Two years later they went out of business. *(Mirrorpix)*

Scoring Merthyr's first goal in the 1987 Welsh Cup Final. Three Welsh Cup winner medals (two for Swansea) were my only silverware of a two decade career. *(Mirrorpix)*

Working in PR for Ladbrokes in 1995. An enjoyable and unexpected role that put me back in touch with football.

With my wife of three decades, Pat, who I so cruelly lost to cancer in 2000. *(Personal collection)*

With Brian Eastick at Birmingham's academy, which we started from scratch. Andrew Johnson (pictured far right) followed in my footsteps by playing for Birmingham, Everton and England. *(Mirrorpix)*

They say home is where your heart is and for me that is in Germany with Andrea and our children. Here I am with her, Sam and Sina; and below, with Isobel and my grandson, Marley, and his youthful uncle and aunt. *(Personal collection)*

a happy period to be going out at Goodison and playing. The players weren't happy about Billy and some of the poor form on the pitch was a manifestation of the resentment about issues like training and his disciplinary regime. We never went out to do anything other than win, but when there's uncertainty about the direction a manager is taking the team it unquestionably has an effect. How can everybody give 100 per cent to a manager they don't fully believe in?

Billy usually seemed immune to the pressure, though; he was as cool as you like. He was never a shouter and if he took it out on players I don't recall him doing it in public. Outwardly he seemed like he could handle everything. I think it manifested itself in what we did during the week that became more and more negative and physical. In other words, he ran us into the ground. The worse we were doing, the more we ran. The more we ran, the greater our resentment.

Yet, Billy was not somebody you took on. It was only talk among ourselves. I don't think anybody really stood up to Billy and said, 'Look, we don't like this and we don't like that.' Certainly I was part of dressing rooms where that happened, but I don't remember any of that with Billy. However, there was a lot of talk among the players about how things weren't right on the pitch and at the training ground. It had all built up from the previous season.

Things came to a head after a 3–0 defeat away at Manchester City on 21 February 1976, a loss which left Everton in fifteenth place. The warning signs had been there for some time. Only a week earlier we had given up a three-goal lead in a friendly with Dundee to draw 3–3, and it meant we had won just four of the previous nineteen games. I was injured and so could only listen from home to radio reports, but it was another poor afternoon. After the game supporters protested outside the players' entrance. Inside the dressing room an argument had broken out, which, if you believed newspaper reports, was little short of a mutiny. This revolt was, according to the *Liverpool Echo*'s Michael Charters, 'unprecedented in my knowledge of Goodison affairs'. However, although I wasn't there I'm sure the scale of it was exaggerated.

Gary Jones and Mick Buckley were said to be the ringleaders, but from my experience they were two of the most unlikely players to lead any sort of rebellion. They simply weren't the sort of lads to stand up and start dictating what we should and shouldn't do. They might voice their opinions to other players, but to actually stand up in front of Billy and read him the riot act? Well, I'm doubtful now and I was doubtful then. By Monday, when I joined the rest of the squad for training at Bellefield, it was talked about a little bit, but it was far from being something that dominated the dressing room.

Our unhappiness, nevertheless, continued and people could see it. One newspaper wrote of 'a glaring absence of team spirit' during the Man City game and accused 'some players' of 'not caring whether they won or lost', suggesting there was a 'disturbed, unsettled atmosphere'. I can honestly say that in almost twenty years of playing professional football I never played for a team that did anything other than try its best. There may have been times when we were poor, but I cannot recall a team where, *en masse*, we didn't try.

I think this dressing room row reflected the rut we were stuck in and that Billy didn't seem to know how to break it. If we lost he'd run us as punishment, if we won he'd run us to keep up our momentum. The players, frankly, had long since stopped responding to such tactics and so the decline continued.

An unlikely boost to all our morale came towards the April transfer deadline, when we signed the teenage midfielder Andy King from Luton Town. He would prove to be a skilful and adroit player, with lovely technique and an eye for goal. But it was his effervescence on and off the field that captured the hearts of Evertonians and ignited the dressing room. Although he was still just a teenager, he was completely full of himself and wouldn't stop talking, even if you threatened him. The lad could play too and score goals. He always thought he was a better goalscorer than me, but I want to put it on record that he wasn't! He was good but not *that* good!

I returned to the team for the final run-in and joined up with my new colleague. At one point we had dropped to sixteenth, but three wins in our last three games took us to eleventh place at the season's end. I finished top scorer with 13 goals from 38 league and cup games, but it was scant consolation either for me or the fans. Having come so close twelve months earlier, we had fallen far short. Worse still, for Evertonians, Liverpool – for whom a golden era had supposed to have ended with the retirement of Bill Shankly – had won a league and UEFA Cup double. An era of living in a red-tinged shadow had begun for Everton FC.

A DIFFERENT ROAD

*

HAVING COME SO CLOSE TO LIFTING THE LEAGUE TITLE IN 1975, Billy and the board had not capitalised on that position of strength and invested in the team. Twelve months on, they hadn't learned from their mistake then, albeit that we faced it from a different context. Now, we needed to rebuild from a position of weakness; we needed fresh impetus, more big characters, like Andy King. But there was nothing. History repeated itself and there were no new additions to the Everton team. Instead several decent young home-grown players, such as Dave Jones, Ken McNaught and Ronnie Goodlass, who had been on the fringes, were promoted to the first-team squad and given more regular berths.

Just why we didn't do any big transfer business doing those two crucial summers is a question only Billy can answer. If he had the money and he wasn't signing players then it was down to him. But if he didn't have the money it was down to the board, and the club. So perhaps you can't blame Billy totally for what happened. But if they gave him the money eventually – which they did – you have to ask, was that money there at the beginning? And if it was, why didn't he spend it? There must have been players out there. If he had the money halfway through the season, why did he not have that money at the beginning of the season?

It frustrated me then, and it frustrates me now. From the supporters, pressure was still mounting on Bingham even before the 1976/77 season kicked off. Fans would tolerate his brand of football while there were good results, but the dull football and poor results encountered in the previous campaign were not good enough for Evertonians.

Yet the team that had been so poor for most of 1976 confounded our critics when we went to Loftus Road on the opening day of the season. Queens Park Rangers had finished the previous campaign just a point behind Liverpool and had, of course, humiliated us ten months earlier. But now we turned the tables, winning 4–0. I scored twice.

Although we lacked consistency, by early October Everton were third. We were playing good football and scoring lots of goals; I'd scored seven in the first five weeks of the season. Yet I don't think Billy ever eased up. He was a very precise, calculating man and I don't think it would be in his nature to change the way he managed the club. However, I think the players maybe got to a stage where we thought, 'Well, whatever is happening from the management we've got to take control.' I think it was a subconscious thing that happened, where we collectively we got to grips with our own game, and played the way we wanted to play regardless of what was being said to us.

We were performing well at times, but I don't recall thinking at any point that we might have cracked it. The foundations of our progress were probably quite fragile. Despite our good form, as players we weren't convinced by the direction we were heading and I don't think the fans ever were too. Unless there's a strong sense of belief and leadership – as there was at various other points in my Everton career – good runs can quickly come to an end and be forgotten … and so it was in the autumn and early winter of 1976/77.

Another defeat to Liverpool in mid-October and more losses that month and in November left Everton languishing in mid-table. This included a defeat to Leeds and a 4–1 hammering at Newcastle United (we'd lost 5–0 there the previous season). Our toils even had a hint of farce about them, and when West Bromwich Albion beat us at the Hawthorns on 27 November, one of their goals was a direct result of a Jack Russell running onto the pitch and panicking our incredulous back four into conceding a goal! 'It's a dog's life for Everton,' quipped one newspaper headline after that one, but it was no laughing matter. At Goodison the cushions would come flying down from the Main Stand as disappointed fans made their displeasure known.

To address the decline, shortly before Christmas Billy brought in two big signings, Bruce Rioch and Duncan McKenzie. Both were excellent acquisitions. Quite why they – or other players of their calibre – hadn't been signed at the start of the season was baffling.

Bruce was a hard Scotland international midfielder who had forged his reputation at Aston Villa before joining Derby, where he was part of the team that pipped us to the 1975 League Championship. He gave us a toughness that we probably lacked, but as with Kingy he could also go up the field and score goals, which we probably lacked as well. Spreading the goal burden had been an issue since I joined Everton: would things change now?

Duncan was the polar opposite. He was a maverick in an era of maverick players. He was renowned for his party pieces, such as leaping over Mini Coopers and throwing golf balls the length of a football pitch, and he carried his showmanship onto the pitch. I got on well with him and played well with him too. He was the same sort of player as Trevor Francis, not in the same class but a similar type: skilful, quick and mercurial. I found him reasonably easy to play with too; it wasn't hard for me to fit in with him.

The received wisdom at the time was 'Sign McKenzie and You're Fired', perhaps because Brian Clough had bought him during his ill-fated 44 days at Leeds. But Duncan McKenzie did not get Billy Bingham sacked. Duncan immediately became a crowd favourite and combined goals with an impressive repertoire of skill.

But equally, he was unable to save the manager. Results in the league remained very poor. Our last league win had been over Derby on 20 November and the winless run carried on in the league for three months. With football such an important part of the festive season, with games coming thick and fast, this added to the burden facing Billy. On 27 December we lost 4–0 at Manchester United, making it a miserable Christmas for every Evertonian.

I think we had got to the point where, although he was manager, as players we were playing for ourselves – and the club and fans, of course – rather than the manager because because we knew he was on borrowed time. It was sad, but it happened.

Shortly after Christmas I was called in to meet the chairman, Alan Waterworth. As players we had little to do with the club's executive management, so it was an unexpected summons. I didn't know what he wanted, but he came straight to the point.

'Bob, now please be honest with me: what is your opinion of the manager?'

As a person who sometimes struggles to contain his emotions, it wasn't something I was going to be able to lie about, even if I'd wanted to.

'Billy's got go,' I said simply. 'He's lost the dressing room, lost the players.'

That was pretty much the extent of the conversation. I wasn't the only player called in either: I think Colin Harvey, who'd returned to the club as a youth coach, might have been another, too. A few days later, on 10 January 1977, Billy

81

was sacked as manager of Everton Football Club.

'I've had pressures from every quarter, and I have tried to do the job as well as I could,' he said. 'Some people may debate whether that was the right way, but it was the best I could do.'

There wasn't any immediate sense of relief at his departure. You couldn't say it was like a fog lifting. There was an inevitability about it. We all knew it was going to happen. I've got no animosity towards him at all. He was OK. He bought me, brought me to Everton; for that I'm always thankful. I think many of my teammates probably shared such sentiments.

Was I responsible for Billy's sacking? Of course not, but when you use the old cliché about nails in a coffin, that conversation with the chairman was almost certainly one of them, if not the final one. The process of his departure had started twenty months earlier, during that ill-fated title challenge. Players always give new managers the benefit of the doubt, and they either buy into their philosophy, how they want to do things, or they start to ask questions. By the end of that 1974/75 season when we didn't win, I think questions were creeping into the players' minds, and the questioning of the manager's approach continued over time. What he wanted from us was not what the players wanted. You have to get the players on board with what you want otherwise you're never going to succeed.

Because of his natural aloofness, I don't think he had any natural allies in the dressing room. Although he was charming, Billy was standoffish too and always had the 'I'm the manager, you're the player' attitude. He'd let you know about that too. As such it was always very difficult to get close or have any sort of bonding with him. I think that also played a little part in his downfall. If he'd had one or two players always on his side, it might have pulled some of the others around. You look at when Howard Kendall came in, and he had players who would have done anything for him. But I'd be surprised if anyone described themselves as having such a close connection with Billy.

There were, of course, some external factors that didn't help. Both Liverpool and Everton had lost defining managers around the same time, and while Bob Paisley was exceeding the achievements of Bill Shankly at Anfield, Everton were falling short of the heights they had reached under Harry Catterick. Everton hadn't even beaten Liverpool for five years, never mind outperformed them in the league. In the pressurised world of Merseyside football, such things matter a great deal.

Billy wasn't a bad manager and his subsequent record as Northern Ireland boss, whom he twice took to the World Cup, attests to some of his qualities. Maybe history has dealt with him a little harshly; maybe his hands were tied when it came to transfer funds. He spent £1.3 million in his time at Everton, but recouped £1 million. But it was true that he had lost us. The hardest thing a manager has to do is stand in a dressing room and get a squad of twenty men to believe in him. They have to believe in his ideas, and act on them. It's a massive challenge, but also the key to any sort of success, especially with older pros. The younger ones are more pliable, but if you don't get the older players on board– you will struggle like mad.

7

MANCHESTER

'It's not whether you get knocked down, it's whether you get up.'
Vince Lombardi

IN THE WAKE OF BILLY'S SACKING, THE EVERTON BOARD MOVED TO
appoint the Ipswich Town manager, Bobby Robson, as his successor. Robson had
transformed what was a hitherto unheralded provincial club into one of the most
attractive and potent forces in English football. Later, he'd prove his pedigree at
the highest levels. As England manager he took the national team to the World
Cup semi-final and would find success in Europe with PSV Eindhoven, Sporting
Lisbon, FC Porto and then Barcelona. But after reportedly agreeing terms on a
ten-year deal with Everton, Robson changed his mind and the search went on.

Who would I have liked to see succeed Billy? I think Brian Clough would
have brought an edge that the club needed. He would have energised the players
and brought the sort of commitment and innovation on the pitch that would
have made us contenders. His record, even at that stage, was phenomenal. But I
don't think the Everton directors would ever have been able to work with a Brian
Clough. Cloughie was the type of manager who would want total control and
no interference, and the directors of Everton would not have been open to that.
The board were a bit like the FA – who later overlooked Clough for the England
job – in a lot of respects: conservative, and controlling. They wanted the kind of

manager that would toe the line, and I'm not sure Cloughie would have fitted their mould.

Billy's eventual successor was more their type: decent, hard-working, un-controversial, but a surprise appointment in many ways. Hired from Newcastle United, Gordon Lee was an outsider and defied Everton's recent tradition of hiring past players as manager. As a player he had been a centre back at Aston Villa, before turning to management with Port Vale. A winning spell in charge of Blackburn Rovers led him to St James's Park, where he was relatively success-ful; Newcastle had got the better of Everton during his spell in charge and had turned us over a couple of times.

I didn't know much about him, other than he came across as being passionate and committed, but he had garnered a reputation – perhaps after selling Malcolm Macdonald to Arsenal when Newcastle manager – for producing somewhat dour teams. But it was newspaper talk, and that was something I took little notice of. My view is, he was probably very brave to sell Macdonald. I'm a centre-forward and usually I stand up for fellow centre-forwards; but Macdonald – who had topped me at Newcastle one year, leaving a scar that remains to this day – was not one of them. Indeed, looking back, having worked with and gotten to know Gordon quite well and how he liked his players to be honest and fair, I know that such antics would never go down well with him.

Gordon's biggest problem was that he wasn't media-friendly. He always had a problem relating to the press, and they gave him an image of being sour-man-nered. Physically he was very gaunt, looking a little like Uncle Fester from *The Ad-dams Family* or the 1990s sitcom character, Victor Meldrew, which I think added to this perception as an austere disciplinarian. Even though he really wasn't like that at all, in his introductory press conference he lived up to the caricature that, according to some people, he had become.

'I'm no Messiah,' he proclaimed.

> *I'm also not that lucky so-and-so some rather unintelligent observers want to make out. Lucky at Vale, Blackburn, Newcastle, and now here? I don't think luck lasts that long.*
>
> *You say you remember me as an honest defender? I accept that and take it as a compliment. That's what I was, someone who gave the lot*

and all the time. I cannot tolerate dishonesty, I just will not have it. I can smell it.

No, I'm just a simple man with a fairly basic philosophy. My parents back home in the Staffordshire village of Hednesford had ten of us to bring up, and made sacrifices to do so. I remember the lessons of honesty, hard work, and self-assessment I learned there... not smoking or drinking, they have stayed with me all my life.'

If you took your impression of Gordon from that, you'd think of him to be miserable to the bone. But he was the total opposite of how he came across in the media. He was somebody completely in love with football, a passionate man obsessed with the game. He thought about football 24 hours a day. Sometimes he was a little bit too intense, too focused on the game rather than the real world. But he was honest and down to earth; a man that you could get behind and believe in what he was saying. That's an important thing as a player, that you can believe and trust in what a manager is saying to you, that you have a sense of doing the right things and going in the right direction. It was just unfortunate for him that his image was such that people got the wrong impression of him.

Gordon settled straight into the Everton manager's job. I think the key to that and to his early success at the club was the rapport he immediately built up with Steve Burtenshaw, who had been retained from Billy's coaching staff and became Gordon's first-team coach. Steve was a former Arsenal coach and had had a spell in charge of Sheffield Wednesday. It was a good move by Gordon to keep him; the lads responded well to Steve, who had a very nice, easy manner about him. He knew the game and knew his stuff. Their personalities complemented each other well, too: Gordon could lose it at times, whereas Steve was able to calm things down.

The immediate legacy Gordon inherited was poor league form. The frustration of sinking to eighteenth place was offset somewhat by strong showings in the cup competitions. We had navigated a tricky FA Cup third-round tie against Stoke City in Billy's last game, but more pressing was the League Cup, in which we were in the midst of a two-legged semi-final against Bolton Wanderers.

The first match, under Steve Burtenshaw's caretakership, had typified the malaise we were facing until the new manager came in. On an edgy night at a packed Goodison we were leading 1–0 through a Duncan McKenzie goal, but had seemingly done enough to hold on to the win. Then, two minutes from the end, David Lawson took more than the six steps goalkeepers were in those days allowed to take with the ball; an indirect free kick was awarded inside the area, from which Bolton equalised. Our hearts sank.

Four weeks passed before the second leg. There was no upswing in form during Gordon's first days: we lost his first two league matches and progressed to the FA Cup fifth round only after Third Division Swindon took us to a replay. Evertonians, however, kept the faith. Their hunger for success and loyalty knew no bounds. When we went to Burnden Park on 15 February we played in front of more than 50,000 spectators, a colossal crowd in such a relatively modest venue.

It was a terrific atmosphere that night at Bolton. I'll always remember getting off the coach and as we walked up the steps to go in the door there were crowds of people wanting autographs. When I reached the top step, somebody pushed an autograph book into my hand, and I was about to sign it when the doorman stopped me.

'Turn it round the right way, it's bad luck to sign it upside down,' he said.

I'd never heard of such a superstition, but I stopped and turned the book around the right way before signing it. Bad luck, good luck – you might think it's all just silly superstition, but luck would turn out to be on my side that night.

The game's only goal came on 24 minutes. Ronnie Goodlass broke down the left and whipped in the ball; it really had a lot of pace on it. I recall managing to raise my head slightly back because it came at such a speed. I didn't have to head it, I just had to let it hit my head, because the pace of it sent it goalwards. It was a case of trying to direct it and keep it under control because there was so much pace on the ball. That's all I thought about, keeping it under control with the header, because if not it could have gone anywhere. I knew that if I got it on target I had a good chance of scoring. The ball flashed past Jim McDonagh and into the Bolton net.

That gave us the advantage and from there we should have put the game beyond Wanderers. In the 65th minute we were awarded a penalty when Duncan McKenzie was brought down by Sam Allardyce, but Duncan then stepped up and missed it, shooting wide of McDonagh's post after pausing in his run-up.

Given how things had recently gone for Everton, that put us on edge. I suppose some supporters might have expected a capitulation. But that didn't happen. We dug in, held off Bolton pressure and the trill of the referee's whistle signalled we were Wembley bound.

There was great excitement in the dressing room later. It would be Everton's first visit to Wembley in nine years, and the first time most of us would play at the home of football. Bottles of bubbly materialised – these things tend to appear when you need them and it turned out that the Bolton boss, Ian Greaves, had sent a crate of them in for us – and we had a glass or two before embarking on the coach journey back. There were a few crates of beer awaiting us and we discussed the reality of it. Wembley. A cup final. A chance of silverware. At last.

It was, in the midst of what had been until then a difficult season, a moment to savour. Semi-final victories always are, because they don't come along too often. But amid all the joy I couldn't help but think of that little incident on my way into Burnden Park. Maybe if I hadn't turned the book around and had signed it upside down – or the doorman hadn't told me – we might have lost. That's how your mind works as a footballer. It may all be nonsense, but either way ever since I make sure that autograph books are the right way round before I put my name to them.

The final was three weeks later against Aston Villa, who had only been promoted to the top flight at the start of the previous season after eight years in the Second and Third Divisions. They weren't a bad outfit and had Andy Gray – who would end the season collecting the 'double' of PFA Player and Young Player of the Year – leading their line, but they held few concerns for us. We felt that we were a stronger unit, despite the struggles we had encountered under Billy. Being a Birmingham boy there was added impetus for me to get one over them. For Gordon too, I'm sure there was a great incentive to win. Having served Villa for such a long time as a player, six weeks into the job at Everton he was leading out his new club against them at Wembley.

But after such great expectation there was disappointment for everybody. It was probably one of the worst games Wembley has ever witnessed. It didn't feel very much like a game at all. It was a horror show and ended goalless. 'The trouble at Wembley,' recorded the *Daily Express*, 'was that nerves hit some players and then it looked as though fifteen minutes from the end both teams decided on a draw and moved on to safety-first tactics.' It was, added the *Liverpool Echo*, 'The final ruined by tension.'

Four days later we met again at Hillsborough for the replay. Martin Dobson was missing with a hip injury and we perhaps lacked some of the composure he brought to our team. The game looked as though it would be heading for another stalemate when, ten minutes from the end, Roger Kenyon, who was playing his first match since Christmas, ran the ball into our net.

It was inexplicable, as a lot of incidents were at key moments for Everton over those years. How on earth do you explain that? Roger was one of our most ex-perienced and dependable players and yet he made such a big and basic mistake at such a huge moment. The pitch, it must be said, was horrible – a complete quagmire and mud from it covered my shirt and hid my number nine – and I think the ball just got stuck under his studs.

Big Roger's error focused some minds and galvanised our attack. We sent waves of attackers forward as we tried desperately to gain an equaliser. These efforts were rewarded in the dying seconds. In a congested penalty area, Duncan McKenzie laid a pass off to Jim Pearson, who scooped in a cross. The ball was touched on and I rammed home a shot from close range. It was a bit of a tap-in, if I'm honest, but the range of emotions you feel at such a moment almost defy explanation. Relief, ecstasy, elation; you feel all of these things, but putting words onto paper to describe what you went through in front of 55,000 screaming people, under floodlights, will never do full justice to the moment.

It was nearly another month before we played the second replay. This time the venue was Old Trafford. After the two disappointing matches that had preceded it, both teams provided a much better encounter. For a lot of the game it looked as though Everton would be lifting the League Cup for the first time. We opened the scoring on 38 minutes. Chris Nicholl fouled me midway in his own half and from the resulting free kick Goodlass hoisted the ball in. Ken McNaught rose to head downwards and I reacted first to side-foot home.

I don't think at any stage the thought occurred to me that we might have cracked it; that the game was ours to take. Villa fought well, and we didn't really settle. Not until that final whistle went would I have felt comfortable that we'd done enough. It was a case of having to battle it out. If we'd have scored another goal then it might have been enough, but Villa were too good a side not to respond to such a slender lead. My goal was never going to be enough on its own.

But when the equaliser came; well, what can I say? It was another of those moments – a freak – that dogged my Everton career. Chris Nicholl, a centre-half who had probably never scored a goal from outside the six-yard box in his life, took possession ten yards inside our half. He dodged a tackle by Jim Pearson and then let fly with a speculative shot that flew past our defence and curled in beyond David Lawson. It was, for him, a once-in-a-lifetime strike.

Briefly we were in disarray. Within a minute Brian Little was played in; nobody tackled him and although Lawson came out he seemed to shoot through his body to put them in front. It was unbelievable.

More drama came within a minute. A corner was swung in and Mick Lyons was first to reach it; Dobbo flicked the ball back and Lyonsy forced the ball over the line with his head. We were saved!

Extra time beckoned and with its conclusion penalties would be used for the first time to decide a domestic cup final. I think fear of losing played on both team's minds; that and the sheer physical and emotional exhaustion of playing at such a high tempo. This was also our fourth game in just eleven days.

And then, ninety seconds from this impending shootout, another of those freak moments. A sweeping cross-field ball was played to Gordon Smith on Villa's right wing. His cross deflected off Ronnie Goodlass, wrong-footing Terry Darracott, who should still have cleared it. Lawson scampered after the loose ball but wasn't quick enough, and Brian Little tapped home the winner at the far post. We were destroyed. It was a conspiracy of errors. Even now it just makes me shake my head and wonder, why? How?

We were utterly flattened, but I don't remember any finger-pointing. Nobody blamed Terry or David. If you listen to stories of the great Everton teams of the 1980s, or Liverpool too, the players would completely slaughter each other even when things were going well. Some of those players say it was a symbol of how comfortable they all were in each other's company. Maybe that was the case. We didn't have that. Maybe we were poorer for it. Perhaps if there had been that openness it would have lifted all of our standards.

*

THIS EPIC AND ULTIMATELY UNSUCCESSFUL STRUGGLE AGAINST
Villa was set against a backdrop of a league revival and progress in the FA Cup.
Any lingering concerns about relegation were pretty much allayed by the end
of March, with results including a 4–0 win over Spurs and a 2–1 victory over
Arsenal.

In the FA Cup momentum was gathering and there was a growing feeling
among us that despite the adversity we'd encountered in the league that maybe,
just maybe, it could be our year. In Gordon's first game in charge at Goodison
we came from behind to beat Swindon Town 2–1 in a fourth-round replay. Next
we travelled to Cardiff and again came from behind to win 2–1; I grabbed the
equaliser on 51 minutes and Duncan got the winner a minute later.

They were teams we could easily have slipped up against, but we managed to
dig in deep and get ourselves out of trouble and get through to the next round.
You always feel, once you've overcome opposition like that, that maybe you can
go all the way to the final.

Three days after the first League Cup final replay we faced Derby County at
Goodison in the quarter-final. It was an attritional game, without much to divide
the two sides. Gordon had dropped Duncan MacKenzie, replacing him with Jim
Pearson, a more industrious player, which, I suppose, set the tone. The deadlock
was broken in the 57th minute, when Andy King darted across the penalty area
and floated in a cross to the far post. Mick Lyons leaped and connected with the
ball and it fell to my feet. I swept it home from close range.

Derby put on a lot of pressure, but it came to nothing. On 78 minutes I was
tripped by Colin Todd and from the free kick Terry Darracott moved possession
towards the goalmouth, where it met Jim Pearson's flying body, and he headed
home our second.

On Monday lunchtime we huddled around a radio at Bellefield awaiting
our destiny. The semi-finals were strong that year and there was no easy draw.
Leeds had beaten Wolves, Manchester United had beaten Villa, and in the other
quarter-final Liverpool had beaten Middlesbrough. That was the draw nobody

wanted. Liverpool were so good and so dominant that nobody wanted to play them, while the football romantics were rooting for divergent paths that would lead to what might have been the first all-Merseyside FA Cup final. That wasn't to be, however, and the dulcet tones of the BBC's Bryon Butler told us that we would be facing Liverpool on 23 April 1977.

The venue was to be Maine Road, which was not, as I've said before, one of my favourite stadiums. But that was irrelevant anyway, because the week before we faced our great rivals, disaster struck. We were playing on the Baseball Ground's usual mudbath in a league match. We'd come from 2–0 down to lead 3–2 when, with just six minutes to go, I got through the inside channel on goal and took a right-footed shot. I came down awkwardly on my left ankle, and I felt pain. It was muddy, my footing went and I crumpled over and I knew as soon as I did that it was going to be a two, three-week job. Ankle injuries don't mend quickly.

There was talk of recovery, a fitness test, but I was not in contention; I was never going to make it. It was sorely disappointing because we owed Liverpool and, after the League Cup defeat, owed our fans. I could only watch from the dugout alongside Gordon, Stevie, Jim McGregor and Bryan Hamilton, who was substitute that afternoon.

Our record against Liverpool was very poor. Since Everton had last beaten them – when I was still a Birmingham player – in 1971 our record was played 11, won 0, lost 6, drawn 5; goals for 1, goals against 12. But that afternoon there was a definite sense that they were for the taking. Whether it was complacency or merely an off-day, Liverpool could not find their rhythm. Even when they went in front – which they did twice, first through Terry McDermott, then Jimmy Case – we sensed that we could get back, which we did through Duncan and then Bruce Rioch.

Bruce's goal seven minutes from the end passed the attacking impetus back to us. Gordon responded by putting Bryan Hamilton on in place of Dobbo. Although he'd never found his best form at Goodison, Bryan had a reputation as a goalscoring midfielder from his Ipswich days and Gordon evidently smelled blood. I think we all did.

With minutes remaining, Ronnie Goodlass cut in from the by-line and played a centre; Duncan's diving header flicked it into the path of Bryan, who was running into the six-yard area, and he deflected the ball past Ray Clemence and into the Liverpool net. It was the most important goal of his life. Everton were 3–2 in front. We rose from the bench in joy. The Liverpool players – as we had ten days earlier when conceding that late winner to Villa – knew they were finished. Only the grace of God would save them.

But God didn't save them. It took a man who seemed to think he was God to do so. In the melee stood the referee, Clive Thomas.

Clive was an international referee, an uncompromising Welshman who thought more of himself than any other referee I ever encountered. Clive was Clive. You took him as he was, but I've never known a referee who liked the focus on him like he did. He made decisions that defied comprehension. This is somebody who, a year later, in the last minute of a World Cup game between Brazil and Sweden, awarded a corner and, in the time between the ball being crossed to the head of Zico and crossing the goal-line – the flicker of an eyelid – blew for full-time. Clive did that sort of thing because Clive could. He was the referee and his authority was absolute.

And so it was that afternoon in Manchester. With the Liverpool players on the ground facing defeat, Clive ruled out Bryan's winner.

On the bench there was disbelief; utter and absolute disbelief. Gordon was apoplectic. He was just in front of me. Everybody got up but Gordon went onto the pitch. He was not happy. He was remonstrating with the linesman and officials. Nobody was happy; we were dumbfounded, we could not understand it. The linesman didn't give anything; the flag never went up. It was all in Clive's mind.

In the dressing room afterwards there was anger, there was shock, there was disbelief. Clive compounded this by refusing to give a proper explanation. During the match he had told Ken McNaught that Hamilton had 'obviously handled the ball'. Afterwards he pompously proclaimed there had been 'an infringement of the rules of the Football Association'. The following Monday he said that Hamilton was offside, despite the fact that his linesman had not flagged. He later told the authors of a book about the Merseyside derby, 'From the angle of the cross there was no way Bryan Hamilton could have controlled the ball without the use of his arm. In no way could I say that from behind I could have seen the ball make contact with his hand or his arm. But I was 100 per cent certain that he couldn't have controlled it any other way. So I disallowed it. For handball.' In other words, Clive Thomas denied Everton a place in the FA Cup final for imagining an infringement.

All through my career there were referees that you could have a chat and a rapport with, but that was never the case with Clive. He was so full of himself that he didn't really want to listen. It wasn't the fact that you couldn't talk to him, it was just that he disregarded anything you said to him anyway, because he thought he was completely and utterly right in everything he did.

This was an era where players tended to get on with things. If you watch the BBC footage of that game on YouTube at full time you won't see hordes of Everton players surrounding and berating Clive. Jim Pearson puts his arm around him and has a word, but that was it. That's the way things were, at Everton at least.

I think it's probably an easy statement to make that Everton were 'too nice', because history shows that we didn't win anything. Some would say we should have been like Liverpool or Leeds. I would have liked to have won in the way that we played and the way that we were; to be true to ourselves as a bunch of lads. You can't suddenly develop a different personality as an individual or a group. We weren't like that. We weren't a Leeds. We weren't a Liverpool with all the bitching that went on. We were who we were. And we were good enough to have their success. It just didn't happen for us – in large part because of incidents like that semi-final.

Bryan's disallowed goal is a massive incident in Everton's history. It robbed us of an opportunity to have played in an FA Cup final against a team – Manchester United – that we were more than capable of beating. Liverpool had gotten out of jail for free and knew it. They hadn't played well and there was no way that Bob Paisley was going to let them play like that again in the replay. When we met again at Maine Road four days later there was really only one team in it. Paisley's Liverpool didn't pass up second chances and won 3–0.

Our season was all but over that evening. I returned for the final few games of the season, and Everton finished ninth. I'd scored 25 goals in 50 league and cup appearances, my best return yet as a professional footballer.

8

GOODISON

IN THE SUMMER OF 1977, GORDON ENTERED THE TRANSFER MARKET
and bought astutely. It was what we'd waited for the previous two summers, but
it never happened then. In an attempt to redress the long-standing goalkeeping
problem, he bought the Scottish goalkeeper, George Wood, from Blackpool. I
didn't know too much about Georgie beforehand, but he turned out to be as
good a goalkeeper as anyone that I played alongside at Everton. He wasn't of the
Peter Shilton standard, but few were and, with respect to David Lawson and Dai
Davies, he represented a marked improvement.

The acquisition that got me most excited was the QPR winger, Dave Thomas.
I first saw Dave at a schoolboy international at Wembley when I was fifteen. For
some reason I just noticed him on the pitch when they came out and picked out
his name from the team sheet. He had a style and a verve that attracted me to
him as a player. He could do things on the pitch with the ball, like juggling it with
both feet, that few other players at that level could manage. I remember thinking,
'He's got some ability, this lad. He's going to be a player.' Sometimes you can recognise players who are going to make it to the very top and so it was with Dave.

We played together for the England Youth and under-23 teams and I followed his career, from Burnley to Loftus Road and a short spell in the England team. Now here we were some ten or eleven years later playing together at Everton.

We called him Tizer, after the soft drink, because he was so bubbly. He had two magical feet. I've always said about Tizer that while Glenn Hoddle also had two terrific feet, Tizer had the same qualities and could do anything with the ball, but also do things at speed, which Glenn couldn't. Glenn was a little bit of a stroller, directing things in midfield, pinging balls around. Tizer had the same sort of technical ability but could do it at pace with both feet.

He was a magical player; he really was. There's the old football saying of 'landing a ball on a sixpence', but Tizer could really do it; he could land it wherever you wanted it, which, to a centre-forward, is the ultimate gift. He played in rubber-soled boots, no matter what condition the pitch was in, and without shin pads too. You can imagine some of the pitches then that he played on – the Baseball Ground and so on – but his balance was absolutely phenomenal. You can't do that without having great balance and good feet, and he did, for the whole of his career. He was a joy to play with, an absolute joy.

Gordon's first signing back in February, a few weeks after becoming Everton manager, had been another player who, like Dave, had been part of the England set-up in the mid-1970s. Mike Pejic was the son of a Yugoslavian immigrant and part of Stoke City's League Cup-winning team in 1972. He was a hard-as-nails left-back who had all the attributes you could want from a great defender: tough, hard-working, very aggressive, but also technically very good. We used to call him 'Farmer Pej', as he lived on an isolated farm in North Wales, where Kevin Keegan had once lived, and would turn up to training in a mud-splattered jeep and wellington boots. He's exactly a year older than me, but even in his mid-60s you can still see that supreme fitness and toughness. He hasn't changed at all. He has taken up taekwondo and competes at international level, in 2014 coming third in the World Championships in Mexico. Can you imagine? Back then you had to work hard to get past Pejjy, and he had a very good understanding with Tizer down the left.

Billy Bingham had started to introduce some promising young home-grown players to the Everton team and Gordon continued this process. There was Dave

Jones, a good, solid local defender who would go on to have a successful managerial career with Southampton, Wolves and Cardiff City. Dave perhaps suffered at
Everton because he rarely got the chance to perform in his natural centre back
position, usually playing at right-back. He did a fair job there and was very solid
in what was maybe his second-best position. You do wonder how he might have
fared with a decent run in central defence, but he was up against Mick Lyons, our
captain, Roger Kenyon, Ken McNaught and then Mark Higgins.

Mark was the son of Bolton's FA Cup-winning defender, John Higgins, and
would go on to captain Everton. He was a good, solid dependable lad, who was
technically very good. He came in at the start of the 1977/78 season – Ken
McNaught had been sold to Aston Villa and Roger Kenyon suffered a serious
injury in our second game of the season – and performed straight away. He was
a fine player and never let anyone down. It was very sad that he himself would
succumb to serious injury when Everton were on the cusp of mid-1980s success
and he was unable to share in it.

On the fringes of the team was Neil Robinson, a full-back who was born and
brought up within a stone's throw of Goodison Park. Neil was a decent enough
player and I'd play with him later at Swansea, but that wasn't what set him apart.
Neil was a vegetarian. It was quite unusual back then. In the 1970s everything
was meat or dairy-oriented, and by the time we met up again at Swansea he was
not just a vegetarian but a vegan. It must have been extraordinarily difficult for
him to get by from day to day in any ordinary circumstances, but as a professional
footballer? He even went to the length of not wearing leather boots: he wouldn't
have leather on his feet and so his boots had to be composed of some other
material. Of course, the other players had a bit of fun at his expense. He was
always the odd one out – the oddball – because of that, but he had his principles
and he stuck by them and it was admirable. He was fit and strong and healthy: a
really good, likeable lad.

I think Gordon wanted a certain type of player and personality at the club.
He liked the game played in the right way. Some players he just didn't take kindly
to. Bruce Rioch was one of them. Off the pitch he was a lively, engaging and
likeable member of the dressing room. On it he was something else. He was one
of the most terrifying players I've ever seen on a football pitch. He would go into

tackles at 100 miles an hour from a standing start. He could be frightening. But the thing was with Bruce, he would kick you in training as well. You were happy if you were on Bruce's team in five-a-side, because he wouldn't back out of any tackle. Bruce was one of those players where tackling was just part of his make-up, but he could be scary at times. I've seen him go thigh-high and knee-high into tackles.

We played Middlesbrough in a League Cup tie in October 1977, when he took out their left-back, Ian Bailey. It was horrendous; it was one of those where you turned your eyes, even as a teammate, and thought, 'Bruce, that's awful.' He was about five yards away, and went flying in and took the lad out. Ian was taken off on a stretcher. Bruce wasn't even booked. Nor was he challenged in the dressing room, not even by Gordon. But Gordon dealt with it in his own way. He played Bruce just one more time and then sold him back to Derby County a few weeks later.

Things had normalised during Gordon's first six months in charge. The over-training, the lingering unhappiness, the loss of faith in the management had been eradicated. We still worked hard on the training ground, but the sort of over-exertion that exhausted our bodies and patience had gone. There was a rapport with the managerial team. We liked Gordon and he formed a good duo with Steve Burtenshaw. Man for man, this was the best Everton team I was part of. If that team had come together earlier we would have won the title, without a shadow of a doubt. As it was we were to come close during the 1977/78 season, but not quite close enough. For me the season would be the most memorable of my career and the one that most Evertonians remember me for.

WE KICKED OFF THE 1977/78 CAMPAIGN AGAINST NEWLY PROMOTED Nottingham Forest at Goodison. In their dugout was the man I admired so much, Brian Clough, and he demonstrated just what a good job he had done at the City Ground, building a team that was fresh and bubbly and energetic. Forest stunned Goodison, convincingly beating us 3–1, and setting a marker for the rest of the campaign.

I was powerless to change the outcome of this match, watching as I was from the stands. I was serving a one-match ban for the one and only sending-off of my competitive Everton career, having received a red card against my old club Birmingham at the end of the previous season. I'd been booked earlier in that game for an overzealous challenge on my brother, Dave, but was simultaneously waging a running battle with Malcolm Page, who was elbowing and kicking me throughout the match. The referee did nothing and, as sometimes happened in those cases, the red mist descended. I snapped and elbowed him in the face. He lost a tooth, and three others were left hanging out. It's not something I'm proud of but that was the way I was. Howard Kendall likened me to the Incredible Hulk, saying I could snap with provocation, and he was probably right.

I returned for the midweek fixture at Highbury, which was seldom a happy venue for me or my teammates. We never played well against Arsenal, who, a bit like Leeds at the time, made it difficult for you to play against them, but had some quality players to complement their tactical rigour. Richie Powling's 33rd-minute goal separated us and left Everton propping up the table.

That defeat marked a turning point and saw us embark on a 22-match unbeaten run that would extend until after Christmas. I opened my scoring account in a 5–1 victory at Leicester City in the fifth game of the season and goals were in abundant supply for me and my teammates who, in sharing the scoring burden, would make Everton the season's leading First Division scorers.

Central to this was Dave Thomas and his supply of crosses. He was brilliant and crucial to our emergence as the division's most potent goalscoring force. When we returned to his old club Queens Park Rangers on 8 October, Gordon rewarded him with the captaincy for the day. I would walk away with the headlines, but it was Tizer who repaid the boss with a superlative performance.

We started the match in fifth place and I'd scored twice in the preceding seven days, in a 1–1 draw at home to Manchester City and then a 3–1 victory over West Bromwich Albion. Confidence was not in short supply and I opened the scoring on eight minutes. Tizer initiated the move, playing the ball inside to Martin Dobson from the left wing. Dobbo took one touch and found Andy King in space, who drilled the ball across the area. All that was left for me to do was to guide the ball past Phil Parkes from six yards out. Ten minutes later Andy found Tizer on the left wing; thirty yards from goal, he took one touch and then with his second delivered a cross of such precision and pace that all I had to do was glance it inside the far post. Phil Parkes stood rooted to the spot; there was nothing he could have done. My hat-trick arrived shortly after half-time. This time Tizer took a free kick that found (with his usual unerring set-piece accuracy) Andy King; he drilled it across goal and I scrambled it in, with David Needham close-by. If I'm honest, he probably got the last touch, but I raised both arms in an instinctive celebration and Dave wasn't going to argue himself an own-goal. Duncan McKenzie added a fourth, and then my own fourth of the afternoon came with 22 minutes remaining. Mick Lyons chipped a cross into the area and I had time, space and confidence; I was never going to miss, and didn't. Having started the week with just a single league goal, I'd since scored six goals in seven days. The plaudits were all mine, but Dave Thomas had been the unsung hero of the day – as he was on many others that season.

Notwithstanding our awful 5–0 defeat there two years earlier, Loftus Road was always one of my happiest hunting grounds. On the train back North, we had a few beers and there was great talk and excitement among the lads. Would this be our year as title challengers? Could we maintain our form? I was reflecting quietly on my own four goals while Andy King was mouthing off and bantering away. He always had a word for everybody and his larger-than-life personality made our dressing room hum. On and on he went, messing around, trying to bait me.

'You weren't half the forward you are today until you started playing with me!'

'The fans all love you, but you're nowhere near as good as me!'

'There's no better finisher at Everton Football Club than me, sorry, Latch!'

On and on he went for the whole length of the journey. I wasn't rising to it, though. I just ignored him, but Andy wouldn't shut up.

In the end I had enough of him and walked down the carriage, picked him up and hung him from a coat hook. His feet weren't touching the floor! The lads fell about laughing as Andy dangled there and the train made its way back to Liverpool.

In what seems a rather antiquated gesture, my hat-trick brought me the reward of a case of Scotch whisky. Can you imagine giving a top-flight footballer a crate of spirits as a reward for sporting prowess today? I think it probably says a lot about football back then, when alcohol consumption was a big part of the dressing-room team-building. I've never been a whisky drinker, so it was shared out among my teammates, but I had to pose for the obligatory photo.

It would not be long before more whisky was coming my way. When we met Coventry on 26 November my tally stood at eleven league goals and I'd made my England debut, of which more later. People remember this match for the scoreline, but what they overlook is that Coventry were level on points with us at the start of the day and a very good team. They had lost just three of their opening sixteen matches and won half of their away games. Although we took an eighth-minute lead through Dobbo, for a lot of the first half they were the only team in this game.

Then, shortly before half-time, Mick Lyons launched a long pass forward and I ran from behind the Coventry defence, beating their offside trap, and headed past Jim Blyth and into the bottom corner of the Gwladys Street net. Two minutes later Dave Thomas sent in a typically pinpoint free kick and I headed home our third of the afternoon at the near post. There was no let-up as Jim Pearson and Andy King made it five.

The grand finale came two minutes from the end. Martin Dobson hit a perfectly weighted ball for Tizer to run on to. He was still deep in our own half, but in acres of space. He just ran and ran and ran, the full length of the pitch. As he approached the by-line, he looked up and floated in a beautiful cross. I was unmarked at the back post and finished with a left-foot volley to complete my hat-trick. I didn't score many volleys during my career, but that is one I will always savour. The headlines were all about me, but again the credit really belonged to Dave. I'd scored three times but he contributed four assists.

Goodison was rocking and the fans sang: 'We're going to win the league'. On ITV's *Big Match*, Brian Moore proclaimed, 'That's the goal of a Championship side.'

And we players believed them.

*

ONE OF THE GREAT CONTROVERSIES OF THIS ERA CONCERNED Gordon Lee and his so-called preference of the solid over the spectacular. The stereotype for some people is of the gaunt-faced manager overlooking a team of tireless runners, who would outwork their opponents into submission. There was no place for mavericks and virtuosos in this austere new world.

Of course, it was all complete and utter nonsense. His treatment of Bruce Rioch attests to the spirit in which he wanted the game played. We were top First Division scorers that season, played some lovely football and had great attacking players in our line-up each week. But this view, embellished over time, has for some reason become part of Goodison mythology.

At the heart of this perceived conflict between workmanlike and free-spirited players was Duncan McKenzie. Duncan was an extravagant player, a virtuoso on and off the pitch. The supporters loved him and rightly so. He was terrific off the pitch as well in terms of entertainment. I'll always remember we went to Europe on tour and he stood up at the back of the plane, telling jokes for about two-and-a-half hours nonstop. He could reel off stories and jokes off the top of his head. He was good at impersonating people too. He was just all-round fun.

But he wasn't Gordon's ideal player; we all knew that, Duncan he knew it too. He could be frustrating. Any player like that can be frustrating at times. But they can also bring a great deal to the team, something extra that you don't have, that other teams don't have. That's always useful in situations where you need to produce something out of the ordinary. It's the consistency of performance that remains open to question. If he has consistency of performance plus his maverick ways, a little bit of magic here and there, you take it, because he's giving you something that other teams haven't got. Trevor Francis was very much like that, and Duncan was too – or he was sometimes.

Yet Gordon played Duncan more often than he left him out. I worked well with him and there was only really one period – which coincided with that free-scoring autumn in 1977 when we were just off the top of the table – where he was really absent from the team. So it wasn't that Gordon came in and bombed him straight out. Yet because their personalities were poles apart, where one was very charismatic and the other very blunt, a perception was cast that the player and the manager were somehow at war.

I think over the years Duncan has made more of this rift than there was back then. Duncan is a raconteur. He'll exaggerate stories and he's very good at doing it to humorous affect in order to sell himself. Duncan is terrific; he was a very good footballer, but he would make the most of things and I think over time this has damaged Gordon's reputation and legacy.

Gordon's image and the way he's been talked about, not only by Duncan but by other players, is not what I recall on a day-to-day basis. I liked him; I connected with him well. I think generally most of the other players had respect for him. You've got to connect with coaches, the manager, otherwise – as I wrote earlier – things will start to fall apart.

Gordon was more honest and openly emotional than Billy Bingham, who kept things to himself most of the time. Gordon would share his thoughts with you, sit down with you at any time and start talking about football. Billy had other interests outside of football and could talk knowledgably about all sorts of things. Gordon was just a football man through and through; it was just 24 hours a day, his obsession. It could get a little bit overbearing and he could be eccentric. I'll always remember the story of him driving up to Newcastle to do some scouting and he was so focused on his mission that when he arrived there he realised he was still wearing his carpet slippers!

He had a tendency to get lost in his own trail of thought. We were in Majorca on a mid-season break and the Duncan McKenzie dilemma was playing on his mind. He'd invent these scenarios – 'Who'd win a game: eleven Duncan McKenzies or eleven Terry Darracotts?' – and talk through them, like some nutty professor. It was endearing, it was part of his personality. Anyway, we were at breakfast sitting around and Gordon was buttering this piece of toast, pondering the question of the day: eleven Duncan McKenzies or eleven Mick Lyonses – who'd win? He was just talking through this problem, and buttering his toast; talking and buttering, and the layer of butter got thicker and thicker and thicker. He would get lost in a thought pattern very easily, and he'd be distracted for a long time over something as simple as that.

Duncan was a bit bemused and he just laughed it off. For him it was mostly just a source of entertainment; he'd just wrap it up in a story and it would be even bigger and greater than what it was. It was fodder for him, but would backfire on Gordon.

I was aware of our supporters' ambivalence towards the manager. This was an era of flamboyant managers, like Ron Atkinson, Tommy Docherty and Malcolm Allison. But Gordon never fitted the stereotype or some supporters' expectations of what a manager should represent. It's something that saddened me, because if I ever talk to fans of that era I'm always telling them, 'You've got it wrong about Gordon. He's not like how he was portrayed in the press and the media.' Some accept it, most don't. You're never going to convince everybody he wasn't this dour, sour man that came across. He seemed as though he lacked flair. But what he did not have in personality or charisma, he made up for with passion and belief.

Because of his honesty, commitment and personal warmth, I had more of a connection with him than I ever did with Billy. Billy might have had the same feelings, but he didn't show it. Gordon showed it; he showed his enthusiasm for the game every day, and that had an effect on me personally and I'm sure on other players too. These are the qualities that the media never saw. Even to this day people still have the wrong impression about Gordon, but he was truly a lovely man; very passionate about football, very passionate about the club and about what he was doing. He instilled that into most of us and it took us to the brink of greatness.

*

AT CHRISTMAS 1977 WE WERE SECOND AND UNBEATEN SINCE August. Confidence swelled in our ranks. And yet we knew how hard it would be to be crowned champions. At the top of the table were Brian Clough's Nottingham Forest, who had stunned us on the opening day of the season. They looked well organised and had very solid and good technical players; they played good football and were scoring goals. Above all they were tight and didn't give much away. That as much as anything through the 1970s was the key to success; certainly it was Liverpool's. They didn't ever look like they were going to crack.

There wasn't much in it at that stage, but it meant there was little margin for error. There could be no slip-ups.

On Boxing Day Manchester United came to Goodison. They were twelve places and twelve points below us. A week earlier they had been turned over 4–0 by Forest at Old Trafford. This wasn't a vintage United side. In goal they had the novice Paddy Roche, deputising for Alex Stepney, and up front was the teenage forward Andy Ritchie. We were not complacent, but we felt we had little to fear.

How wrong we were. The game was a freak. United hit us for six. Every time they went up our end they scored. Once you start leaking soft goals, very often you can't stop. Myself and Dobbo grabbed a couple of consolations, but it shattered us. We lost 6–2. You can't put it down to the fact that we all over-ate and drank; we didn't. Gordon made sure that we did the right things and – a little like Billy – was very strict like that. When you're on a run you don't expect to get turned over 6–2 at home. The following day we went to Leeds – where we never got anything – and lost 3–1. From being two points behind Forest, within barely 24 hours we suddenly found ourselves five in arrears.

It was a gap that we never looked like making up. There was a time in March where we were just a point behind Forest, but they had four games in hand. All season they lost just three league games and were undefeated at home. We waited for a slump, but it never came. They finished nine points ahead of us and seven ahead of Liverpool, who were runners-up.

Although we spent most of the rest of the season in second place, eventually finishing third, history shows that from Christmas onwards this was never a fully fledged title challenge. Instead, for Evertonians at least, the 1977/78 campaign has come to be remembered for something else.

That season the *Daily Express* had offered a £10,000 prize to a player who could claim thirty league goals. Although the contest may seem parochial by today's standards, it generated enormous interest. The 1970s were a difficult era for strikers to score a lot of goals. The statistics support my claim. In the 1960s, the thirty-goal mark in the league had been beaten on nine occasions, but by the end of the 1976/77 season only Francis Lee had achieved it, needing 13 penalties to score 33 goals in the 1971/72 season. To a goal-hungry public, the prize carried some resonance and to a publicity-hungry newspaper – the *Express* was a far larger and more significant publication then than it is today – it had value too.

By New Year I was nearly two-thirds of the way to reaching the magical total. At the time I didn't give it any real thought; I was just focused on Everton's title challenge. Indeed the first months of 1978 represented something of a lean patch, in which I scored just twice in the first nine league games of the year. My mood was typified by a comment that I made at the end of March when I was on 23 goals (with eight games remaining). 'How do I rate my chances?' I was quoted. 'Well, the odds started to turn against me a few weeks ago, but I just want to score as many as possible. I'll start thinking about 30 if I get to 29.'

The goals returned soon enough, and a brace against Manchester United – a game in which I'd been knocked out having clashed heads with Terry Darracott and played on while concussed – brought me up to 25. Yet it was only four games out that I really started to give the *Express* prize proper consideration. We were facing Bobby Robson's Ipswich Town at Goodison and I was up to 27 goals. That day I did something I'd never done before: I took a penalty.

It came on 63 minutes with the score goalless. Martin Dobson had been hauled to the ground by Russell Osman while challenging for a Neil Robinson cross and it was I – not Andy King with the absent Trevor Ross ,our regular taker – who claimed the ball.

I sometimes look back at my career now and think, 'Why didn't I take penalties?' I suppose I always felt I could score goals, so why did I need to take penalties? I also believed that it was fair for the goals to be shared out among the team. And to be honest, I didn't really consider them proper goals. *Proper* goals, in my view, took place in the penalty area, with opponents jostling for possession. A penalty was a bit like a free punch. So I didn't take penalties, I let other people score and claim their moment of glory.

It's probably not the sort of single-mindedness you would expect from a centre-forward, but it's the way that I thought. Looking back it seems silly; if I'd started taking penalties from the start of my career at Birmingham I could maybe have added another 20 or 30 per cent to my career tally. Certainly I would have passed the 300-goal mark.

Up against me was Paul Cooper, a former Birmingham teammate who was renowned as a penalty-saving expert, although the thought didn't cross my mind. I took the ball and planted it down the middle of the goal. If Paul had stood still he'd have saved it, but he had already dived. Although he got a hand to it, he couldn't stop goal number 28, the only goal of that spring afternoon.

'It's the first penalty I've taken and I was feeling a bit nervous about it,' I admitted to reporters afterwards. 'So I just tried to keep my shot down and whacked it, so the prize is still there to go for, although it's not going to be easy.'

Suddenly my goalscoring odyssey became something of a media frenzy. It was strange because although the *Express* had created the prize, other newspapers, TV and radio stations became interested in the story. Pat and the children were called up to pose with me for photoshoots, and all sorts of interview requests came in.

Fame back then was different to how it is today, with camera-phones and social media so ubiquitous. Now you can't go to the toilet without someone knowing what you're doing. It was easier to control and although Pat was private and quite protective of the children, exposing them to the odd press photo was never an issue. In fact, I'm not sure that Izzy and Richard were ever totally aware of my fame until their late teens, by which time I was coming to the end of my career.

We travelled to Middlesbrough a week after the Ipswich win. I had a total of 270 minutes to get the two precious goals. But after 90 goalless minutes at Ayresome Park, I was still on 28.

More frustration came three days later when we travelled to the Hawthorns to play West Bromwich Albion. Again I was not on the scoresheet. George Telfer got our goal in a 3–1 defeat.

It meant that everything rested on the final day of the season, when we faced Chelsea at Goodison. There was an added poignancy to the occasion, because that week marked the fiftieth anniversary of Dixie Dean's haul of sixty league goals, an immortal achievement that will surely never be surpassed.

I'd been lucky enough to meet Dixie – or Bill, as he preferred to be known – on several occasions, and he was a lovely, humble man. I was in awe of him and his achievements. He is the true legend of Everton Football Club and it was through him that I realised what I needed to do in order to carry on the tradition of Everton number nines. He had been the original number nine, first wearing the numbered shirt in the 1933 FA Cup final, and his successors included Tommy Lawton, Dave Hickson, Alex Young and Joe Royle. It was a lofty tradition and one he made me very aware of. In that respect, he was one of the most influential figures during my Everton career.

'If Bob gets the two goals he wants, it will be a wonderful way to mark the fiftieth anniversary of my record,' said Bill in the week of the Chelsea game.

> *I'd like him to know that I send him every good wish and I think he can do it, especially against this Chelsea lot. Needless to say, I'll be rooting for him because I've been an Evertonian since I was a kid. I still am and I always will be. The last time I went to the other place (Anfield) was when I was paid to play there!*
>
> *You've got to give credit to what he's done. The Everton team has been chopped and changed this season because Gordon Lee has been trying to find his best side, but he has kept scoring regularly. An early goal would obviously help him. When I needed three in that last match of 1927/28, I got the first one after about fifteen minutes.*

Such words meant the world to me and filled me with confidence and hope. When I woke on the morning of the day of destiny, 29 April 1978, I always knew I was going to score the two goals I needed. I don't think I can think of another situation during my career where I knew for certain something good was going to happen. But I certainly woke up that morning not feeling nervous for the first time ever over a football match. There's always some nerves or butterflies bouncing around, but I woke up that morning feeling mentally calm. I knew with utmost certainty that I was going to score the two goals, no matter what went on in the game.

Everyone was behind me and urged me on. My wife and children, the Goodison staff, my teammates, but above all Everton's fantastic supporters wished me luck and encouraged me. Perhaps for the first time since Dixie completed his great odyssey fifty years earlier, Evertonians were coming not to see their team win, but to see one man reach a target. Nearly 40,000 people packed into Goodison to see the game and goals weren't long in coming – just not for me.

Martin Dobson, Billy Wright and Neil Robinson all appeared on the scoresheet within the first 55 minutes, but not me. Teammates were setting up chances, almost tripping over themselves to hand me opportunities to reach the target, but nothing was forthcoming. On 72 minutes, Mick Buckley crossed into the box, Lyonsy flicked it on and I rose above Steve Wicks to head the ball into the Gwladys Street net. Goodison exploded.

Even though time was running out, I still had no doubt at all that another goal would come. Three minutes later, from an almost identical situation, possession came to Mick Lyons. He only needed to repeat the old trick, flicking it on to me, and I was certain to score. But instead he'd headed the ball past Peter Bonetti for our fifth of the afternoon. I'd never heard a reaction like it. You could almost hear a groan echo around Goodison Park. Mick, who is perhaps the biggest Evertonian to pull on that royal-blue shirt, was bereft. Never in my life had I heard a player celebrate a goal with the word 'sorry' before.

'Just get back in your own half,' I told him. But Mick didn't listen. He wanted to make amends – and he did. A few minutes later he backed into Mickey Droy and went down in the penalty area in a way you wouldn't normally expect from as honest and whole-hearted a player as Lyonsy. The crowd howled for a penalty, and the Chelsea players protested as the referee pointed to the spot. I had my chance.

Dobbo took me aside as the Chelsea players continued to protest. 'Just keep your head down and blast it,' he whispered. I knew exactly where I wanted to put the ball – to Bonetti's right side. There were no nerves. At the referee's whistle, I blasted the ball with my right foot. The roar of the Gwladys Street signalled that I'd fulfilled my task. I ran to the fans and sank to my knees. Fans and players raced towards me. I'd done it.

The final twelve minutes were played out to a carnival of songs from the Goodison crowd. They were great moments. We'd had a good season: we hadn't won a trophy, but we had restored some pride at a time when Everton and Evertonians badly needed it. We had given those people and that great football club something to remember. The final whistle heralded a massive pitch invasion. I was so relieved and joyful that we'd made so many people happy. Those memories have lived with me ever since.

There was a chaos of celebration after the final whistle. There were people – officials, players, fans – everywhere. Who knows what it would have been like had we won a trophy? It certainly felt like it that afternoon. Champagne flowed and I drank it like it was water – I certainly drank too much of it because I had to drive back to join friends and family at the Pheasant Pub in Hightown.

I was blotto, three parts gone to the wind, but I knew I had to get out of Goodison and get to Hightown to see Pat and my family. Everybody wanted a piece of me. It was lovely, but I needed to get away, so I took a back route, which I knew would get me past the press pack and to the car park.

As I was making my escape, a lift door opened onto an atrium and there – with his family – was the great man himself. Dixie.

'Well done, lad, I'm very pleased for you, very happy.'

I was gone at that stage, I'd had too much to drink. Dixie wasn't going to get any sense out of me. So I thanked him and shook his hand, anxious – perhaps too anxious – to make my leave.

He turned to leave to go back to his family and get in the lift. I was about to go down the stairs. He half-turned back to me and the sixty-goal hero still had this smile on his face.

'Just remember one thing though, lad.'

'What's that, Bill?'

'You're only half as good as I was.'

And with that, he was gone.

9

WEMBLEY

'Surrender to what is, let go of what was, have faith in what will be.'
Sonia Ricotti

I BELONG TO A GENERATION OF FOOTBALLERS FOR WHOM PLAYING for your country represented the very pinnacle of your profession. Footballers plotted their careers not to maximise their earnings but to attain playing success and in so doing enhance their chances for playing for their country. I suppose in the same way that today's players aspire to play in the Champions League, my generation strove to represent their countries. As an English professional footballer, there was no greater honour, no greater deed you could do, than to wear the Three Lions on your chest. It was the high point of your career – pulling that England shirt over your shoulders. It was hard to come by too – or at least a little bit harder than it is today.

To be involved in the international scene was a source of great enjoyment and pride, but for me it was elusive until I was nearly 27 years old, by which stage – looking back – it was probably too late for me to fully feel part of the national team set-up.

There was a crossover between my playing career and that of England's World Cup winners and I played against most of those players, starting with Jack Charlton in the 1972 FA Cup semi-final against Leeds. He was like a giraffe, all legs and neck. To some, the class of 1966 had been something of a burden. I think for the England teams that played in the 1970 World Cup and, more especially, tried to qualify for the 1974 tournament, it was hard living in their shadow and with the expectation England's only ever success in a major tournament brought.

For me 1966 was an inspirational moment, and one that we sadly have not built on over the years. I remember that July day as a fifteen-year-old. When Martin Peters scored England's second goal to put us 2–1 ahead, I ran out the back door and in the excitement fell over and tore my jeans! There was disappointment when the Germans made it 2–2 and the sinking feeling – 'Oh no, this can't happen' – and then relief and ultimately elation. For me it was a source of wonder and pride.

I had my own direct involvement with this golden generation. I had, of course, been involved with the England set-up at youth level, but when I made the step up to England under-23 towards the end of my time at Birmingham, in autumn 1973, Sir Alf Ramsey took an active involvement.

I was in awe of Alf; I think we all were. This was a man who'd won the World Cup. His pedigree was such that you looked up to him and you drew inspiration from what he was saying; you respected him and listened carefully to what he told you. Somebody who had achieved what he had, you have to give the greatest sort of respect to.

I wouldn't say from the coaching point of view he did anything out of the ordinary, but in terms of his management, and being able to put a team together, he was very good. He was of that era where managers would map out what they wanted, then have others actually put it into practice. He would retain overall direction of how we were going to play. Then there'd be two or three under him organising the sessions. Yet Alf would be there directing, watching over; if something wasn't right he'd be sure to step in.

I felt that I was ready for the England team by the time I came to play in the First Division for Birmingham in 1972. I was as good as any striker in that squad, and probably scoring as many goals. But Alf wouldn't risk me. I still dream about coming off the bench in the crucial and infamous World Cup qualifier against Poland in October 1973 and scoring. But Alf was conservative. He stuck with what he knew and didn't take his chances on in-form players from outside his squad. Instead he placed great emphasis on reputation, which you needed to build up over several years. Instead of calling me up to the full team, he expected me to prove my mettle for the under-23s.

My England under-23 debut came at Fratton Park against Denmark in November 1973. My younger brother Peter, who had broken into the West Brom team, had made his a month earlier, against Poland. I lined up in attack with Trevor Francis and Charlie George and scored England's equaliser in a 1–1 draw with eleven minutes remaining. Two months later Peter and I lined up in the same England under-23 team in a goalless draw against Wales at Ashton Gate.

At the end of the 1973/74 season, not long after my transfer to Everton, I embarked on an end-of-season tour with the England under-23s. The national team set-up was in a state of flux after Alf Ramsey had been fired the previous month. We travelled to Turkey, Yugoslavia and then France. This was a very different Europe to the one we know today, where we enjoy free movement, are linked by direct flights and mostly united by a common currency.

Turkey was a footballing backwater, far removed from the country that would finish third at the World Cup less than thirty years later. And yet, although we weren't playing at full senior level and only 9,000 fans turned out on a soaking day, the noise, vociferousness and intensity of the Turkish supporters was something that has stayed with me – much more so than the game, which was abandoned at half-time with the scores goalless, owing to a waterlogged pitch.

We then travelled behind the Iron Curtain, to Zrenjanin, which is in the east of modern Serbia, but was then part of Yugoslavia. Tito's country was arguably the most Western-oriented of all of the old Communist bloc and on the surface it seemed pretty normal. Nothing really stood out that accentuated the differences between West and East, as it had in East Germany, which I'd visited a few years earlier, where the repression of every aspect of people's daily lives was so patently obvious. Yugoslavia seemed quite a normal place to be back then; I suppose Tito had it under such control that there wasn't much disturbance going on. We lost 1–0 in front of a sparse crowd and then journeyed straight to France. I somehow lost all my luggage on the way and when we lined up in Valence I was reunited with Dave Thomas, the elusive winger who'd left such an impression as a schoolboy international and with whom I'd go on to form such a potent footballing relationship. A 2–2 draw marked the end of my involvement with the England under-23s.

Indeed it marked the start of a hiatus of more than three years of my involvement in the national set-up. That period coincided exactly with Don Revie's tenure in charge of the England team.

Revie was the controversial and charismatic former footballer of the year who, as Leeds United manager through the 1960s and early 70s, transformed his club and arguably the face of English football. He was the all-encompassing 'boss' of his team, his influence extending beyond the usual team selection and training to include diet, team bonding, kit design and input into the commercial running of his club. He was loved by Leeds fans, to whom he brought unprecedented success, but loathed by many others who decried his team's brutal, win-at-all-costs mentality. There were also allegations of corruption and match-fixing attached to his name. In 1974 he was appointed Alf Ramsey's successor as England manager.

Revie called up eighty current, past and prospective England players for a get-together early in his reign as manager. I was one of them, but that was the closest I came to any sort of international recognition while he was in charge. He never spoke to me. He never, as far as I knew, came to see me play. As far as Don Revie was concerned I might as well not have existed, despite scoring 67 Everton goals in his three years in charge of England.

I think everybody within the game knew what type of character he was. From a personal point of view it was sad that he must have held a grudge against me, and I'd love to know why. I can't think of one occasion that I said anything personal about him. Maybe it was because of my connections with Everton, a club that he came close to managing in 1973 only for a deal to break down at the last minute. He never selected any Everton player during his three years in charge, not one. Most likely it must have come down to a personal dislike from him towards me. For what reason I will never ever know.

Revie left in the summer of 1977, having signed a lucrative tax-free deal to manage the United Arab Emirates. Underlying that decision was on-field failure and a falling-out with the FA's prickly and dictatorial chairman, Sir Harold Thompson. Revie might have been a lot of things, but at least he was a football man. Thompson, an Oxford professor who had played at a high level as an amateur, had taken a dim view of the England manager because he had the temerity to ask him to refrain from smoking cigars in front of the players at breakfast. In another incident at an official dinner, when Revie and his wife were seated with Thompson, the England manager objected to Sir Harold's habit of referring to him by his surname. 'When I get to know you better, Revie, I shall call you Don,' Thompson responded with a sneer. Revie retorted, 'When I get to know you better, Thompson, I shall call you Sir Harold.' Such quick-wittedness would not have gone down well with the FA hierarchy.

As players we had little dealings with such figures. I don't think they ever came out to the hotels where we stayed or to any of the training practices. We were isolated from all that bureaucracy and the chaps in blazers. But, although the coaching set up was good, there was a strong feeling among us that the game in general was run in an amateurish and haphazard way. It was a bunch of amateur people running what was a professional game. The fact that it took until 2012 for a national training centre to be built – an idea first advocated in the 1950s by Walter Winterbottom – is telling of how the FA was run.

My view is – and was – that there should be two set-ups within the FA: a professional part, with responsibility for internationals and oversight of the Premier League and Football League, and an amateur FA to look after the grass-roots game. This could easily be split and breed a more coherent and responsive way of running football in England, as I see in Germany. We have a national centre now, but it's all too late; the boat has sailed for us, and we're not going to get on it. Not in my lifetime will we again scale the heights that we did under Alf Ramsey. There's too much political and economic influence in other areas of the sport for the FA to ever establish any true authority over the national game.

Back then, Brian Clough was the bookmakers' and overwhelming public favourite to succeed Revie, but he was always going to be too much of a maverick to convince the FA bosses. Instead they opted for a safe pair of hands to oversee the remainder of England's qualifying campaign for the 1978 World Cup. They wanted a man to quell the storm that had surrounded Revie's departure and, in the words of Thompson, bring 'honesty, devotion and cooperation' to the job. Their choice was Ron Greenwood, and his caretaker appointment would eventually be made permanent and last five years.

*

RON HAD A REPUTATION AS ONE OF THE GAME'S GREAT THINKERS.
He had been a widely respected coach at Arsenal before becoming West Ham manager in the early 1960s. He produced some good cup sides, winning the FA Cup in 1964 and the European Cup Winners' Cup a year later. He also oversaw the rise of the Hammers' World Cup-winning trio of Geoff Hurst, Martin Peters and Bobby Moore. In the league, however, West Ham were perennial underachievers and by the time the call came from the FA he was in semi-retirement.

To me he was a very nice man; very much a football man and knew the game intimately. He was very knowledgeable, but also very quiet. He never used to rant or rave, but was nevertheless a strong character and knew what he wanted. He struck me as someone who didn't want to be at the forefront and was more comfortable working behind the scenes. He was the antithesis of some of today's managers, such as José Mourinho; he didn't relish the focus the job brought, he just wanted to do his work quietly and get on with it.

The qualification process for the 1978 World Cup finals in Argentina was very tight. Just one country would emerge from a group consisting of England, Finland, Luxembourg and Italy. It was a system that placed huge emphasis on the fixtures between the two favourites, England and Italy, and also against Luxembourg, against whom we were expected to win comfortably and boost our goals-for tally. In Revie's last competitive match, in March 1977, England put five past Luxembourg at Wembley, but we were by then playing catch-up having already lost against the Italians in Rome. Italy, meanwhile, were picking up wins and goals, including nine in their two matches against Finland. The game that really killed England came in October under Greenwood when they could only manage a 2–0 win in Luxembourg.

It meant that when England faced Italy on 16 November 1977 we needed to win comfortably and hope Luxembourg somehow staved off a massacre in the lions' pit when they travelled to Rome three weeks later. Leading the line for the country for the first time that night, was me.

If I'm honest I thought the chance had passed me by at the age of nearly 27. I had always viewed playing for England as the absolute summit of my career, but when the call finally came it was with a minimum of fuss. Gordon Lee approached me at Bellefield one morning and told me, quite simply, 'You're in.' Ron Greenwood had phoned him to advise of my call-up and a few days later I received a letter from the FA with all the logistics of attending an England match. There were caps afterwards, of course, but no other fanfare.

It was the first time I'd ever been called up by England and I was straight into the starting XI. I suspect Ron felt he needed something drastic in order to take England to South America. I was joined in the England starting line-up by two other debutants, two wingers from either side of the Manchester divide: Peter Barnes of City and Steve Coppell of United. Kevin Keegan was nominated by Ron to play in the 'hole' behind me. Maybe because it was one of those all-or-nothing matches, it was a bold, attack-minded formation that immediately captured the imagination of the capacity Wembley crowd.

I'd played at Wembley before, but going out there in front of more than 90,000 with the country's hopes pinned on your shoulders was truly nerve-wracking. Although there was always tension and nerves jumping around before ever match, for the first time I was really, truly nervous going out, walking out that first time with the Three Lions on my chest.

Within eleven minutes we'd taken the lead when Trevor Brooking sent in a fast, dangerous cross and Keegan glanced a looping header over the head of Dino Zoff and into the far corner of the Italy net. Wembley roared, and we laid into the Italians.

People remember the England teams of the 1970s for their failures, but they forget just how many very capable players we possessed. If tournament qualification had been more straightforward in those days, there's no question that we would have regularly challenged in the latter stages of World Cups and European Championships.

Ten minutes from the end, as Trevor Francis was warming up to replace him, Kevin sent Trevor Brooking clear with a through ball that the West Ham player eased past Zoff to seal a 2–0 win. 'We set out to restore pride and respect in our football and we got the verdict from the crowd at the end,' said Ron afterwards.

'We played with a lot of emotion and freedom for the first time in a long while. I am proud of English football and proud we showed millions of people up and down the country we are not down and out as people seem to think we are.'

I hadn't scored and had been largely subdued by Italy's man-mountain defender, Claudio Gentile. With about twenty minutes to go I was substituted for Stuart Pearson and was deeply disappointed. Like any player, I desperately wanted to stay on the field. Nevertheless my performance drew some praise in the newspaper write-ups the following day.

However, a 2–0 win over Italy was not enough. After England's lacklustre display in Luxembourg, Italy needed just a single-goal victory over the Duchy to surpass England's goal difference. Italy scored three and England's slim hopes of qualification ended.

*

FROM BEING FRUSTRATED BY ALF RAMSEY'S CONSERVATISM AND mystified by Don Revie's apparent grudge, I suddenly found myself at the heart of the England squad. Maybe it was because of my age – I was 27 at the time of my second international – or form – I was in the midst of my thirty-goal season at Everton – or maybe I was just helped by a new manager with new ideas, but I suddenly seemed to fit in with England's plans.

At the same time it was a frustrating time for the national team. Failure to qualify for the Argentina World Cup meant that England's fans would have to wait until at least the summer of 1980, when the European Championships were to be hosted by Italy, to see their country in a major tournament. That would be staged 31 months after my international debut, which is a long time in football.

As England players we were given around £400 per call-up – which was roughly a week's basic wages – and were well looked after by the FA. Of course, we got the obligatory caps too, that was an important part of the experience. Mine are mostly in a box at my daughter's home, although I donated one to the Everton historical collection. Yet earning mementoes was never the point. It was the playing. It's not what I got for it. It's like my whole career, it's not what I earned, it's that I did it, I played; that was my driving force. That was me.

From a social perspective, there were good times with the England team too. Because I was always so family-oriented, when I was playing my club football I wasn't big on that side of things unless I was on tour. With England? Well, to a greater or lesser extent we were on tour the whole time. Back then it was very good, the social side. We had a reasonable amount of freedom. Liverpool players dominated the ranks of the England team, and I'd meet them in a pub on a Sunday afternoon. We'd be picked up in a limo and driven down to London, but we made sure it was stocked up with a few crates of beer and the driver would have to stop every now and then for the inevitable toilet breaks. We'd go out for something to eat then head out with the others; train on the Monday morning and afternoon, then go out on the Monday night. Tuesday we'd train and stay in for the evening; Wednesday morning there'd be a bit of light training, then we'd play the game on Wednesday evening.

The away trips were always good fun. We'd generally go out after games for a few drinks in whatever European capital we wound up in. I remember walking around from bar to bar in the centre of Stockholm at midnight in June and marvelling at the fact it was still light. These trips were sociable. You were in good company. The press and fans would never give you any trouble. It was before the days of the tabloid rotter or football being seen as a celebrity culture. We enjoyed ourselves but never went mad. We went to the same places that ordinary people went. We were able to.

It amazes me now, looking back, that that's the way things were. Because we were allowed freedom we didn't abuse it; we just had a good time.

There were some big personalities in the dressing room, but Kevin Keegan stood out above all others. Kevin was super. I have to say that even though he previously played for Liverpool. He is a lovely guy and was a super, super footballer. Kevin was probably the easiest player I've had the fortune to play with. He was just everywhere; when you needed him he was there, and he encouraged and drove you on and just kept going. He was a dynamo, and by his sheer will and effort to keep going and keep everybody else going, he kept the team ticking. He was a top player.

Outside of the dressing room we hardly saw him, apart from training, because he always had commercial interests to fulfil. We were all fairly significant players in our own right, but you knew where you were with Kevin. He's about the only player of whom I was really conscious that he was a major, major star, way above me.

Although Kevin had played for Liverpool, generally there was a pronounced gap between the northern and southern-based players and their earnings and commercial expectations. The London players would be quite open in talking about their salaries and sometimes we'd do a double-take when we heard what some of them were earning. For many of us playing for Everton or Leeds or Manchester United or Liverpool, being paid to play football was our dream, and although we knew we had to earn a living, the money was really a secondary consideration.

When I was with England I was approached by a colleague of Mark McCormack, an American lawyer and probably one of the first super-agents. He had revolutionised professional golf and was trying to do the same in football. His sports marketing and TV rights agency IMG is now one of the most powerful operators in global sport. He approached me around that time and offered me a marketing contract.

If I'm honest, it scared me. I was wondering, why have they come to me? Kevin Keegan I could understand, but why me? It was during my thirty-goal season, but in my mind it didn't connect. Part of my reaction was down to my naivety and not being in an environment where recognising your commercial value was normal; I just could not accept why they would want to work with me. In my mind there was an ongoing battle between defining myself as an ordinary bloke who was just doing his job and the view of others, which was that I was a star doing something quite extraordinary. I couldn't reconcile those different views of my life. Even today it's very hard for me to accept how people see me as being something different to how I see myself. I played football and scored goals, but so what? Why is that something that people see as extraordinary?

Part of it is a matter of self-confidence. I've never been a confident person. I was never naturally confident at school or growing up. I was a very shy boy; extremely shy, in fact. So ever since I found fame I've always had to really portray an alter-ego of myself. On the pitch I was fine, but I sometimes reflect that I could have been a better player if I'd had a bigger ego. If I'd had an ego like John

Toshack's, for instance, I probably would have been.

Besides Kevin Keegan, the other stand-out players in that England squad were Trevor Brooking and Peter Shilton. Trevor was such a good player, so elegant – a little like Martin Dobson – and embodied all the qualities that you would expect from an international footballer. Shilts, who vied for the top goalkeeping spot with Ray Clemence, was at times almost unbeatable. Playing alongside him only emphasised what Everton were missing with their lack of a top-class keeper.

What I also understood from sharing the same dressing room as them was how ordinary, relatively speaking, most of the Liverpool players were. They weren't the superhumans that their medal haul suggested. This isn't written with any sense of sour grapes, but I came to realise that Liverpool's success was predicated by having a winning set-up, a winning formula, rather than individual players that were immeasurably talented. Their performance level was greater than anybody else's and they would turn in a performance week in, week out, whereas maybe other teams – including Everton – would have their off-days. Their big secret was consistency; nothing more. When you stack the Liverpool players up against players from other clubs in the England dressing room they really weren't that much better.

I missed England's next match after my debut, a friendly against West Germany in Munich's Olympiastadion in February 1978, due to injury, but when England faced Brazil in a friendly in April I was back in the starting line- up. Brazil were a rough, tough team, far removed from the Samba footballers who had wowed the planet at the 1970 World Cup. In a 1–1 draw I was kicked all over the place and agreed with the universal assessment of them as 'butchers'.

My first England goal came on 13 May 1978 in a Home International against Wales; it was a near-post header from a Peter Barnes cross, past my former Everton teammate Dai Davies. I found the Home Internationals terrific; I really enjoyed them. They were very competitive as well. I really do think we've lost something by not having them any more. Britain has probably lost that internal battle and sense of self.

None of the four home nations have lost more from the passing of the home internationals than Scotland, and none of the four nations valued them more at the time than the Scots. We were the Auld Enemy and they wanted to win at all costs. As well as the fans there was great rivalry between the two sets of players and you could say things in the dressing room you probably couldn't say towards them today. But you knew it was just banter; there was nothing malicious in it. I'm sure a lot of that has gone out of the dressing rooms these days.

I was left out the day that England beat Scotland 1–0 at Hampden in front of 88,000 on the eve of a 1978 World Cup that their manager Ally McLeod infamously had bragged that they'd win only to be knocked out at the group stages. Twelve months later I was in the team that faced them at Wembley and there were probably nearly as many Scots as English in the stadium that day. I would have loved to have gotten on the scoresheet against my Everton teammate George Wood, but although I didn't manage that I couldn't help but be delighted by the 3–1 win.

I was a regular through most of 1978 and 1979. During that time England won all three of the 1978 Home Championship ties and topped the qualification group – consisting of Denmark, Bulgaria, the Republic of Ireland and Northern Ireland – for the 1980 European Championship Finals in Italy, having dropped just a solitary point. After we beat Bulgaria 3–0 in Sofia in June 1979, their manager Tzvetan Ilchev marvelled: 'This is a new England. They are still physically strong but they no longer concentrate on power. They have ideas, sophistication, a team who play modern football.'

As much as I liked Ron Greenwood, I always felt – and still feel – that the right man for the England manager's job would have been Brian Clough. We would have come a damn sight closer to winning something with him than we did without. We more than likely would have qualified in 1978, and in subsequent World Cups would have done better under Cloughie than anybody previous to Sir Alf.

Clough was someone I could only admire from afar but like most players from the time wanted to experience playing for him. The players that came under his charge at Nottingham Forest, like Trevor Francis and Tony Woodcock, would always be very guarded when talking about him. We'd hear the odd story of him turning up in the dressing room in his squash kit and saying something inspiring. I think the unpredictability of not knowing when he was going to appear or not – because he didn't always appear – kept his players on their toes. What he said went: nobody argued with him. He had total authority. But his teams played football the right way and the man was a football genius, that was indisputable. How many managers could go into the clubs that he went into and turn them into winning sides? Yet all geniuses are slightly flawed and I'm sure he was no exception. Clough was great at Derby and Nottingham Forest, but how would he fare on the bigger, international stage? Maybe he would have become a complete political nightmare for the FA.

I never felt inherently part of the England set-up. It seemed quite a transient relationship. I don't think you feel like you belong until you've played about 25 or 30 times. I think you've got to be there for three, four years plus to feel really part of it. By the time of my debut, nearing the age of 27, that opportunity had probably passed me by. In the end I managed twelve caps at a time when there was some meaning attached to playing for your country a dozen times, but from a career point of view it happened too late for me. Had my debut come maybe three or four years earlier, I would maybe have got those fifty caps.

My last international came against Austria in a 4–2 defeat in June 1979. Thereafter my Everton form declined and I was troubled by injury. I was completely out of it – it was as if I'd dropped off the radar. It's like being laid off at work: you just get let go; nobody really tells you. I felt saddened that I'd been part of the 1980 Euro Championship qualification team and felt that I had put in enough work to warrant a place in the squad. My club form wasn't good, but I felt I could perform on the international stage, as I had done during the 1978/79 season, when my form wasn't always as it should have been for Everton. That was one thing about Alf Ramsey – and which I found frustrating as an outsider looking in – that no matter how your club form was, if you did it internationally for him he'd stick with you. That, unfortunately for me, didn't happen with Ron Greenwood.

10

BERLIN

'Falling down is part of life. Getting back up is living.'

Anonymous

ONE OF THE FIXATIONS OF MODERN FOOTBALL IS PLAYER SALARIES, as if a weekly pay packet is some sort of indicator of a player's ability. Since the advent of freedom of movement at the expiry of a contract under the so-called 'Bosman system', combined with the enormous revenues from broadcast deals, player wages have entered a different stratosphere. Footballers are paid sums that are beyond the comprehension of the supporters who pay to watch them. Although I don't for a minute begrudge what any modern player earns, it is also a great shame in many ways because today's icons have – through their wealth – become removed from their fanbase.

During my time at Everton I became increasingly conscious of my rights and value as a player. I was the club's PFA rep at a time when the organisation was undergoing a profound change. When I'd started out at Birmingham the vision and mentality of the PFA was grounded in a different era, rooted in the philosophy that the players were servants and the clubs were the bosses. There was still this idea that we had to knock on a chairman's door and ask, 'Can we have this? Can we have that?' You were just a chattel, an item, in many respects. Maybe it was a reflection of British society, where unions were across the board becoming more militant and confrontational with employees, but during this decade the relationship between players and clubs started to fundamentally change.

As PFA rep I was a conduit of information between the organisation and the players. But across football, players started to take more control over their destinies and careers. There was enhancement to freedom of contract, with the implementation of a tribunal system for out-of-contract players, and the process that would culminate in Bosman was under way. As an organisation the PFA evolved and developed and it is still led by an old teammate of mine, Gordon Taylor, who was of that era where players began to take more responsibility for their futures.

Gordon was the key figure who took the PFA from being a small operation that existed solely within the confines of clubs to a major international organisation. I think it's something he was always destined to do and even as a young player he took a great interest in the welfare of those in the same profession as him.

Personally I think the balance has been lost in football. It has gone from everything being in the club's court, to the players holding all the cards. I can't see there being a middle ground again. In the space of a generation footballers have gone from being serfs to lords of the manor.

My thirty-goal season was set against a backdrop of a long-running contract dispute with Everton. I'd been naive when I joined the club, accepting what was put in front of me – which was the same as I was on at Birmingham – and, as an institution that shared many of John Moores's patrician values, Everton were a club where players were expected to accept their lot. My naivety was compounded by an era of spiralling inflation and high taxation. I was far from the stereotype of a greedy player exploiting a situation for their maximum personal gain. Like most of our fans, I was just a young man supporting his family. I needed a pay rise to keep up with the cost and pressures of modern living. I think my performances in the number nine shirt merited it too.

Everton, however, wouldn't budge. There were a few reports in the media that I was looking to leave the club. I want to stress that I never wanted to leave Everton. I loved the club by then, but I was left with little option other than to use the press to issue empty threats and to fuel speculation and put pressure on the management. There was a lot of brinkmanship going on from both sides, but I never formally requested a transfer, although if you believed everything you read in the *Liverpool Echo* there were at least three occasions when I 'demanded' a move. That was never the case. I might have issued verbal threats about wanting to leave, but as far as I was concerned they meant nothing. I never wanted to leave Everton and I suspect the club selectively leaked or inflated my empty threats as part of this ongoing dispute.

Kevin Keegan's departure from Liverpool to SV Hamburg in 1977, which probably made him the best-paid footballer in Europe, opened many players' eyes to our earning potential and served as a warning to chairmen, who suddenly realised they could lose their best players to European clubs.

Whereas Billy Bingham was unyielding on contract negotiations, Gordon Lee was a great help. He championed my cause to the board and even dropped a few hints to journalists that I was looking to leave, which were complete nonsense! In fairness, it was a pragmatic approach to take for the simple reason that it would have cost Everton far more to replace me than to keep me. Eventually the Everton board saw sense, and shortly before Easter 1978 I signed a new three-year contract that would take me to the end of the 1980/81 season, when I would be thirty.

That 1977/78 season was, financially, the most successful of my career. My basic wage was £400 per week, but with bonuses and endorsements it rose to just over £50,000 for the year. That was a good living at a time when the average annual wage was around £5,000. But in today's terms? It's the equivalent of about £250,000. In other words, the equivalent of what I earned in a year when I was Everton and England's centre-forward, Wayne Rooney now earns in a week.

That £50,000 sum was net of the majority of that £10,000 prize from the *Express*. Of that sum, £5,000 was split between the Football League Jubilee Provident Fund and the Professional Footballers' Association Benefit Fund and I got to keep the other £5,000. But I never wanted to keep all that money to myself and it would have been wrong not to recognise the efforts of all of my teammates. So I kept £1,000 for myself and put the remaining £4,000 into the players' pool for everyone to share. It meant the rest of the squad got £192 each.

However, a few months later I had a letter from the taxman demanding his share of the £10,000. This was the start of a legal and accountancy nightmare that would last for years. At first, the taxman would not accept that I did not receive £10,000. The Football League and the PFA supported my case and the Inland Revenue accepted that I was not in receipt of that full amount. But then they wanted tax on the £5,000! My teammates – or former teammates as they now were, because I was by that time a Swansea player – became involved and had to give statements to the effect that I put £4,000 into the players' pool. Eventually the taxman took me to court for the tax on £1,000. My defence was based on the fact that it was a prize and prizes should not be taxed, but the taxman won. I had to pay him, but with legal and accountancy fees I ended up paying out more money than I actually received. With hindsight, I should have given it all to charity, but then hindsight is a wonderful thing.

As a leading professional footballer in the 1970s there weren't so many endorsements and sponsorship deals as there are today . Some players now collect sponsorship deals like kids collect football stickers, giving them a wealth and fame that transcends their sport. You look at David Beckham and he ceased to become a player in the middle of his career; he became a brand. He's unique though: if I were playing today, you wouldn't catch me parading around in my underwear, not least because I don't have the body for it!

I was certainly never a fashion icon, although I did have my own foray in the fashion business. Formby became the base of my own short-lived *haute couture* empire – or at least a clothes shop – Bob Latchford Menswear. I'd go down and help out after training, but I wouldn't say I ever curated my own collections. Pat went around a couple of trade fairs to get an angle on what was out there and we stocked the shop that way.

The actual shop itself and the clothes were OK, albeit by the standards of the day – they were proper 1970s clothes, big collars and flared trousers – but when you talk about location being all-important, we discovered within a few months that we'd got it all wrong. If you'd put that shop somewhere else, like Church Street in Liverpool or Lord Street, Southport, we probably would have made a success out of it. Suburban Formby, however, didn't have the same footfall. In the end, we lost quite a bit of money before Kevin Sheedy, who was then a Liverpool player, took over the lease and made a profitable return from some other enterprise.

If you look at photos of me during my Everton years, there's quite a transition from season to season. Beard, no beard, bubble perm – I had them all. It always embarrasses me when I see photos of my 1970s self, it was such an awful decade for fashion. I can't say, however, that I was ever a fashion victim. I was never attuned to what was 'in' or not, it was just coincidental that I looked the part in a decade when, with hindsight, you wouldn't want to.

That said, I had a beard when no one else had a beard. That was an image thing, because I wanted to look rough and tough and scary and I thought a beard would add to this impression. I had long hair as well, which, again with hindsight, gave me the look of the Yorkshire Ripper. Then there was the perm. The un-forgettable perm. That was just one of the fads that swept the game, like beards now – everyone has a beard today. I'd go to a local hairdresser in Formby and have curlers and tongs and all sorts, but I never had the best hair in the Everton dressing room: that was Gary Stanley. He was a playboy, an absolute playboy.

*

DURING THE SUMMER OF 1978 GORDON TRADED IN ORDER TO TRY and bring a winning mix to Goodison. Jim Pearson was sold to Newcastle United and Mick Buckley to Sunderland. More controversially, Duncan McKenzie was sold to Chelsea. There was, of course, an inevitability about this sale, and what Gordon perceived as Duncan's waywardness almost became a point of principle for him. The supporters were not too happy. When Duncan returned to Goodison in November with his new Chelsea teammates, Duncan scored for the Londoners to be greeted with an ovation from the home crowd.

Duncan's replacement was Blackpool's Micky Walsh. He had made his reputation as the winner of the BBC's Goal of the Season award and was a prolific lower-league scorer. He cost a lot of money, but never really lived up to his £325,000 fee. Geoff Nulty arrived from Gordon's old club, Newcastle. You could understand why he bought him: he knew him and he was a good, solid, all-round, no-flair player; typical of what Gordon liked. The boss liked his players technically good but he didn't want them doing silly things, like Duncan would do occasionally. Geoff was down to earth, a grafter, and got on with things: a Gordon Lee type of player. He just wanted them to get on with playing football.

At the same time these two new arrivals were emblematic of Everton's problems in the era. We could never build on success. These weren't players of the calibre of Tizer or Martin Dobson or Mickey Pejic. They were good players, good honest pros, but they weren't going to give us something extra, something more to add to what we'd already got. It was as if we were constantly taking one step forward and two back.

In September Gordon signed Colin Todd from Derby County for £300,000. This was more like the sort of player that Everton needed. He was experienced. He'd won League Championship medals with Derby in 1972 and 1975 – the same year he was decorated with the PFA Player of the Year award – as well as 27 England caps. Colin was one of the best defenders of his generation. Yet at Everton we saw only glimpses of the form, which once saw Todd likened to Bobby Moore. For reasons that we – and Colin – could never quite grasp, one of the finest centre backs of the era was deployed in an unfamiliar right-back position.

The 1978/79 season got off to a flying start. We won four of the first six games, including victories in the opening three fixtures against Chelsea, Derby County and Arsenal. On 29 August we faced Wimbledon, just elected to the Football League, at Goodison. We didn't underestimate them; we knew what they were capable of, that they were fresh and bubbly and out for a scalp. But we burst their bubble that night, beating them 8–0, equalling the club's post-war record for its biggest victory.

It was a strange night. Goodison was less than half-full and it was just one of those games – like when Manchester United had come to Goodison the previous Christmas – when absolutely everything went in. When we were 4–0 up we were awarded a penalty at the Gwladys Street end. I'd scored two by then and Martin Dobson had scored twice as well. We both wanted the hat-trick and ended up arguing over who was going to take the penalty. I came out on top and was very cool and calm about taking penalties by then, and simply side-footed this one into the net. But the whole thing was completely out of character and went against what I'd done in my previous twenty years of playing football. I've no idea what

129

got into me. It was really odd behaviour. Dobbo reached his hat-trick, of course – and I ended up scoring five. That was my only five: I scored a four, and a few hat-tricks, braces and plenty of ones. So I've gone five, four, three, two, one in my career. It added a nice symmetry to my goalscoring.

*

THIS WAS AN ERA WHERE FOOTBALL WAS BESET BY HOOLIGANISM. Barely a Saturday passed without stories emerging of trouble at football stadiums. Travelling Everton supporters had been caught up in a few nasty incidents that year, at Newcastle on Good Friday, and against Chelsea on the opening day of the 1978/79 season. At the so-called Battle of Kensington High Street, Chelsea hooligans barricaded an underground carriage and indiscriminately attacked Evertonians. Police were taken by surprise by the scale of the incident and by the time they arrived with reinforcements several fans had been stabbed and many more needed hospital treatment.

I played most of my career against a backdrop of what seemed like – if you believed the press and politicians – endemic football hooliganism. It might seem strange, but as players we were largely removed from it. A lot of it was taking place outside of the grounds so in many respects it didn't really affect what was happening on the pitch. I never encountered hooliganism getting out of control, where the game was actually stopped. But you were always aware that at any time something could go off.

Racism was also starting to have a deeper impact on English football as more and more players of Afro-Caribbean heritage broke through to the First Division. It's tough enough anyway to make it as a professional footballer. But in the late 1960s or 70s, if you were black it was even tougher. People may be complaining today about abuse but to be playing back then as a player of colour must have been horrendous. You have to admire the players who actually got out there and played, like my Everton teammate Cliff Marshall. You start saying anything derogatory now and you're in trouble. But back then nobody gave a toss. There was real vitriol and hatred. It must have been very difficult for those players in the early days.

One match that was guaranteed to be virtually trouble-free was the Merseyside derby. I realise that the relationship between Everton and Liverpool supporters has soured in recent years and that some believe the 'friendly derby' to be dead. Back then, while there was great intensity to the rivalry, it *was* friendly and families were split between red and blue. As players, the passion across Merseyside ahead of a derby permeated your every thought leading up to that big game.

Of course, it was a problem fixture for us as Everton players. We had failed to beat them in 362 weeks and faced the indignity of that winless streak extending to seven years if the Goodison derby on 28 October 1978 passed without an Everton victory. Nobody wanted that to happen. This was all against a backdrop of near-continual Liverpool success. They were reigning European Champions and were picking up domestic trophies for fun. For Evertonians misery was being piled upon misery. As an Everton player I had never scored against them and on a personal level wanted that streak to end.

It would be one of the most memorable days of my Everton career. Goodison was a 53,000 all-ticket sell-out. We were missing Mick Lyons through injury so Roger Kenyon stepped in for a rare start. We were still unbeaten in the league and Europe and second in the league. It was a chance to draw blood in what we hoped would be the race for the league title.

Surprisingly, for a derby, it was a really good game. We had lots of chances and played well throughout. On a different afternoon we could have had three or four goals. I think I probably had my best chance of scoring against them while in the blue of Everton. Played in one-on-one with an onrushing Ray Clemence I tried to loop a header in from the edge of the penalty area when I should have tried to blast it. But maybe it wasn't meant to be.

The game's decisive moment came on 58 minutes. Mickey Pejic looped a long high ball forward, which Dobbo got his head to. The ball fell to Andy King, who hit the ball sweetly, first time, from the edge of the Liverpool area and into the top corner of the net.

A hoodoo had been broken. It was a great afternoon and it became a great evening. We celebrated in the way that we knew best: lots of alcohol and lots of talk of doing it all over again. We drank because that's what players did then, but we drank to switch off and forget. If you're in a stadium with 50,000 people baying for you to win and you actually go and do that, the adrenaline rush, the energy that that gives you is phenomenal. We didn't need reasons to drink on a day like that, but if you're looking for an excuse one of them would be to switch off.

When we challenged for the league title in 1974/75, Derby County ultimately lifted the League Championship almost by default. I don't mean that to sound ungracious or to diminish their achievement, but it was a Championship that seemed at times as if nobody wanted to win. Four years later we were challenging again, but this time were against two opponents of formidable quality. Obviously there was Liverpool, the reigning European Champions, but also Nottingham Forest. The champions were unbeaten in the league in almost a year, a run that would eventually extend to an unprecedented 42 games. In February 1979 they boosted their already formidable line-up with Britain's first £1 million player, my old friend Trevor Francis. He was – and would prove – to be worth every single penny Brian Clough paid for him.

In short, it was becoming harder than at any time of my career to become league champions. That's not finding excuses; it was the reality of the situation. Derby had won the title with 53 points and when Liverpool won it in 1977 they did so with 57 points. But by 1977/78, the benchmark was 64 and by the end of 1978/79 it would rise to 68 points. There was no room for slips.

We remained unbeaten throughout November 1978 and continued to shadow Liverpool at the top of the league. Dave Sexton, the Manchester United manager, heralded us as 'the best football side we have met so far', when we played them in September. 'They have a good mixture of strength and skill and it is not surprising they get results playing like that,' he added. Yet the top slot continued to elude us. A visit to West Bromwich Albion was called off at the start of December because of bad weather, and the following week only Liverpool ending Nottingham Forest's record-busting 42-game unbeaten streak prevented Everton from drawing level at the top. Only two days before Christmas did we lose our record as the First Division's only unbeaten team, when we lost 3–2 at Coventry. On Boxing Day a single Billy Wright goal was enough to see off Manchester City and maintain pressure at the top.

This was Britain's winter of discontent – with strikes, power cuts, mounting piles of rubbish and bitterly cold weather – and it unsettled us too. Games fell victim to the ice and cold, while restrictions on electricity usage limited night games. Only at the end of January 1979, after a gap of a month, did the league programme resume for Everton. We topped the table for a week after beating Bristol City on 10 February, but from there on our title challenge slipped away. We drew far too many games and won just five matches after Christmas, losing seven and drawing the rest. I was troubled by injury and my goals dried up – I managed just three of nineteen (only eleven of which came in the league) – after Boxing Day. Gordon entered the transfer market again and signed Brian Kidd and Peter Eastoe, but they could not bolster our flagging challenge. In the end we finished fourth on 51 points, far behind champions Liverpool.

The problems we faced then under Gordon were not dissimilar to those we encountered under Billy. As players we were not responding to what was going on in the training ground or what we were being told in the dressing room. I don't think Gordon had lost us, but he'd certainly started to lose the fans. The flying cushions had again become part of the Goodison match-day experience. More concerning was the fact people were staying away. When we played Birmingham in our penultimate home game the crowd was barely 23,000-strong. The title had long been lost by then, but we were still fourth. These days that would be celebrated.

The turning point, I think, in Gordon's managerial reign was the loss of Steve Burtenshaw, who became QPR manager at the start of the 1978/79 season. It took some months for this to manifest itself, but a key part of the balance at Goodison had been lost. As I've discussed, Steve and Gordon complemented each other very well. Gordon was so intense, so wrapped up in things, whereas Steve was an easy-going cockney and we responded well to him.

In his place Gordon promoted the youth coach Eric Harrison. I've not got a problem with Eric. I got on well with him; he was likeable, had a good character, was a good coach, and knew his stuff. He showed his calibre as a youth coach later in his career when he was credited with the emergence of Manchester United's golden generation of Ryan Giggs, Paul Scholes and David Beckham. But for me he was the wrong person at the wrong time to promote as first-team coach at Everton. Looking back, we needed somebody of the calibre of Steve

Burtenshaw, an experienced first-team coach who knew how to handle players, from senior players to young pros. And we lost the balance between Gordon and Steve's personalities.

His knowledge as a coach and of techniques weren't Eric's problem. Personally I just don't think he was ready to be a first-team coach. For me he was a youth coach – an outstanding one, as history would show – but he wasn't cut out for his promotion. Certain people fit into certain niches in terms of coaching. Some people can coach at a certain level, be terrific, then they can try to coach at another level and be absolutely useless at it. I think every coach knows where they feel comfortable and players sense that too. I didn't get the feeling that Eric was ready for that job.

The Everton dressing room contained a lot of senior professionals. It is difficult to impose yourself on such an environment and, looking back on it now, I can understand what Eric did and why he did it, but he went about things in the wrong way. He started to dig out all the senior pros and have a go at them. In some respects his mentality was a bit like Gordon's: he could be very aggressive, in fact, in Eric's case, extremely so. But in any relationship you need a balance and we lost that when Steve left and Eric came in. In some ways he was too similar in temperament to Gordon. This need not have been a problem, but sometimes in a managerial partnership you need to play out in the dressing room a good-cop, bad-cop scenario and we lost that. He wanted to be seen to have the authority, especially with the younger pros that were there. But at the time you don't see that. You just see someone who is angry all the time, bollocking you for no reason. At times it was upsetting. Sometimes it ended up in shouting matches. Usually, it just rubbed people up the wrong way.

That disharmony started to manifest itself in the second half of the 1978/79 season. As had happened under Billy, our failure to mount a sustained title challenge left a sour taste, a hangover if you like. Gordon couldn't change things. It became, again, a snowball effect. Things, however, got much worse.

The 1979/80 pre-season was a disaster. Players were so fed up they were starting to leave. Dobbo turned down a new contract and dropped down a division to return to Burnley. Others were soon to follow.

In one pre-season game at Hertha Berlin all the anger and frustration boiled over. Colin Todd was being played out of position, again at right-back. We knew he wasn't happy about this, and we were aware of the madness of the situation. He'd played all his life as a centre-half, and was a terrific central defender. In that position he was one of the most difficult players I ever played against. That afternoon something snapped. The game was going on and all of a sudden Toddy was walking across the field. He got to the touchline, took his shin pads off, threw them down, took his shirt off and proclaimed, 'I'm not playing there. That's it. I'm not a full-back and I'm not playing there any more.'

It was chaos in the dressing room at half-time. People were shouting and arguing and suddenly Eric started on Dave Thomas. Tizer was one of the most unassuming and placid members of the Everton squad. I don't know why Eric chose to have a go at him, but he started ranting about his rubber-soled boots.

'You should be wearing fucking studs; get your stockings up, get your shin pads on.'

Tizer for the first and only time I'd ever known, blew it. He swore – Tizer never swore – he was swearing, and his boots came off, his shirt came off.

'Fuck this and fuck you; I'm not playing.'

This was pre-season.

As chaos descended I sat there thinking: 'This is not right; we've suddenly gone from being a harmonious bunch of players, to having rucks during friendly matches.'

Tizer was sold by the start of the new season, Toddy had left by the end of August. Both were retrograde steps and indicative of the way things were heading.

I too had the chance to move. There was talk of a swap deal involving the Wolves midfielder Steve Daley, which I wasn't happy about, and he moved to Manchester City instead. Although deep down I didn't want to go, I'd asked in the heat of the moment for a transfer again, and Gordon accepted my request on the understanding that it would be on the club's terms. In other words, it meant nothing. But at the time Aston Villa were casting around for a centre-forward to replace Andy Gray, who Wolves had bought with the money they received for Daley. With what was going on at Everton, given the circumstances if it had been any club other than Villa, another top club, I would probably have given it serious consideration. Goodison wasn't a happy camp. There was too much disharmony. I'm big on emotional connections and although I loved the Everton supporters, I felt I had started to lose that in the dressing room. It was dispiriting to see players of the quality of Dobbo and Tizer leaving the club. It wasn't good.

But I couldn't go to Villa. Of all the clubs, being a Birmingham City boy, they were the one I could not join. Looking back now, it was probably a bad career move: I would have ended up in a League Championship-winning side and winning the European Cup. And I could have been the one scoring the goal in the European Cup final and not the man who eventually replaced Gray, Peter Withe.

Instead I continued at Goodison, and despite the disharmony I was proud to be an Everton player; it wasn't long before I came off the transfer list. I missed the opening stages of the 1979/80 season with a knee injury that lingered from the previous campaign. That had occurred not in the First Division on some mudbath, but on a rock-solid artificial pitch in Libya. You wouldn't credit it.

During the 1978/79 season we'd been taken there on a mid-season break for reasons that were never fully explained to us. Libya was becoming an international pariah under Colonel Gaddafi, but we went there most likely for a payday for the club, although we never saw any of the rewards. My recollection is that there was absolutely nothing there. I went to Egypt with Everton, which was a great trip, full of culture and history and hospitality. But Libya? It was just the weirdest place that you could imagine wanting to go and play a game of football. The texture of the pitch was like carpet, it was dreadful, and when I went up for a corner I came down heavily, twisted and the keeper landed on me. The resultant injury jeopardised but didn't quite end my involvement in the remainder of the 1978/79 campaign, but I was still hobbling and limping when I came back for pre-season.

I returned to the Everton team as a substitute in our second-leg UEFA Cup tie against Feyenoord in October 1979, but I was unable to stave off a 2–0 aggregate defeat. We had started the league season slowly, winning just two of the opening ten league games. Things picked up slightly after my return, but we lacked a rhythm and found it difficult to string together a run of results. Only once all season would we win back-to-back league games.

Although league form was poor, relegation was never something that was talked about. I never felt at any stage, even when we were not playing that well, that we would be relegated, ever. I always felt we were capable of staying in the First Division, even though things were going badly. I wasn't playing well, the mood wasn't good, but I never felt at any stage that relegation was an issue.

Gordon was well aware that things weren't right, but – like Billy before him – he seemed powerless in the teeth of adversity. In a newspaper interview halfway through the season, he said: 'If we had kept the players who wanted to go – Thomas, Pejic and Colin Todd, plus Martin Dobson – and if we had continued to play the way we did last season, we would have done better.' Talk about stating the obvious…

I remember one morning at Bellefield, after training, when one of the young apprentices came into the dressing room and told me Gordon wanted to speak. I went into the manager's room and Gordon was in the shower, stark bollock naked. I leaned against the door.

'Latch, what's wrong? Tell me what's wrong.'

'Gordon, you know what's wrong, don't you?'

He made a sort of groaning noise. 'Yeah, I do,' he answered.

But that was it. He knew and I knew, everybody knew what was wrong, but he didn't do anything about it. Whether he could or he couldn't change his coaching staff I simply don't know because I never pressed him on it; but he knew what the problem was.

On 1 March 1980, while watching Everton fall to a 2–1 derby defeat at Goodison, Dixie Dean collapsed and died of a heart attack. He was 72 years old and had been in a frail condition having undergone an amputation of his left leg a few years earlier, but he remained until the end a great character and a huge inspiration to me. When he was buried shortly after, it was an enormous honour and privilege to join Mick Lyons and Brian Labone as one of his pallbearers.

That derby encounter really was an afternoon to forget. The game itself was marked – and marred – by a horrific challenge by Jimmy Case on Geoff Nulty. Back in those days there were some hard, vicious tackles that went about, and went unpunished as well; severely unpunished. That afternoon, Jimmy scythed through Geoff, shredding his cruciate ligament. There's always anger when that sort of thing happens, but more so because it was a Liverpool player that did him.

Jimmy was a hard, nasty type of player, the sort you knew you had to be wary of. You got to know who these players were and that you had to protect yourself when you were facing them. There was real disgust at Jimmy's actions. He wasn't sent off; I don't think he was even booked. When Geoff, who was 31, learned the extent of the injury the following Monday, he knew immediately that his career was over.

I had been missing from that fateful game through injury, but I returned a week later for our FA Cup quarter-final against Ipswich Town. Ipswich were a really good side, challenging for the league title, and would go on to win the following year's UEFA Cup. They were very formidable opponents and only a month earlier had turned us over – humiliated us – 4–0 at Goodison.

Whatever the struggles we'd had that season in the league, Evertonians got behind us. Goodison was rammed. The official attendance was cited at 45,104, but it was a time when the stadium could hold nearly 53,000 and I could not see a spare seat in the house. The terraces were heaving, swaying with masses of the expectant and hopeful. I'd scored in every round so far, against Aldershot, Wigan and then Wrexham in the fifth round, and I had a good feeling going into the game. It was a testy affair, but we held our own, and John Gidman, our athletic full-back, was given licence to roam up the field and almost scored with a thirty-yard pile-driver.

John was instrumental in our opening goal on 28 minutes. Taking possession on the left wing, he sent in a swirling cross. I lurked at the back post and the ball came in with such pace that I had to lean back and just take some of the speed out of the ball, to cushion it past Paul Cooper. I ran to the Main Stand terrace, fists clenched with joy. On 77 minutes we were awarded a free kick on the edge of the Ipswich area. Andy King tapped the ball to Brian Kidd, who simply leathered it into the back of the Gwladys Street goal. Goodison went wild with cries of 'We shall not be moved!' Although Kevin Beattie pulled a late goal back, we would not be moved.

It set up a semi-final at Villa Park with West Ham. Our opponents were then in the Second Division and we really fancied our chances. It said a lot about the season I was having that I only started from the bench, but from the dugout I could see that we had the measure of our opponents. We took the lead two minutes before half-time through a Brian Kidd penalty and had West Ham cold. I couldn't see a way back into it for them.

The game turned in the 63rd minute. For reasons only he can explain, Brian got involved in an off-the-ball tangle with Ray Stewart that developed into a fight. It was inexplicable and inexcusable and cost us dearly. He was sent off. Seven minutes later Trevor Brooking broke down the left and cut in from the by-line to set up Stuart Pearson for an easy goal. Gordon, to his credit, still went for the win, bringing me on in place of Gary Megson, but from a winning position we were now left with a replay at Elland Road the following Wednesday.

This was never one of the happier grounds I visited and it was with some trepidation that we made our way over the Pennines. Brian was suspended and so I got my chance up front. It was a tight and fraught game that finished goalless after ninety minutes, but we should have had it won by then. In the first ten minutes of the second half the referee disallowed goals from myself and Peter Eastoe, each for handball, and another from West Ham's Billy Bonds on the pretext of a foul. In extra time, Alan Devonshire put West Ham ahead with a superb solo goal. We had to call on all of our reserves to try and retrieve something and we did just that. Billy Wright broke down the right flank and sent in a low, hard cross; I dived at the near post, made a connection and the ball flew past Phil Parkes into the back of the net, right in front of the Evertonians. It was a brilliant moment. I climbed onto the security fences, my hands aloft, as supporters charged forward trying to touch me.

We were heading for a second replay, but then one of those freak moments that typified this era for Everton struck. Just ninety seconds from the end, a long cross from Ray Stewart was headed back across our penalty area, and who should be there but the left-back Frank Lampard snr, who headed home the winner. He hadn't scored in a year and I don't think he'd scored with a header in his entire life. It was unbelievable.

I sometimes think about Mario Balotelli and his famous T-shirt emblazoned 'Why Always Me?' That's how I felt back then. But it kept happening to Everton over my time there. Carlisle, Clive Thomas, Chris Nicholl and now this. It wasn't just one thing, it was a catalogue of misfortune.

It was a long, sorry journey back to Merseyside. Mostly it was silence: contemplation, regret, the odd drink. We drank when we won to steady ourselves, now we drank to drown out what had happened. Maybe some talked about what we could have done, or should have done, but it was all very muted. We knew we'd let ourselves down, and in doing so we'd let the club and the fans down. But it wasn't through a lack of effort; it wasn't through a lack of trying. We were playing against a Second Division team that we were more than capable of beating. It was not a good feeling. It was not a good time. We just wanted to forget.

We finished the 1979/80 season nineteenth, a single place and four points off relegation. I ended the campaign with thirteen goals, but just six in the league. I, and my teammates, were well aware that it wasn't good enough.

*

BEHIND THE SCENES THE DISCORD CONTINUED. ANDY KING – AMONG Gordon's most consistent performers during his three-and-a-half years in charge – fell out with the boss and was sold to Queens Park Rangers. Ostensibly his motivation was to get a place in England's 1982 World Cup squad, but the Second Division seemed a strange place to try and realise such an ambition. Others remained unhappy and tried to leave. Attempts to deal in the transfer market and sign players like Bolton's Peter Reid met with frustration. Optimism was rock bottom. Our opening attendance for the 1980/81 season at Goodison was just 23,337.

Gordon did at least try something new and invested his faith in youth. He opened the new season with the five almost untried youngsters Gary Megson, Steve McMahon, Kevin Ratcliffe, Joe McBride and Graeme Sharp in his line-up to face Sunderland. Sharp was signed from Dumbarton for £120,000 by Lee the previous April aged only nineteen, and it was the one time I played alongside him. In so doing it formed an unbroken link, lasting thirty years, between some of Everton's most famous number nines – Alex Young, Joe Royle, myself and Graeme. He was raw then, but you could see straight away that he had all the attributes you would expect from a great centre-forward.

Ratcliffe was the other lad that stood out a mile. He had presence as a defender, but also as a man. Even as a teenager you could tell that once he established himself he would be a leader. The success that followed for him never surprised me at all. McMahon too was a good little player, a hard worker, who achieved great things, but in a Liverpool shirt.

What this young team lacked in experience it made up for in desire, and for a few months we clicked, rising as high as third in the league. Gordon even won the Bell's Manager of the Month award. I think what Gordon did then, in giving such an array of young players their opportunities, helped Everton later more than it did in 1980.

For me, the goals briefly returned: braces against Blackpool and Coventry and a hat-trick against Crystal Palace. But then, in mid-November, disaster struck. Playing against Sunderland at Goodison I pulled my hamstring. It became the worst injury of my career. It was so persistent. I went through the rehabilitation process several times, but every time I got near to sprinting – because sprinting was the one thing you had to do to see whether the hamstring was OK – I'd pull up again. I spent many lonely days in rehabilitation with Jim McGregor.

In my absence Everton laboured. Crowds, by the end of the season, were down to 15,000. A home defeat to Stoke City witnessed the lowest league attendance since the war. The board announced that Gordon's position was 'under review'. With his contract expiring at the end of the season we all knew what lay in store.

I'd still go and watch my teammates when we played at home, but it wasn't the same. It was difficult and frustrating. In total I was on the sidelines for just shy of six months.

I returned on the May Day bank holiday, as a substitute at Wolves. I replaced Peter Eastoe as we played out a goalless draw. It confirmed a finish of fifteenth place, three points clear of relegation. Everton had won just one of their previous twelve games. Hours after the end of the match Gordon was sacked. I hadn't foreseen it then, but it was to be my last game for the club too.

EVERTON'S BOARD MOVED DECISIVELY AFTER GORDON'S DEPARTURE, appointing in his place Blackburn Rover's brilliant young player-manager, a man who had taken Rovers from the Third Division to the brink of the First in just two years. His name was familiar to me and every single Evertonian, for my arrival seven years earlier had heralded his departure from Everton. It was Howard Kendall.

The scale of the task facing Howard was immense. As one newspaper put it, 'They're not asking much from Howard Kendall – only a three-minute mile, a century before lunch and a successful assault on Everest.' The club was in the doldrums and needed significant investment and changes. It was period of economic decline in the city of Liverpool, with the effects of deindustrialisation and mass unemployment particularly harshly felt.

Howard's first task was to take the team on an end-of-season tour to Japan. I, however, wouldn't be joining them. I had contracted to go to Australia for May, June and part of July to play for Brisbane Lions. I was able to take Pat and the children, play at a different pace, earn some money and regain some fitness after the frustrations of the 1980/81 season.

It was also a time to ponder the future. I was thirty and my contract had expired. It had been a testing two years. I felt that I'd stagnated. I'd lost my place in the England team. I wanted to play and I wanted to play to the same standards I had set earlier in my career. I knew I was capable of it. I was aware of my age and fitness and how talented the emerging Graeme Sharp was. I could see that Everton's striking future more than likely lay with him. All these things went through my mind. But above all, I felt that after seven and a half years the time was right for something different.

When pre-season started at Bellefield I met Howard and had a full and very frank conversation with him. He wanted me to stay. He made a concerted effort for me to stay. It's always nice to be wanted. But my mind was made up and I told him that I needed a change. We parted amicably.

*

WHEN I LOOK BACK ON MY CAREER AT EVERTON IT EVOKES THE first line of Charles Dickens' *Tale of Two Cities*. It was at once the best of times and worst of times.

Leaving Everton rejuvenated me. For the next few years I felt fitter than I had been in years. The goals would come back too. But I should probably never have left. It would have been nice to have stayed at Everton until my mid-thirties, to have helped Graeme Sharp progress, and to have shared in some of the colossal success that lay not too far in the future. Hindsight is a great thing and few people then could ever have imagined what was going to happen next for that great football club.

For me, though, I had a new start and the 1981/82 campaign would herald some unexpected pleasures.

11

SWANSEA

'I may not have gone where I intended to go, but I think I have ended up where I needed to be.'
Douglas Adams

JOHN TOSHACK HAD BECOME ONE OF THE BIGGEST NAMES IN football during an incredibly successful spell as Liverpool's centre-forward through the 1970s. Towards the end of that decade, as injuries increasingly held him back, he became Swansea City player-manager at the age of just 28 and helped instigate a football revolution in South Wales. In just four seasons Swansea rose from the Fourth Division to, in 1981, the First. And Toshack wanted me to lead Swansea's forward line in the top flight.

I'd met Toshack during his time at Anfield. The Everton and Liverpool players were never especially close, but there were inevitable interactions due to the proximity of the two clubs, with Stanley Park separating Goodison and Anfield and Bellefield being around the corner from Melwood in West Derby. I think Tosh and I had some photographs taken together one year ahead of a derby match.

So I knew of him, but I wouldn't say I particularly knew him well. There was no close bond that made my move from Everton to Swansea an inevitability. In fact the main reason for my move to South Wales was pragmatic above any other:

they were the only First Division club that came in for me, and I wanted to stay in the top flight. I had very little choice. I could have stayed at Goodison but, as I've articulated, there were good reasons to move on. I'd done my time at Everton.

I was aware of Swansea's meteoric rise through the divisions, from bottom to top. I think everybody in football was; it was a bit of a fairy-tale story. What Toshack had done at the Vetch Field in football terms was remarkable, but his powers of persuasion and charisma were evident too. Without such qualities, how else could you persuade players like Tommy Smith and Ian Callaghan to leave the European Champions for a team in the third or fourth tier?

Tosh had a very quiet, persuasive manner about him. He was a good communicator in terms of his vision and what he wanted, and how he saw things. We met soon after my return from Australia, a period I had enjoyed very much and which revitalised me. Once he showed an interest in me the transfer happened very quickly. Swansea agreed to pay a fee of £150,000 and I agreed a contract with Tosh myself. Of course, there was no agent involved. It was all very smooth.

I suppose the biggest burden fell on my family. Richard was ten, Izzy thirteen and we had to find them schools and somewhere nice to live. We didn't have that long, just July and August. Schooling was a problem not just in terms of the disruption that was caused – no child wants to change schools and no parent wants to move them except as a last resort – but because all the Welsh state schools taught Welsh and so our options became immediately limited. Learning Welsh is great if you're Welsh or going to live in Wales and have your career in Wales; I can see the benefit of learning the language then. But Pat and I could see no benefit from them learning Welsh, or having such an educational focus on the language, which meant that we eventually put them in a small private school.

We rented a house at first before settling in Mayals, a village near the Mumbles on the coast, west of Swansea. Having lived in Southport and Formby for the previous seven years it was great to be near the beach again. We soon discovered what a lovely part of the world southwest Wales is, a really beautiful place to live with friendly people, but very remote too. The M4 can seem like an eternal highway and you can feel a little bit cut off.

By the end of the 1980s Toshack had reached the summit of the club managerial ladder when he managed Real Madrid. Having worked with some fairly big-name managers at Everton, Birmingham and England I could see straight away his pedigree as a boss. There was no denying that he had the ability and the know-how to win and he had a winning mentality that was inherent from his time at Liverpool. A lot of his managerial formula was based on what Liverpool did. It was very simple but a winning formula. You could see what he had learned from Bill Shankly and Bob Paisley and then put into practice with his own personality on it.

At the same time Toshack was spending big money at Swansea. I was a senior player and a big name, but even I wasn't one of one of the most expensive players. He spent £350,000 on Colin Irwin, a Liverpool reserve centre-half, for instance, and £175,000 bringing the forward Alan Curtis back to the Vetch Field after an unsuccessful spell at Leeds. These were big sums and Swansea were not a wealthy club or playing in a big stadium or in an affluent part of the country. Yet as a player there were never any doubts about Swansea's economic model or how Tosh was able to build this team, at least not at first. As a player you never think too much about the financial side of things because that's for the boardroom to deal with. We were all just delighted to be playing in the top flight.

Tosh had built a team simmering with experience and yet supplemented by some promising young players. My forward partner was Jeremy Charles, who, like his uncle – the Welsh football legend, John Charles – was just as adept playing at centre-half. His father Mel was another forward/defender who had represented the Swans in the 1950s, before playing for Arsenal and Cardiff. Jeremy was probably not of the calibre of his forbears, but he was, nevertheless, a decent player. We were aware of his heritage, however, and his uncle would be a daunting presence in and around the club. Not only was he a living Swansea and Wales legend, but one of the greats of European football. He was imposing in every way and boomed with a very deep Welsh accent.

On the wing we had Leighton James. He had been at Burnley with Dobbo and liked to moan, but everybody ignored him. Technically he was a decent winger and I've always been lucky to play with at least one good out-and-out wide man wherever I played. When you're playing with a winger you want consistency and that ability to deliver quality balls in a place where you knew you'd be. Obviously a good winger has to beat men, go past men, be able to play balls in under pressure. But it was the final delivery that was crucial. Dave Thomas was the master, nobody could touch him, but there were plenty of others whose assists helped me keep the goals coming and Leighton was one of them.

Later Ray Kennedy was added to the squad from Liverpool. He was a player of top pedigree and although he was probably not as mobile as he once was, he still had all the ability. He reminded me of Trevor Brooking, the way he moved and played, a very elegant winger-cum-midfield player. He was probably not of the same calibre as Trevor but he had that sort of quality about him.

Tosh regularly went back to Liverpool to prise away players that had dropped out of the first team, or those unable to quite make the breakthrough. It was the biggest open secret in football that Liverpool's reserves were the most potent source of talent in the country. Howard Kendall would use them to good effect to bring in Alan Harper and Kevin Sheedy to his up-and-coming Everton team too. Tosh brought in the ball-playing centre back Colin Irwin for a club record fee (that stood for 27 years). Colin's progress had been disrupted at Anfield by the emergence of Alan Hansen. Liverpool rarely changed their team and it meant Colin stayed in the reserves. He had good mobility and could bring the ball out of defence. He also brought Max Thompson, who'd had a spell at Blackpool after leaving Liverpool. Mad Max, as we called him, was a different sort of centre back, limited but giving everything he had in every game. Off the pitch he was a tearaway and would do some crazy, unpredictable things, which is why his nickname was such a good fit.

John Mahoney was a good, hard-working midfield player. He was the engine of our team; he'd keep us going. He was Toshack's cousin and our driving force; he'd get stuck in and encourage us. You always need somebody there like that who's just keeping you going, ceaselessly, endlessly, keeping you going.

While I was at the Vetch Field I also came into contact with my first foreign teammates, the Yugoslav international defensive duo of Ante Rajković and Džemal Hadžiabdić. Besides the occasional South African footballer, English football had largely been closed to overseas players until the late 1970s. It started to change when Tottenham brought in two Argentine World Cup winners, Ricky Villa and Ossie Ardilles, and soon other clubs began casting their scouting nets beyond Britain and Ireland. It was an interesting experience and the pair of

Yugoslavs certainly brought different approaches to the game and different mental approaches too. The full-back, 'Jimmy', as we called Hadžiabdić, was a decent player; Ante, who played at centre-half, went missing now and again. They spoke reasonably good English and certainly added something to the dressing room.

Could I have ever imagined that a generation later you'd have teams in the First Division or Premier League where English players were a minority? And sometimes fielding starting line-ups without a single Englishman? It was hard to conceive back in the early 1980s that that was going to come about. But it wasn't too hard to see what was going to happen when Sky eventually entered football in 1992 with all the money. And it's just snowballed from there. They keep talking about trying to do something to boost the numbers of English players in the top flight, but I can't see how they're going to do it. The percentage of English players is just going to continue to fall and English managers in years to come will be looking at Championship players for the national team. We're already at that stage with Wales and Scotland. There's a lot of razzmatazz around English football now and foreign players – of which these two were early pioneers – have added to that. But, as with everything in life, when you gain something you normally lose something too.

HAVING BEEN SO FRUSTRATED WITH INJURIES IN MY LAST YEAR AT Everton, I finally felt back to my best going into the 1981/82 season. The spell in Australia had brought me almost up to peak fitness going into pre-season, and I was refreshed by my new surroundings and teammates. No player relishes pre-season, but I was enjoying my football again. Physically I felt ready for anything at this stage, as if I was in my early twenties. Between the age of 30 and 34 I probably felt as strong as – or stronger than – I did between 20 and 24. I was as physically fit as I ever could be, or ever was, and always felt I could score.

I think Tosh saw that in me as well. On Fridays we trained at the Vetch and I'll always remember going out the door to go home on the eve of the opening day of the season when I bumped into him.

'Latch, see you tomorrow,' he said. 'Oh, and by the way, Latch, two tomorrow will be OK.'

I just smiled at him.

The opening day of the 1981/82 season brought Leeds United to the Vetch Field. They were accompanied by 23,489 spectators and the *Match of the Day* cameras. These were the days when just three games were shown on the highlights programme, so it always brought a sense of occasion. Pinned up on the dressing-room noticeboard was a good-luck telegram from Toshack's mentor, Bill Shankly. I was wearing an unfamiliar shirt – number eleven.

It took just five minutes for us to open our account in the top flight. I dummied a cross and the ball ran to Jeremy Charles, who side-footed home. Derek Parlane brought the scores level with a diving header and Leeds might have been ahead at half-time had it not been for some inspired saves by Dai Davies, with whom I was now re-united.

But in the second half we took over. A minute after the break Charles headed down a Robbie James cross and I volleyed home from twelve yards. On fifty minutes I had a second with a tap-in at the near post. Five minutes later I completed my hat-trick with a towering header from a Leighton James free kick. Alan Curtis completed the rout on seventy minutes with a run and then a fierce shot that swerved past John Lukic in the Leeds goal. Swansea City five, Leeds United one. It had been a stunning start to the season.

A win the following Tuesday over Brighton took us top, albeit after just two games, but our good start continued through September. Victories over Tottenham, Notts County and Sunderland took us to third by the end of the month. Only a 4–1 hammering at West Brom, where we conceded three goals in five minutes, brought us down to earth.

One of the advantages of playing for one of the four Welsh teams competing in the Football League in this period were the opportunities it afforded in terms of playing in Europe. Swansea, like Cardiff, Newport and Wrexham, all competed in the Welsh Cup against a plethora of non-league teams, and the occasional wildcard from over the English border (for reasons that escaped me even then, Shrewsbury, Hereford and even Kidderminster Harriers all featured in the competition). Winning it afforded progress to the European Cup Winners' Cup, and as the strongest team in the principality we had a good chance every year.

I joined Swansea when they were reigning Welsh Cup holders and one of my first playing tasks was to travel back behind the Iron Curtain, to East Germany, where the poverty and narrowness of life had so shocked me as a teenager. We faced Lokomotiv Leipzig and after a 1–0 defeat in the first leg in Wales we headed east.

There hadn't been any major changes in the country. Maybe there was a little bit of economic regeneration, but nothing substantial. Arriving and departing from West Berlin and then crossing over to the East highlighted the stark differences in the divided nation. It was almost like Las Vegas had landed in this oppressed, pallid place; compared to the East, West Berlin was like a paradise. There were lots of soldiers standing around the stadium, which added to the harshness of our surroundings. The game was instantly forgettable. We conceded two goals in the first 22 minutes, virtually killing the game, and when Alan Curtis was sent off on 41 minutes we knew we had no chance. Jeremy Charles scored a late goal, but it was only a consolation.

On 3 October we were back in front of the *Match of the Day* cameras, this time at Anfield, where we were up against the reigning European Champions and Tosh's former club, Liverpool. It was an emotional afternoon, particularly for him, as his great mentor Bill Shankly had died four days earlier. Tosh had been in constant contact with Shankly ever since he became a manager and you could see how the older man's ideas were impressed upon the Welshman's style. Tosh caused a bit of a stir when, ahead of the minute's silence, he stripped off his Swansea tracksuit to reveal a Liverpool shirt. Some felt it was an overture for Bob Paisley's job, but that was just Tosh, paying his respect.

I was enduring an eight-year scoreless streak against Liverpool, which had unfortunately coincided with my time at Goodison. And yet I never had any problems scoring against Liverpool for the other clubs I played for. And so it was that day.

We took the lead on fifteen minutes when Phil Thompson conceded a penalty and Leighton James converted. In the second half Anfield was further silenced on 57 minutes when I stole in front of Thompson and slammed the ball into the roof of Bruce Grobbelaar's net. I clenched my fists in celebration and yelled with delight into the dumbstruck Kop end. If only I'd managed to do that in my

Everton days!

Yet Liverpool were never a team to give much away, particularly at Anfield, where they had lost just five league games in the previous five seasons . Two minutes after my goal we gave away a needless penalty and Terry McDermott tucked it away. Four minutes after that McDermott fell easily when running away from goal and scored the resultant, highly contentious penalty kick. With this being the first season three points for a win were awarded, it felt like we had dropped two points. We remained in third. Liverpool dropped down to thirteenth.

A week later we beat Arsenal 2–0 at the Vetch Field. A week after that we travelled to the Victoria Ground. Stoke City had just three wins all season, while we were in sight of the top. Tosh had just further added to our squad by signing another of my former Everton teammates, Gary Stanley, although he was only named on the bench. Yet it was Stoke that led at half-time thanks to a Peter Griffiths goal. Tosh changed things around, bringing on Gary for Leighton James. The new boy transformed the game. On 67 minutes he scored our equaliser, then fourteen minutes later sent in a cross that I rose to head home for our winner. It sent Swansea top, the first time in sixty years a Welsh club had led the First Division.

The mood was euphoric after the game. I think in our minds we quite fancied our chances of staying there. Inwardly, I believed we had a terrific chance of winning the First Division title. Speaking afterwards the Stoke manager, Ritchie Barker, likened us to Brian Clough's Nottingham Forest team that was promoted to the top flight in 1977 and won the title a year later. 'Forest didn't blow up when they were in a similar position and there's no reason to believe Swansea's start was just a flash in the pan,' he said.

And yet a week later we travelled to Coventry and lost 3–1. We were so underwhelming. It was bitterly disappointing.

We reached the top of the table again a week before Christmas when a Robbie James brace secured a 2–1 win over Aston Villa at the Vetch. And yet when we faced a Southampton team that included Kevin Keegan, Alan Ball and Mick Channon on 28 December we fell to a 3–1 defeat and dropped to third. This was still beyond the wildest expectations of most pundits, many of whom had tipped us for relegation. We were nine points clear of ninth-placed Liverpool at that stage.

When we faced them the day after New Year's Day 1982 in the third round of the FA Cup, many expected us to confirm our superiority, but we were given a rude awakening in front of a packed Vetch. Liverpool ran out easy 4–0 winners. And yet there was no let-up in the league. At the end of January we beat a Manchester United side that were top of the league and kept on winning. I, unfortunately, dropped out of contention with an Achilles injury, but my teammates carried on valiantly without me. When we played Wolves at Molineux on 20 March, Andy Gray and Wayne Clarke missed open goals for the hosts, but when we broke against the run of play we weren't so wasteful. Ian Walsh headed home an Alan Curtis cross for the only goal of the game. It sent us top for the third time that season. We had twelve games remaining, but, ominously, just six points separated the top six.

I had been there twice before at that stage of the season with Everton, in 1975 and 1979. I knew just how hard it was to sustain that winning momentum. But now I was more experienced, wiser, and with a manager in Tosh for whom winning had become a habit as a player with Liverpool and with Swansea – whom he'd led to those rapid promotions – as a manager.

A week after going top again we faced Bobby Robson's Ipswich at the Vetch. A close game was decided by Eric Gates's volley for Ipswich two minutes from the end. It was a cruel blow. We then faced West Ham at home in midweek. I returned to the team in my now-familiar number eleven shirt for the first time in two months. Whether it was fatigue, or bad luck – West Ham were a bogey team for Swansea – I'm not sure, but we didn't click. The Belgian international Francois van der Elst scored from an early long-range shot and whatever we did was not enough to get anything from the game.

From being top, dropping six points at home in just four days killed us. We went top three times that season and every time we lost the next game. It was as if we got to the summit of a formidable mountain and suddenly the air became too thin and we lost concentration and slipped back down again. We'd crawl back up there but couldn't find a safe footing. Again, it's hard to put your finger on why, because we had a lot of experience.

In the end, as they always seemed to be in this era, Liverpool were irresistible.

When we went top after that victory over Wolves we had 56 points from 30 games, they had 51 points from 28 matches. During the run-in we took 13 points from a possible 36. They took 39 from 42 and were record-breaking champions. We had finished a still-creditable sixth, five points and two places ahead of my former club, Everton. We had exceeded all expectations except our own. An unlikely title had been ours to win, but we'd fallen short.

*

THE 1981/82 SEASON WASN'T DEVOID OF GLORY. IN FACT, FOR THE first time in my fourteen years as a professional footballer, I ended it with a medal.

The Welsh Cup might have been considered a slight distraction from the main business of the league programme, but when there are trophies at stake and the competition is underpinned by some of the fiercest rivalries in British football. It wasn't to be dismissed. You also wanted to win because it was an avenue into Europe.

Tosh used the competition as an exercise to give some fringe players match time in the earlier rounds, when we faced the likes of Colwyn Bay (who took us to a replay after a schoolteacher named Paul Philips twice put the non-leaguers in front). In the semi-final we faced another North Wales team in Bangor City, although they surrendered home advantage in the first leg to play at the Vetch. They took a lead but couldn't hold on, and goals by Leighton James and Alan Curtis brought us a win. A goalless draw in the second leg saw us through to the two-legged final against Cardiff.

I'd played in derbies on Merseyside and experienced them as a fan in Birmingham, but the Swansea–Cardiff derby was something else. Considering Wales is such a small country with a small population and the Welsh can be very nationalistic, it is surprising that between themselves they don't like each other one bit. That rivalry isn't just between Cardiff and Swansea, but also between the north and south of the country.

As a Swansea player you were always conscious of this bad blood; you always knew what the reality was. They really don't like each other, but until you're down there I don't think you appreciate just how bad it is.

The irony was that Tosh, adored by our fans and the man responsible for the renaissance of the club, was a Cardiff boy and former Cardiff player. In fact the last time Cardiff and Swansea had met in a Welsh Cup final in 1969, he scored three of Cardiff's goals in a 5–1 aggregate win. As manager he was quite professional about it all. He didn't put any more emphasis on it than any other game. Maybe that's something he was quite good at, that he took each game as it came; nothing was made out to be greater than the previous match. I think it was a Liverpool thing. The contrast with someone like Billy Bingham, who when the Mersey derby came along, you knew things were going to be stepped up, was significant. With Tosh we did our usual things. He tried to cool things down, keep things calm. Everything was taken seriously and prepared for but nothing became bigger than the previous match, or the next-but-one game either.

Whereas we had exceeded all expectations at the Vetch during the 1981/82 season, finishing sixth in the top flight, Cardiff had had a nightmare season, which ended with relegation from the old Second Division. We still had league games to play but, conscious of local pride and the avenue into Europe, Tosh picked his strongest sides. The first leg at Ninian Park was a tight affair, which we thought we'd won through a Robbie James strike only for the goal was ruled out for offside.

We met in the second leg at the Vetch the following Thursday, and although it wasn't a capacity crowd it was an electric atmosphere, with thousands of Cardiff fans making the journey. Some, unfortunately, were bent on making trouble and there were scores of arrests, with a policeman being struck by a dart. The following day's newspapers had a full spread of the arsenal of weapons they had seized and a picture of the copper with the dart.

As players we were mostly oblivious to these running battles. We just focused on the match in hand. And yet when Gary Bennett gave the Bluebirds a surprise lead, it looked briefly as if my poor cup luck was continuing. The lead lasted just a few minutes though. A looping cross by Alan Curtis was headed back across goal by Robbie James and I struck a powerful volley past Andy Dibble to level the scores. Shortly after I was given a lucky break when a defender air-kicked what should have been an easy clearance. It put me through on goal and I hit the second – and the winner – past Dibble. It meant, at the age of 31, I had won my first trophy; and what a way to do so!

This meant qualification for another European Cup Winners' Cup campaign, and we were drawn against Braga, who had finished runners-up in the Portuguese Cup, the following August. It was Swansea's seventh attempt at European football, but they had never won a tie. That unwelcome record was vanquished in the home leg, which we won 3–0 thanks to a Jeremy Charles brace and an own-goal. When we travelled to Portugal for the second leg there was all sorts of skulduggery taking place, with the Braga stadium closed to us when we were meant to be training on it, and Braga trying to play unregistered players, which delayed kick-off by ten minutes. Tosh knew how to play these kind of matches and told us to slow it down and keep it tight. We did just that, and although we lost on the night to a late deflected goal, it was enough to see us through.

In the first round proper we were handed a good draw, against Sliema Wanderers of Malta. Our opponents were amateurs, unused to playing on grass or under floodlights, so we held the advantage; although two years earlier they had almost held Barcelona to a draw at the Nou Camp in the UEFA Cup, falling only to a penalty. Tosh picked his strongest side, but our opponents were really poor. It was a massacre. We won 12–0, a club record result. I only scored once and was substituted; my replacement Ian Walsh then grabbed a hat-trick in eleven minutes. Sliema's players mustn't have been the only ones having an off-day! The result was so emphatic as to be embarrassing. It got to the stage where we could barely look our opponents in the eye. We just wanted it to finish and get away. We won the second leg 5–0 in Malta. I didn't play, but Tosh picked himself – two years after his previous game – and scored the fifth in the final minute.

Our next opponents were of a different calibre altogether. Paris Saint-Germain's team included several stars of the 1982 World Cup, including Ossie Ardiles, who had taken a year-long loan from Spurs in Paris following the outbreak of the Falklands War. Tosh described them as the best European team to ever appear at the Vetch and he was probably right, and yet a disappointing crowd of less than 10,000 turned out to see our tie. It was a tight game that we lost 1–0 to a goal from the Chad striker Toko.

In Paris we were acutely aware of the size of the task facing us. PSG were such a good side. Things might have been different were it not for the inspired form of the veteran French international goalkeeper Dominique Baratelli. He brilliantly saved Jeremy Charles's early header and was equal to everything we threw at him all night. Shortly after Jeremy's miss, Kees Kist gave the French the lead. It left us needing two goals to win it, but that was beyond us. Luis Fernandez scored PSG's second with fifteen minutes remaining and that ended our European dream.

*

THE 1982/83 SEASON STARTED WELL FOR SWANSEA IN THE LEAGUE. We won two of our first three matches, drawing the other, to shoot right up the table. I scored the twelfth hat-trick of my professional career in the 4–0 rout of Norwich City. Nothing seemed to have changed. I think we all went into that season thinking we could have another good campaign; that we could be up there again challenging. There was no way of foreseeing what was going to happen at that early point, how things were going to go.

And yet there was something not quite right. Maybe the fans had a handle on it. When we opened the campaign the Vetch was less than half-full – just 11,712 turned out. I didn't really find that frustrating, but it was very different to, say, Evertonians, whose loyalty you could be pretty much assured of. At Swansea when things were going well they were there. If things started to tail off I think they went missing. But it was all new to them because they'd never been in that position in the First Division. Maybe Swansea fans had simply become so accustomed to winning that when the club found its level some of them didn't appreciate that victories every single week were not guaranteed.

It said much about the new season that that early run was about as good as it got for Swansea, not just for that season, but probably the next quarter-century. Early in the campaign the club were handed a transfer ban after they missed an instalment due to Everton for the transfers of Gary Stanley and myself. The club had spent more than £2 million on transfers under Tosh, but recouped just £800,000. This, combined with a loss of gate receipts when attendances fell, was clearly having an impact on the club's finances and jeopardising its future plans.

As players, like I've said, you tend to be blind to the business side of football, but that was maybe a wake-up call; the point when you started to wonder why the club was not able to service its debts. Then you started thinking, 'What's the problem here?' Those little questions start to be niggly; then little questions become big questions. That transfer ban was probably reality biting and the beginning of the end of Swansea's dream.

Form remained patchy, but I continued to score goals – six in the first eight league games – and yet Tosh dropped me for the ninth match, a 1–1 draw with Brighton. That was the manager's style, though; it was meant to be a short, sharp reminder that nobody was indispensable. It annoyed me but his approach went down less well with other, more confrontational players. When Everton beat us 3–0 at home he said publicly that we 'did not deserve' our wages, which might have played well to the gallery, but was a less than popular tactic in the dressing room. Maybe, subconsciously, it paid off: a week later we beat Southampton 3–2 at the Vetch and I scored the winner two minutes from full time.

John Toshack had it in him to be volatile. He could lose it. Then he'd calm down and all of a sudden things would return to normality. But he had that unpredictable streak about him. In one sense it kept us on our toes, in another it didn't do him any favours. We'd talk about his mood swings and his tempers away from the dressing room. Most of the Welsh lads knew Tosh and what he was like, so there was a degree of acceptance. But at the same time the approach can have a snowball effect. Whispers of discontent soon became louder.

Tosh's outspokenness also earned him the opprobrium of the Welsh FA. At the start of October he was given a five-month touchline ban for bringing the game into disrepute after a half-time dispute during our league game with Watford. Tosh could be very combustible. It wasn't very surprising that he kept getting fined because he was very excitable and the Welsh FA wouldn't have time for that. Halted in the transfer market, now limited in his match-day input, these were great setbacks for our manager. By Christmas we were seventeenth.

Tosh started to lose control of the situation around this time. He'd made Ray Kennedy captain at the start of the season, but Ray had struggled with injuries and form. He was attempting another comeback from injury and had played two reserve games and was due to play a third, but withdrew an hour before kick-off. Tosh's response was to strip him of the captaincy and suspend him for two weeks. Leighton James was another to fall foul of the manager and was given a free transfer. Tosh then called a press conference to announce these decisions and lay into the team for not doing enough. That it came to this was in some respects unsurprising. Tosh overreacted to many things; Ray, being Ray, was a bit blasé about the whole affair. He knew the manager better than most of us and probably saw the whole kerfuffle for what it was. As teammates we'd talk among ourselves about it. The question perpetually on people's lips seemed to be, 'What has Tosh done now?' The falling-out with Ray was just another example of someone losing his grip on what was going on around him.

In fairness, Tosh tried to turn it around. He brought in the former Manchester United goalkeeper and Swans manager Harry Gregg as part of his management team and placed a greater emphasis on young Welsh players. When we played Norwich on 3 January, myself and the two Yugoslavs were the only non-Welsh players included in the starting XI.

For me, the goals continued to flow. In a League Cup tie with Bristol Rovers in October I scored a hat-trick, bringing me up to 250 career goals. When we played Watford on 6 February two bits of history were made. It was the first time a First Division game had ever been played on a Sunday. What seems normal now was extraordinary then. I remember we were asked whether anybody had any religious beliefs or any reason that they couldn't play on a Sunday. There might have been one or two Welsh players, because it's quite a religious principality; but everybody was OK about it. I was also on 199 career league goals, having scored at Notts County three weeks earlier, so was very conscious that I might break that barrier, which I did to give us a 1–0 half-time lead. And yet Graham Taylor's Watford came back strongly in the second half and won 3–1.

Our slide, however, continued. Tosh launched a scathing attack on us in the press, saying that we weren't working hard enough and lacked self-belief. Yet there was no rally and we continued to struggle, while the club's financial problems became more public. Harry was sacked just two months into his reign as Tosh's assistant. Gary Stanley, who had cost £150,000 barely a year earlier, was made available for just £30,000. Max Thompson was given a free transfer.

At the start of March Swansea agreed a £100,000 fee with Chelsea for me. It was purely to ease the club's financial predicament but I felt the move wasn't the right one. I found the manager John Neal uninspiring and that was before I encountered his chairman, Ken Bates. He gave the impression of being a complete Jack-the-lad and frankly full of bullshit. Pat wasn't keen on moving to London and I didn't see myself there and so I stayed in Wales.

With four games left we found ourselves bottom of the table, seven points from safety. Tosh refused to accept that it was an impossible situation, blaming injuries and the congested fixture list, but it seemed as if we were already preparing for life in the Second Division. We took four points from our final four games, but our relegation was confirmed with a 2–1 defeat at Manchester United in the penultimate game of the season. I scored my twentieth league goal of the campaign in the final minute, but it was scant consolation. Nor was winning the Welsh Cup a few weeks later with a 4–1 aggregate win over Wrexham. When we lifted the trophy at the Vetch, just 5,630 supporters witnessed it.

*

RELEGATION IS A DREADFUL EXPERIENCE. YOU ARE A FAILURE AND you feel it in everything you do. Life deteriorates. You get to the stage where you're trying your best – it's not as if you're not putting the effort in – but nothing's working. And this was partly the problem, that nobody knew what to do to put it right, because nobody had been through the experience before. If you've experienced something you know what to expect, and possibly you can then put it right before it gets any worse. But I don't think anybody among us had experienced relegation. We were used to winning and challenging.

Tosh, throughout his career, had never experienced anything like it either. As a player with Liverpool, then as Swansea manager, it had always been success, success, success. You looked to the management to try and put things right, and when they couldn't you tried to do it as players; and we couldn't. It wasn't as if the effort wasn't there; it was, but the application and the understanding and know-how to try to turn the corner was lacking. We simply couldn't do it.

12

HERE, THERE & EVERYWHERE

'Glory is fleeting, but obscurity is forever.'
Napoleon Bonaparte

I'D SCORED 34 LEAGUE AND CUP GOALS IN THE 1982/83 SEASON, including 20 in the First Division. All this was in spite of Swansea City's relegation. But my own achievements in front of goal were scant consolation as we faced the realities of life in the Second Division. This posed a problem for a club that had significantly overspent. There were no parachute payments in 1983 as there are now and the Swansea fans had already shown themselves to be fickle even when we were riding high. There was talk of new investment, which came to nothing. Instead there was an exodus of players. Dai Davies left for Tranmere. John Mahoney called it a day and retired. Robbie James joined Stoke for a knockdown fee.

The start of the 1983/84 season was a nightmare for Swansea. It was almost as if we were doomed to fail from the outset. We didn't win a single pre-season friendly. In the European Cup Winners' Cup we were again sent to East Germany, but lost narrowly on aggregate to Magdeburg. We were winless until the sixth league match of the season, by which time we were bottom.

Tosh started playing younger players like Dean Saunders and Colin Pascoe. Although they were very promising and would enjoy good careers, it wasn't the

160

answer. He was looking for a solution but the younger players were never going to be it. You only had to look at the goal tally – we were letting in too many goals. He persuaded Emlyn Hughes to come out of retirement, but that didn't work either. Things went from bad to worse and not one person, from management to players, could find a solution to it. We drifted. As I said, the effort was there, it was more that the application and the understanding of what needed to be done was lacking. The impetus to change things didn't come from management, nor did it come from the players either. Ultimately we were all in it together; it's a team game, so as players we must assume part of the blame. You share the success but you've got to share the failure, and we all failed, from top to bottom.

It reached crisis point for Swansea in late October. The bank advised that there was no more money; we were £2 million in debt and losing £10,000 each week. The chairman and vice-chairman resigned. They were followed on 29 October by Tosh.

At this stage I was approached to take over as manager from Tosh. I hadn't considered management at this stage and the place was in chaos. There was no proper leadership. I asked for some assurances and some indication of what had happened to the club and where the future lay, but no one would – or could – give me any. And so I said no.

Instead Doug Livermore took charge and did the best he could. But the exodus continued. Jeremy Charles joined QPR and Alan Curtis Southampton for bargain fees. It looked like I might be on my way too. Sunderland were interested and I travelled up to Manchester City for talks with Billy McNeill.

I had a good feeling about this move. Billy had managed my brother Peter at Celtic and I'd heard good things. It was in the north west, where as a family we had some roots, and it was in the First Division. We met and there was a rapport and everything was agreed. I mentioned that if City – bearing in mind they were getting me on a free transfer – could come up with an additional £5,000 signing-on fee it would be greatly appreciated. For me it wasn't a deal-breaker, just something that would help with the logistics of a move back North. I left, thinking a deal was done. A few days later I got a phone call telling me the deal was off. To this day I have no idea why.

Unbeknown to me, Howard Kendall was weighing up a move to bring me back to Everton. Howard was under huge pressure as Everton manager and had been given a vote of confidence by his chairman Philip Carter. He was desperate to allay Everton's goal drought and help ease the burden on Graeme Sharp. He wanted experience. He had three options under consideration: Ipswich Town's Paul Mariner, Andy Gray, who was then at Wolves, and me. Mariner was out of his price league, so it was a straight choice between Andy and I. He plumped for Gray and I was never any the wiser until three decades later, when Howard revealed in his autobiography that I had been an option.

Andy helped save Howard's job and was one of the catalysts for Everton's extraordinary mid-1980s revival. He did so as much through force of personality as through his feats on the field. Would I have made such an impression? We were very different characters, but I know – I'd proved – I still had it in me to score goals. I'd have loved to have gone back and gone out on a high at Goodison, but it wasn't to be.

Instead, Swansea's decline continued. In a bizarre twist Tosh returned as manager just after Christmas. One of his first acts was to pick himself for the Boxing Day fixture at Cardiff and score one of our goals in a 3–2 defeat. His next was to hand me a free transfer.

Suddenly I found myself on the scrapheap. An English centre-forward that had just scored twenty First Division goals in a struggling team without a club? You couldn't equate that now because there'd be clubs lining up, even at 32, to take you on. In fact in the past five Premier League seasons, only three English players – Harry Kane, Daniel Sturridge and Wayne Rooney – have reached that total. But it didn't have the same resonance back then. Instead I was adrift. If I'd had an agent I probably would have got another club more easily, but that wasn't me, and that wasn't the case.

It's not like today where you can probably get on Twitter or something and tell the world that you're available. The PFA, which was a much smaller organisation then than it is now, looked out for me. But that was it. Instead I sat by the phone at our home near the Mumbles waiting for a call. Waiting, waiting, waiting.

*

A DIFFERENT ROAD

WHEN THE CALL CAME, IT WASN'T WHAT I EXPECTED.

NAC hailed from Breda, a small city in the south of the Netherlands. They are known for the fierce and fanatical support of their fans and had won one national title in 1921 and a Dutch FA Cup in 1973. When they approached me they were in a rare spell in the Eerste Divisie, the second tier in Dutch football, and vying for promotion back to the top flight.

NAC was a semi-pro club. They played at an old stadium. It's only within the last fifteen years they've had a new stadium built. They had a few players like myself who were full professionals, and had a number of players who had jobs and used to come in training in the evening, or afternoons. My old Everton teammate Ronnie Goodlass had had a spell with them in the late 1970s. Perhaps he alerted them to my availability. I spoke to the head coach Bob Maaskant, who was friendly and persuasive, and he told me they wanted to sign me for the remainder of the 1983/84 season.

There was nothing going for me at Swansea, other than a successive relegation. They needed me off their books in any case. There was nobody else in England that wanted me and it was the chance of something new, something different, a different road. I liked Breda's proposal and so I agreed to join for the rest of the season.

Pat remained in South Wales with the children and I'd return every month for a long weekend. I was living in a hotel and then a shared house. This was an era before Skype or email or even cheap international phone calls and so it wasn't an ideal scenario. But I was made to feel very welcome. I used to go and socialise with the club secretary Ton Van der Meer and his family. Bob used to come out to the hotel I was in and we'd maybe share a meal.

Technically the standard in Holland was good. It was all pass pass pass, even from the back. They wouldn't lump it forward. They either passed it forward or they ran with it. We had a full-back who used to do that all the time; he'd never just lump it, and if he couldn't pass it he'd start to dribble out. At first I kept thinking, 'Fuck, if he loses the ball there on the edge of the box...' But they just did it, because they'd been brought up to play football from the back to the front.

It was quite refreshing and certainly a lot different to what I was used to. You had to be a little bit more patient because the ball didn't come to you as quickly as it did in the English game. I think I brought a degree of directness to their play, but I had to adapt my game too to an extent and be patient. The fact I could be a physical player worked to my advantage, as did my professional experience in a league where the majority of players were semi-pros. I was the only foreign player at the club – although they'd had English players like Ronnie in the past – and I remember causing a stir when I first went to a training session. While all my teammates were shielded from the Dutch winter cold in full tracksuits, I strode out in my shorts as was normal for me. They thought that this was the height of eccentricity and it was talked about in the club for days.

The set-up at NAC was quite typical for the Eerste Divisie. There was a core of experienced pros who were supplemented by younger boys trying to make the grade. My teammates included Ruud Geels, the former Dutch international who had been the country's most prolific goalscorer during the 1970s and starred for Ajax and Club Brugge. His former Ajax teammate, defender Johnny Dusbaba, was also part of the Breda squad. He too had been a member of the Dutch national team during an era when they'd twice reached the World Cup final.

Johnny was a funny character. He was of gypsy origin – perhaps one of the most high-profile sportsmen to come from such a background – although he certainly didn't live in a caravan; he had a very nice house just over the border in Belgium, and invited Pat and I to visit him one weekend. Johnny used to sit next to me in the changing room. I'll never forget one incident when we were getting changed at the end of training. For some reason we were the last there and I was last out of the showers. When I came out, Johnny was gone and so were my underpants. He'd taken them! I have no idea why, whether his were wet or he'd made a mistake, but either way I was left with no option other than to go commando! I mentioned this in passing to Bob Maaskant a few days later and he just shrugged his shoulders. 'Johnny's just like that,' he said. 'It's not malicious and he means nothing by it. It's just the way that he is.'

Breda were in the midst of a promotion battle when I joined. My job was to score the goals that would get them over the line and secure that place back in the top flight. We were helped by passionate and noisy fans. Breda played on Friday nights and the atmosphere under floodlights is always better. Because it was the end of the working week, I think supporters were also up for the occasion more than they were on other days of the week. We certainly gave them plenty to shout about. I was only there for the second half of the season, but scored thirteen goals in sixteen league games.

There were two ways of gaining promotion to the top flight: the two automatic spots, or via playoffs. These were played between the best-performing team in the first eight matches, second, third and fourth eight matches – or the 'period champions'. Breda had finished third in the ordinary season, but had done enough to qualify for the playoffs as one of the 'period champions' with VVV-Venlo, De Graafschap and NEC. It seems convoluted, but it added an exciting epilogue to the season. Because our form was so good going into these playoffs it carried us through; we topped the four-team group, winning four games and drawing two.

My goals had made me a local hero and Bob Maaskant tried hard to get me to stay. I loved my time in the Netherlands, although family-wise it would have been tough to remain. I did not like being away from Pat and the children for four months. But in terms of playing and financially it would have been a lot better to have stuck it out. I probably would have ended up better paid than I did on my return to England. Football-wise it would also have been the right choice. On reflection I should have had one more season, if not two, with NAC in the Dutch top flight, for my next moves were to be terrible mistakes.

WHEN MY TIME IN HOLLAND CAME TO AN END I WAS LEFT WITHOUT a club once more. Again the PFA acted as my intermediary and put word around that I was looking for somewhere to play. When an offer came in from Coventry City it grabbed my attention. Coventry were well established in the First Division and, having failed to get a top-flight deal the last time around, I considered it a bit of a bonus that I would play at that level again. They had some good players like Stuart Pearce, Cyrille Regis and Martin Jol. Plus, Pat came from Coventry, so we knew the city. It was agreed that she'd remain in South Wales with Izzy and Richard, who were still at school, while I'd stay with her family and catch up with them after games and during the week.

In many respects it was a relatively easy decision to make, but it turned out to be an utterly forgettable experience. Bobby Gould was manager when I signed and very full of himself, giving orders left, right and centre. He reminded me a little of Billy Bingham and was something of a control freak. I'm not sure whether it was him or the impact he had on the team – which struggled – that made me unsettled, but Coventry just didn't seem the right club for me. I never really got into it. I tried to keep my relationship with the club at arm's length because I knew I'd made a mistake. Yet I did my best in terms of training and when I played. But because of the atmosphere about the place I didn't really want to be there.

After a poor start to the season Bobby was sacked and replaced by Don Mackay. I dropped out of the team and they escaped relegation only by winning their last match against champions Everton, 4–1. At the end of the season there was a clean sweep and it came as no surprise when my contract was not renewed. It was the end of my time as a First Division player.

PERHAPS IF I'D BEEN BETTER ORGANISED OR TAKEN BETTER CARE OF my off-field affairs or had done what I should have done years earlier and hired an agent, I would have had another club to go to after my time at Highfield Road came to its inevitable conclusion. Maybe I should have called time on my career at the age of 34. But I was in denial that it would come to an end in such a way and had given no thought as to what would happen next. Although Coventry was not a good experience I still felt ready and able to continue to play football. My problem was finding a club.

Instead there was a drift, away from Coventry, away from the top flight – but to where?

One afternoon I took a call from Phil Boersma, the former Liverpool player who had been Tosh's assistant at Swansea. Phil is a Scouser with an infectious personality and can be quite persuasive. He was assistant manager at Lincoln City, then in the Third Division, and they were looking for a centre-forward.

'Latchy, come on, get yourself up here and play a few games,' he said. In the end I signed up for the 1985/86 season. I think I was still on about £200 or

£300 a week, which was still reasonably good money, but the move was a disaster. Going to Lincoln, you could say, was out of the frying pan and into the fire. Even Newport, who I joined later, was a little bit better than Lincoln.

Again, Pat and the children remained in Wales, while I rented a flat in Lincoln. Depending on what was happening I'd come back for a few days in the week and, of course, after matches, but it was far from ideal. The road from Lincoln to Swansea is even longer than the journey to Coventry, and the 500-mile round trips were wearying.

When you're living that transient existence you just feel like you're treading water. Treading water, playing football as well as you can, and picking up some money. I wouldn't say my heart was in it. It's not that I didn't try; I tried, but my being, my heart, would definitely have liked to have been somewhere else.

There were times when I looked over at my old club, Everton, who had started to dominate English football, which was terrific to see. I sometimes thought to myself, 'What if I'd stayed on as Howard had wanted?' But a life of regrets and imponderables is not one I lived, so those thoughts never lingered long. I was never invited back to Goodison as a guest for another twenty years and did not have any reason to go back. I just followed all the clubs I played for – apart from Coventry – through the media.

Looking back, I think my confidence was knocked at Coventry and it sent me on a downward spiral, which was compounded by going to Lincoln. Not playing at the same standard with the same amount of success does knock you back. Your expectations become so much lower; you don't expect anything to happen after you've done that.

There's a big danger too for a smaller club to put all its faith in a big-name striker at the end of his career. You can get injured and not find your feet, but the club won't necessarily have the resources to have a Plan B. If it doesn't work out, which it didn't at Sincil Bank, it can leave a bad taste for the manager and for the fans. Lincoln ended the 1985/86 season relegated from the Third Division along with another of my old clubs, Swansea.

I hadn't stayed until the season reached its dismal conclusion, instead agreeing a settlement with Lincoln and parting amicably enough.

It left me without a club once more, but again my unpreparedness either for my next move or life beyond football caught me short. I went home to Wales, rested, trained on my own, and went running along the Mumbles. But I was really at a loss as to what to do next, when the call came from Newport County asking me to join them for the rest of the 1985/86 season. Leighton James, my former Swansea teammate, was there and they were also in danger of relegation (along with Lincoln and Swansea).

Relatively speaking they were just up the road from our home and it was convenient. It was an hour-or-so drive, but compared to most other clubs it was on the doorstep; I could live at home again for the first time since leaving Swansea two years previously.

I was aware of Newport's severe financial problems before I arrived, but perhaps hadn't appreciated the sheer scale of them. The whole place looked like it was on its knees, on its last legs. You looked at it and thought that no matter what you did you were never going to affect what was going to happen on the pitch. The crowds were tiny, averaging just over 2,500, and the results poor.

Newport were stuck in a terrible losing run of eight consecutive matches when I arrived. It seemed insurmountable. But then the board replaced Bobby Smith with John Relish as manager six weeks from the end of the season and form improved. We lost just one of the last nine games of the season and finished five points clear of the last relegation spot, occupied by my previous club, Lincoln. And yet I could see that there was no future at Newport and when my contract ended at the end of the season I left with four goals to my name and no regrets. County underwent successive relegations and dropped out of the Football League in 1988. The following year they were unable to complete their Conference season and were declared bankrupt. My initial instincts about the club had proved sadly prescient.

*

IT WAS 1986 AND I WAS NOW AGED 35. I STILL FELT I HAD SOMETHING to offer football, if only through want of knowing what to do next. Having said that, my poise had been knocked a little by the previous two years and in one sense I was ready to retire. In another, the lack of a plan and the fact that I was still fit told me I wasn't quite ready yet for life after professional football.

I got a phone call from the manager of Merthyr Tydfil, Lyn Jones. His team were in the Beazer Homes Premier League. I'd not really thought about dropping down into semi-professional football but he was a lively Welsh fellow and had a good personality, very bubbly, very passionate and I saw something in him. He invited me up to the club to meet the owner, and they offered me the chance to come and play for the 1986/87 season. I'm not sure what it was, but being such a believer in emotional connections it seemed like a good move. Again, it was only an hour away from our home, so it was convenient.

The club had only been founded after the Second World War, but had been immensely successful from the outset. They won the Southern League Championship five times in their first eight years and were it not for the vagaries of the Football League's re-election system might have entered the league itself. It's always very difficult for a club like Merthyr, because rugby in South Wales is the dominant sport and always has been. Swansea probably find it a little bit easier now, but vying for popularity with another sport was something we were conscious of as players there and also at Newport. Back in that era, Welsh rugby was as good as it got and so it became even more difficult for a small town like Merthyr.

There was no real pressure and expectation on me, even if I was probably the most high-profile player to have graced the park at Merthyr Tydfil. It wasn't like, say, Coventry City, a First Division club where there was pressure on you to perform week in, week out. It was much more relaxed than that: it was enjoyable, it was even fun. Within the town there was excitement at my arrival, but I was relaxed and just happy to be wanted and to play football with a good group of players. All of them had jobs in the real world, such as our captain Ceri Williams, who laid tarmac, and I used to go and train two or three nights a week with them.

They had some half-decent players for that standard. There was Gary Wager in goal, whom many considered the best goalkeeper in non-league football at the time, and David Tong, an experienced midfielder who had played for Blackpool and Cardiff City. It was pretty easy to adapt because I'd played in a similar set-up in the Netherlands, where you had number of players who were semi-pro. I was comfortable with it, and enjoyed the fact that I could live with Pat and the children and not be away for long stretches.

Because I was a former England centre-forward playing non-league there were, of course, one or two people who thought they could make names for themselves by kicking me. One or two tried and I got up-ended a few times, but you have to expect that; you have to expect that they're going to have a dig at you, so you have to take care of yourself and be ready for it when it happens. My teammates watched out for me, however. There was a good bond between all the players there, and that bond extended to protecting each other. We were all in it together and had a good camaraderie among the players, which only helped to bring the success that we would have.

The season started a little slowly, but I was enjoying my football, I liked my teammates, and was scoring goals. For the team it was the Welsh Cup that saw us pull together and realise our potential. After good progress in the early rounds a two-legged semi-final win against Bangor City saw the Martyrs reach the final, where we faced my former club, Newport County, at Ninian Park in what was now a one-off final.

There were 7,100 fans there, although it seemed like much more. Newport, despite their struggles, were playing four divisions above us and went in front through Andy Thackeray. Our fans, however, were in good voice and we were not going to let them down. When Kevin Rogers broke down their left flank and sent in a teasing awkward cross to the back post, who should be there but me to hammer into the roof of the net from close range. Newport came back, as we expected them to, and Thackeray restored their lead with a dipping volley from the edge of the area. But we would not be beaten. Tong put in a cross from the angle of the area and although it eluded my head, Dai Webley beat the defender and goalkeeper to the ball to power home our equaliser.

It was a tremendous achievement holding the league side like that. One thing I'd learned from my years in Wales was that the Welsh boys can drink. I went through different stages of drinking cultures, from Birmingham, to Liverpool, to Swansea; and each one stepped up. I always thought, 'This couldn't get any heavier,' but the Merthyr boys – oh dear me! – they could drink and they did that night.

The players and directors went to the Hoover factory in Pentrebach, where the company had laid on a celebratory meal for us. After that function the party moved on to Strikers, a social club at Merthyr's stadium. There were 500 supporters waiting for us and they carried Lyn Jones shoulder-high into the club.

It was a tremendous evening – as nights out with my Merthyr teammates so often were – but four days later, when we replayed at Ninian Park, we were to surpass even that. When a long ball was played over the top, Dai Webley got in between two defenders and was wrestled to the ground. Chris Baird stepped up for the penalty and planted the only goal of the game into the back of the Newport net.

It was the centennial edition of the Welsh Cup and Merthyr's third win, their first in 36 years. For me, after two Welsh Cup wins with Swansea, it was a third and unexpected piece of silverware to a collection that I still think should be bigger after all those near misses with Everton.

It provided enough encouragement for me to stay for another season. I liked it there and I'd have, at the age of 36, the added bonus of European football, after success ensured qualification for the European Cup Winners' Cup.

We could have drawn anyone in the first round, from Ajax to Young Boys; from fellow minnows like Glentoran to giants like SV Hamburg. We didn't face real giants in the end, but Atalanta were Italian Cup winners at a time when Serie A was by some distance the strongest league in the world. It was our luck – or misfortune – to face them in the opening round.

Nobody gave us a chance, but the town of Merthyr united around us like it had probably never done for a football match before. Unfortunately I was injured with a groin strain and could only watch on the sidelines of jam-packed Penydarren Park. The official attendance was 8,000, but some claimed there were up to 14,000 present. We pulled off one of the great shocks of European football that amazing night in South Wales. Kevin Rogers fired our first goal after 34 minutes, while Domenico Progna equalised just before half-time. At this point most people would have expected Merthyr to collapse, but we held strong and, spurred on by our raucous fans, struck a winner from a deflected Ceri Williams shot. The atmosphere was magical, absolutely electric. Our team became instant heroes and partied all night and into the morning.

I had hopes of being fit for the return in Bergamo and travelled with the team and what seemed like half of the town to northern Italy. And yet I could only watch from the sidelines again after failing to pass a fitness test. There wasn't the expected capitulation, but after two quick-fire first-half goals we didn't have enough to force an away goal and extra time. It had been an extraordinary effort, but time had run out for Merthyr Tydfil.

It was running out for me too, as I neared my 37th birthday. The end came quite abruptly for me during the 1987/88 season. My legs gave out, basically. I just could not get around the pitch, it was as simple as that. Literally from one day to the next. Physiologically it obviously came over a period of time, and maybe, looking back, it was as if the realisation finally dawned in my mind rather than my body. You try to deny it to yourself; you go into deniability mode and think, 'I can still do it', but in reality you can't. I think the manager saw it quicker than I did. Then it was a case of accepting it and retiring.

I'd had roughly twenty years of playing football for a living, which is longer than most people.

Now I had to work out which road I would take next.

13

HOME

'Never look down to test the ground before taking your next step; only he who keeps his eye fixed on the far horizon will find the right road.'
Dag Hammarskjold

AS THEY ENTER THEIR THIRTIES MANY FOOTBALLERS EMBARK UPON a period of uncertainty, fear and ultimately denial that their sporting talent is diminishing. Ahead of many of them lies a decision that is inevitable, although many will put off: where the next path in their life will lead them.

Some will have strong ambitions to become a manager, an aspiration that will be obvious throughout their playing days. For others, coaching ambitions come later, or it becomes something that they fall into. For a sizeable majority, however, it is a big dilemma that is put off and put off. When I was a player few of my contemporaries earned enough money to sustain the rest of their lives. Therefore, the future could not be delayed forever.

The clever ones prepare for life after football. Some go into denial and then get over it, get past it, then continue with their lives. But then there are others that can't get over the denial. As I've written, much of my mid-thirties was spent in a period of denial. There was a huge emptiness looming ahead of me, because football was such a massive part of my life and had always been there: training, playing, scoring goals. It was probably only when the legs went and I left Merthyr that I got over this period. When reality was accepted it was a case then of pondering what to do next with my life.

While I was at Swansea Pat and I had set up a shop near the Mumbles called Rainbow that sold childrenswear. It was my first venture in the fashion industry since the ill-fated Bob Latchford Menswear in the 1970s. This was, by contrast, relatively successful and I think having the business helped stabilise the situation for me after football. If we hadn't have had that focus it would have been a bigger problem coming to terms with the end of my career.

By the end of the 1980s, Izzy and Richard had completed their school education and moved on to university. Although we enjoyed life in South Wales our roots lay elsewhere, so when the opportunity arose to return to the Midlands we took it. We sold the business as a going concern – it is still running to this day – and moved back to Redditch in 1989 after a gap of more than fifteen years.

My new job was as a financial advisor, a career route an increasing number of ex-footballers were following at the time. It was mundane, but mundanity works at times. It didn't bother me being away from the limelight. What I did miss was the day-to-day involvement in a football environment, not just the training and playing, but its routines and camaraderie. It was natural to miss it, as a big part of my life was now in the past.

I did, however, have a spell as a director of Alvechurch, a non-league side local to the part of Birmingham I'd grown up in. They played in the Beazer Homes League Midland Division, but had fallen on hard times. They were rescued by Geoff Turton of the 1960s pop group the Rockin' Berries. Geoff was a friend of mine and asked me to become involved as a director. I turned up at games and lent my support to the club. I even drove the minibus on one occasion. It was a bit of fun, a case of dabbling in the game.

I never considered myself shunned by football, as some do, because it was always my decision to step back from it. As a player I never considered myself as a prospective manager or coach. My problem was that I never thought I could be as good a coach or manager as I was a player, and for me that was a big psychological barrier to overcome. I couldn't accept anything less than being at a high standard, so that always held me back, and steered me away from any thought about wanting to go into coaching, at least initially.

Looking back I was wrong to have that view. It was a bit like not taking penalties, a similar mentality that held me back from achieving more. I was wrong with the penalties, and I was definitely wrong with the mentality that I couldn't be as good a coach or manager as I was a player. I think perhaps if I'd fallen under the guidance of an influential mentor, as I did later with Brian Eastick, it would have given me the self-belief to go straight into coaching and succeed at it.

I was comfortable with this transitional period between professional football and civvy street, but lots of other players struggle with it. In general football is unkind to former players. There is an attitude that when you're finished at a club, that's it, because it's a business. Clubs are not particularly interested in what their old players – even heroes – are doing afterwards, even at the greatest clubs in the world. The PFA are a source of support, where you can go for help, and over the years they have built that side of their union into quite an important part of their work and help ex-pros in all sorts of areas. But even at the best football clubs, you are a commodity where you'll be used, and you know you're being used, and at the end it's 'Goodbye, be on your way'.

Some clubs, of course, are better at keeping in touch and welcoming back their ex-players than others; but to my mind there's little variance throughout the sport. Because of the sheer number of players that pass through each club, they don't have the time or facilities or the manpower to invest time in finding out what their ex-players are doing career-wise afterwards. It's never been done, it never will be done.

*

IN 1994 I HAD A CALL FROM BRENDAN BATSON AT THE PFA. WOULD I be interested in talking to Ladbrokes about a communications job ahead of the European Championships? Of course, I jumped at the chance to meet them and when they offered it to me, I was delighted to accept.

It was a corporate communications role, very different from anything that I'd done previously. Ladbrokes were the official bookmaker for Euro 96, and I served as their front man for the operation. I'd go round the country talking to football clubs, talking to media, just driving up the image of Ladbrokes and betting in football, even though I'm not a betting man. It was a hugely enjoyable job and although it was on the fringes of football, it was a football thing. The European Championships exceeded all expectations, with England reaching the semi-finals and the country swaying to the sound of David Baddiel and Frank Skinner's 'Football's Coming Home'. And it also turned out to be a route back into the game.

Shortly before that tournament, Trevor Francis returned to Birmingham City after eighteen years away, as its new manager. His appointment as Barry Fry's successor came after years of instability and underachievement at St Andrew's, with Birmingham dropping down to the third tier. The club was now in the ownership of David Gold and David Sullivan, well-known West Ham fans, who nevertheless had high ambitions for Birmingham. The chief executive was Karren Brady, then in her early twenties, who blended a mixture of ambition and ruthlessness. It was an exciting time for the club.

Trevor called me when he took over at St Andrew's and asked if I'd be interested in coming back to work as a youth coach. As I've written, a career in coaching had never really occurred to me and I'd not done my badges at that stage. But we met and we talked and he introduced me to Brian Eastick.

Brian, who is nine days younger than me, had been a promising young player at Crystal Palace, appearing as a midfielder for the England Youth team around the same time as myself. He made his career in coaching rather than playing, however, and had had roles at a number of clubs including Chelsea, QPR, Brighton and Charlton, as well as a short spell as Newport County manager and time at the FA's centre of excellence at Lilleshall. He was – and still is – one of the most highly respected coaches in English football.

Brian explained about the new academy system and how he would be creating one at Birmingham, effectively from scratch. The system that had bred players such as myself, Trevor, Garry Pendrey and my brother David in the late 1960s and early 1970s had been left to slide and it was a priority of the owners to recreate those productive days. Brian wanted me to assist him.

It had been 22 years since I left Birmingham as a player but I had no hesitation about returning as the club's head of youth development. While Brian was the overall head of youth, my priority was getting youngsters in.

It was quite shocking, having left a club in the mid-1970s with such a good record of producing its own players, to go back to an institution that had nothing when Brian and I first walked through the door. The previous regime had totally scrapped the youth scheme and all the players from all the age groups had gone. There were no balls, no kit, nothing.

We had to set everything up from scratch. We did not even have a first team training ground; we used to train all over the place, because Birmingham's previous owners sold the old training ground years earlier. That was a big problem not just for us, but for Trevor too, and the club's different teams were all training here, there and everywhere. Eventually Brian and I found a place at Wast Hills, which belongs to Birmingham University. I knew it because I grew up around that part of Birmingham, and after looking around and seeing its potential we were charged with the task of securing a lease upon it. Brian eventually sealed the lease and over the years the club has built the training ground up into the fine institution we know today.

The other problem that we had was acquiring a group of players that had a chance of making it professionally. I'm not sure if it was a symptom of this generation of young players – who had other priorities and distractions away from sport – or the coaching they had received, but many of them were technically very poor. I remember watching from the sideline and seeing youth players encounter difficulties kicking a stationary ball properly. Youth players at a professional club incapable of striking a ball? It was a poor state of affairs.

Other players, however, stood out. Andy Johnson had been released, but fortunately came back when Brian and I took over. I remember being on the touchline with Brian and we were watching him in a game, when he was fourteen or fifteen and playing out wide right, and saying to Brian, 'He's going to be some player.' He was a lovely lad who worked extremely hard and had an abundance of pace; his pace was the thing that excited you about him. And he could finish too. There's not many players at that age where you could say with such certainty that they'd progress to being a professional, but Andy was one. When Brian started to play him through the middle when he was sixteen you could see that he was going to be a star. The fact that he became an England international – and would also follow in my footsteps by joining Everton – I could not have predicted, but he excited me.

The other stand-out player under my charge was Darren Carter. Although he made it as a professional and played in the top flight, for me he has wasted his talent. Whenever I look at Darren now – a solid journeyman player – I think back to when he was twelve years old. He had everything: he was big, he was strong, he was mobile, he was left-sided, he could defend – he was a terrific defender – but he could come out with the ball and play too. But Darren decided that he wanted to play in midfield because he wanted to get up and down the pitch and score goals, which he could do; he had the quality to do it. But what he didn't possess was an ability to manipulate the ball quickly enough to play in midfield at the top level. At the back he was fine, but in midfield you need to be able to play the ball quicker because you're under that much more pressure. He has gone on to play at a professional level at many clubs, but in the wrong position for me. He would have made an outstanding centre back; but he chose to play in midfield and persevered with it. I still feel it was the wrong thing for him to do.

I realised how much I'd missed the routines of football when I returned to Birmingham. It was like putting on an old pair of slippers; it was something I was comfortable in. It was good too, to be among my own people and back in a place and an area I knew well. The city had undergone a bit of a transformation since the era in which I grew up, not always for the better.

It was good to be back in the company of Trevor Francis as well. People sometimes get the wrong impression of him; some perceive him as a bit snobbish or stuck-up, but he's not like that all. The thing with Trevor is that from the age of sixteen he was different from everybody else, and when you're set apart and move in a different environment all the time people see you differently. Some can't take to him because they think he's a bit stand-offish. But he's not at all – he's very friendly, very nice. You can sit down with him and have a really terrific conversation, and he'll be funny as well; he's got a terrific, very dry sense of humour. I could understand him because I knew where he came from; I was there at the beginning.

The owners and Karren Brady brought a greater level of professionalism to Birmingham City. They were very businesslike and ran the club pretty well, according to a tight model. They represented, in the mid-1990s, the new face of football. They were the shape of what was to come, how the owners of football clubs were going to be: business people, creating a better-run, more efficient and profitable organisation and seeing the value of their asset rise.

For all their wealth and grounding in the business world – a world that was very different to my own – I found them to be very approachable. Every time we encountered them they'd take an interest in what we were doing, have a chat, find out what players were looking as though they could step up. David Sullivan came to a youth game down at Tottenham and stood on the touchline with me and Brian. Karren has, of course, gone on to be a significant public figure. I look at her now sitting in the House of Lords, and I don't think you would have got many bets on that happening when she was aged 23. But you've got to hold your hand up and salute her quite remarkable ascent.

I worked with them through what was at once a very difficult and special time in my life, when Pat was dying from cancer. I've outlined this episode of our lives in this book's introduction, the despair and the sadness, but also how that time in our lives brought the best from our marriage and how it was a peaceful and calm period, despite living with such a horrendous reality. I like to think too that it brought the best out of other people in my life.

Cancer affects everybody within your family. I tried to give Pat support every day, and be there, between working of course. You have to remain strong, not just physically strong but mentally strong too, because if you're not it can just overwhelm you. I suppose I was fortunate in the business I was in – football – because it gave me a mental toughness and Pat was mentally strong as well. But it can wear you down. It's a disease that eats away not just at the victim, but those around them too. If you let it, it can destroy you as well.

Towards the end, Richard and Izzy were home a lot. It was so good to have them around, to be together as a family. It was terrible losing Pat, but it was such a special time too; having that closeness over those final years, not just between the two of us, but as a family too.

At Birmingham the club were super, absolutely top-class. Whatever people may think about the Golds, David Sullivan and Karren – and they could be very dominant when it came to business methods and how they wanted to run the club, and we had disagreements at times – when it came to something very personal and important like that with Pat they were very supportive.

*

AFTER MEETING AND FALLING IN LOVE WITH ANDREA WE DECIDED to make a clean break. I left Birmingham City and football in 2001. Part of me needed to separate the two lives I'd led: the past, and a very happy past at that, the footballer, the husband, the father; and the future, which still lay undefined. The way that I saw it I had had one life and it came to an end and I let go of a lot of the baggage associated with it to concentrate on a new one with Andrea.

We ended up living in Salzburg. I had an idealised view of the city, having loved *The Sound of Music* when it came out in 1965 and had been enthralled by stories from my Auntie Mary, who had gone on foreign holidays to the Alps in the 1950s and 60s at a time when few people travelled abroad. She would come home from these exotic places with packets of holiday snaps taken with a Kodak Brownie and wow me and my brothers.

And then, some forty years later, I found myself living in Salzburg, with the mountains towering above the beautiful old city. We relaxed, got to know each other better, hiked, skied and spent a lot of time outdoors. On the one hand it was a little bit surreal, being in the heart of somewhere that I had such a romanticised impression of. On the other I soon learned the Austrians don't actually give a toss about *The Sound of Music* at all. In fact, I think they tried to not really believe that it had happened.

Because I didn't speak German and was not really part of it I found myself on the periphery of society, albeit in a nice way. It was a little like being on a very long vacation. Austria is a lovely country; if you like the outdoor life and a bit of mountain walking and skiing in the winter it's a good place to go.

I'd enjoyed being back in football with Birmingham, but I didn't really miss it once I moved away. Like many jobs, you take comfort in the routine. The only glamorous part of it is actually the finished product, which you see on match day, and hopefully when you win something. What you do to achieve that is just ordinary day-to-day mundane things associated with the sport, run-of-the-mill stuff, repetitive.

I don't think I found it hard walking away from football. Some people might find it difficlt to understand why I did what I did. I was lucky that Richard and Izzy understood what I was doing and why I'd done it. I think they were bright enough to have appreciated my rationale. Whether they totally agreed with it I'm not entirely sure, but they seem to be comfortable with my new life.

All good things come to an end, however, and so it was with our time in Austria. However, our reason for leaving was a happy one. In 2003 Andrea learned that she was expecting our first child. After a gap of more than 30 years I was going to become a dad again at the age of 52. Later that year our son Sam was born in Salzburg.

We had never talked much about going to live in Germany, it was always Italy or somewhere else in Austria. Even though we both enjoyed life in Salzburg the older Sam became we knew a decision had to be made sooner rather than later about our future so with rather heavy hearts we packed up and headed north. In 2005 we moved to a village near Nuremberg in the Bayern province in southern Germany; it's not far from where Andrea and her family are from. The following year our daughter Sina was born. It's a peaceful, quiet, safe, rural environment, ideal for bringing up young children.

I could never have imagined when I was the height of my fame that in my mid-60s I would be a father to two adorable kids, who, I should add, keep me very busy 24/7. Andrea and I keep as active as possible but with two youngsters, as any parent will know, it can take a lot out of you. Our days together are always full and busy. I wouldn't change it or want it any other way.

*

I'D LEFT EVERTON IN 1981 AND ALTHOUGH IT WAS THE CLUB I'D BEEN most synonymous with, a place where I was accorded legendary status, more than two decades had passed and I'd never really been back. There was the 1995 FA Cup final, which I attended as a supporter with Richard, but that glorious afternoon was pretty much the extent of my involvement with my former club.

As I've written, although fans are nostalgic, football is, on the whole, an unsympathetic industry. Clubs don't know how to treat their former players. People don't reach out to you and I was never one to go and impose myself on my old clubs. My outlook was that if they wanted me they knew where I was or they could find me. I was never one to go and say, 'Here I am, what can I do for you?' It's not me. I was always very comfortable being in the background and looking at what was happening from afar, following events without being part of what was going on.

It was around 2003, we were living in Salzburg and Andrea was expecting Sam when a phone call came in from England. Andrea took it, and all of a sudden she was mouthing to me, 'It's someone from Everton.' I gesticulated back, 'No, I'm not interested.'

I was thinking, 'Who the hell is this? I don't want to talk to them. How did they get my number?' I just thought, 'No, whoever it is, I don't want to talk to them.' It could have been any sort of cowboy. But Germans are very straightforward people; they're not very good at white lies. In the end, Andrea said, 'You'd better come and talk, I've already said you're here.'

It was Steve Milne, who was then a trustee of the Everton Former Players' Foundation, a charitable organisation I'd never heard about. It transpired that the Foundation looks after and benefits all players who have made at least one appearance in that famous blue shirt. I was sceptical about what he was saying at first; when you get a call out of the blue from somebody purporting to be an Everton supporter and he starts talking about some charity, my first instinct is to be suspicious.

But Steve was persistent and persuasive. He arranged to come over to Austria to meet me and tell me about the Foundation's work. It raises money for the physical and pastoral care of former football players who have previously been contracted to Everton. It was the first such organisation in world football, but has since been replicated at clubs from Barcelona to Burnley. They wanted me to attend a function, which I was unable to do, but I recorded a short video message and from that point a bridge had been built.

That club was always in my blood. It was a terrific wrench to leave Everton. It had played a major part in my life. Since that call from Steve I've been going back over the past decade and it's re-established that connection. If anything my feelings towards the club are even greater and deeper than they were before.

Everton does leave a mark on you. It's hard to say for any one reason why it does, but it's true, and others say the same.

Evertonians are the most fanatical supporters I've ever come across. In terms of their regard for and knowledge of their former players they are without parallel. They want to know everything about their ex-players, what they're up to, and genuinely want to meet and talk to you. Evertonians make their club what it is. I've never been at a club where they are so genuine in their affection for their ex-players as Everton.

Every time I come across to England and talk to Evertonians they're as enthusiastic now as they were over ten years ago when I first started visiting. I don't know another club like it. Newcastle may come close, but I don't think there's another club to touch these fans, their enthusiasm and love for their ex-players. This isn't just towards me; you name a former player and they will want to see them, want to talk to them. Evertonians know the history of the club; they're steeped in it, and that is a good thing. They'll pass that on to their children and their children's children. The knowledge of what this club is and was will always continue, which I think is terrific. Alan Ball was right: this club touches you in a way that other clubs don't. And that's coming from a Birmingham boy, born and bred. My heart is in Birmingham: that's where I grew up, that's where all the family were and who I played for. But my soul lies with Everton, and always will.

I enjoy my trips back to England to catch up with everyone at Goodison, to watch a game and reminisce with supporters about the football days long ago. But I must confess I enjoy going home to my family even more. Andrea and my kids are fully aware of my life as a former professional footballer, although life in general in Germany is one of being under the radar. I think one day I would love to take my family to one or two of my old stamping grounds. I'm sure they would really enjoy it. Maybe one day!

*

THE ROAD HAS NOW BROUGHT ME TO GERMANY. COULD I EVER have foreseen this, along with the death of Pat and meeting and falling in love with Andrea, who has become my life and my world? But then as a young boy, could I have seen myself being a First Division player, scoring more First Division goals than anyone else in my generation, representing my country, and being the most expensive footballer in Britain? Absolutely not.

They say home is where your heart is and for me that is in Germany with Andrea and our children. Having felt at times I was not always in control of my life I do feel now that I'm where I need to be, firmly anchored and looking forward to what life brings. Whether the road stays in Germany or goes beyond I know I will never be travelling alone, now and for always.

The road goes on and I haven't stopped travelling yet.

APPENDIX

Q & A

Your brothers were goalkeepers and you were a goalkeeper's nightmare; family gatherings must have been interesting. Martin Healy (via Facebook).

Yeah, we were always trying to really outdo each other, even as kids. You tried to be top dog and come out with the best quip. I always liked to keep them down, being goalkeepers. My father was a goalkeeper and that's where David and Peter got it from. As a lad I played in goal as well. So it's not as if I wasn't capable of playing in goal, I just didn't fancy it at the end of the day.

You were always pretty rough when you played against your brothers and were even sent off after being booked for clattering David. Why did you do that to your own brothers? Ian Smith, Melbourne.

They expected it. Back then all goalkeepers expected it, because it was part of the game. So they doubly expected me to hit them, irrespective of them being my brothers. There was probably more incentive for all of us to get stuck in! All of us were ready for it. It would give us something to talk about at family gatherings.

Who was the true football royalty of the 1970s? Was it the Latchford family or the Clarke family? Gary Matthews, Solihull.

Well they outdid us by one, didn't they? There was four of them and just three of us. It's a close run thing; I'm not sure either family comes out on top. I think they both were probably on a par with each other in terms of ability; although individuals within the families enjoyed greater success and maybe longer careers. Collectively as families, the achievements were pretty special. I wonder whether there will be any football families in this country again.

What are your memories of that game at Leyton Orient in May 1972, given that it was incredible to watch? *Sid Smith, Birmingham.*

It was very competitive, very nervy. We only needed a point I think at the end of the day, but we got all three. And I managed to get my head on a cross from Gordon Taylor to give us the lead. Once we got the goal we weren't going to lose it. But it was certainly very competitive, and obviously some Millwall fans that turned up there and caused a bit of trouble. It was quite a night.

There was some big names coming out of Birmingham in the 1970s, like Noddy Holder, Jasper Carrott and Jeff Lyne. Were you ever part of the Birmingham celebrity circle? *Mark Hughes, Liverpool.*

Not really, no; I don't think so. You got to meet them. I don't remember meeting Noddy Holder but I met Jasper and Jeff. I wouldn't say I was ever part of their scene. They were major celebrities and I didn't consider myself a celebrity.

Did you ever fear anybody on the football pitch? *Pat Whitehead, Shropshire.*

Not really, no. There were obviously a lot of very difficult, very hard players around, but I didn't really go out thinking, 'Oh shit, I've got so-and-so next week'. I never thought about it, no; you just went out and played, and that was it. But obviously there was a lot of tough, difficult opponents around.

Birmingham had the best forward line in years, some say ever, when you were there. Why did you leave? *David Taylor, Bunbury, Western Australia*

Because at the end of the day I wasn't going to get any further with Birmingham career-wise and Freddie Goodwin needed to sell somebody to get in the players he wanted. So it got to a situation where Freddy needed to sell somebody and he wasn't prepared to sell Trevor Francis, so I was the next one that he could sell in order to bring players in, which he did. So that combination was the reason I left.

Who was the player that you loved playing alongside the most during your career? *Michael Scripps, Liverpool.*

This is a tough one. There's three or four players I could suggest to you. Dave Thomas, Trevor Francis, Bobby Hatton, and Kevin Keegan. You could pick any one of those for different reasons, but they would all fit the bill.

What was the greatest moment of your career? *Michael Shields, Northampton.*

I would have to probably go with putting the England shirt on that first time; putting the three lions over my head. I'd have to say that was the highlight.

What was more enjoyable, winning promotion with Birmingham, lifting the Welsh Cup with Swansea, or scoring 30 league goals in a season for Everton? *Dai Jones, Swansea.*

They're all pleasurable but for different reasons. It's a little bit unfair to pick out one against the other. In the moment it was the most pleasurable thing in that time period, and to pick out one against the other – I find these sort of questions difficult to answer with any honesty.

Who was the best coach you ever worked with? *Marge Riley, Liverpool.*

When I was playing football? I may have to go with Freddy Goodwin. He really turned me into the player I became. He took hold of me and turned me into a real player. Brian Eastick, though, who I worked with at Birmingham's academy, was technically the most accomplished coach I encountered in football.

Was the late equalising goal you scored against Aston Villa in the replay of the League Cup Final at Hillsborough the most emotional goal you ever scored? And if it wasn't, which one was? *Gerry Byrne, Nottingham*

Certainly I would say that it was close. The other one in the semi-final against West Ham at Leeds was probably just as emotional, if not more. It was a much better goal too. It was certainly an emotional feeling but in terms of the quality of the goal and the emotions afterwards, West Ham would probably cap it.

When you went around Ray Clements in the morning kick off Derby game, he dragged the St Christopher necklace off your neck; what happened to that? *Ray Jones (via Facebook)*

I don't think you weren't allowed to wear anything even in those days. I don't remember wearing any sort of necklace when I played. Someone's dreaming there!

Who outside of football inspired you, and in what way? *Liam Magee (via Twitter)*

I'd have to say my father, Reg, because he was such a very honest man, and he just wanted all of us to be ourselves and be true to ourselves and be as honest to yourself as you could.

Were you gutted that you had to share the 30 goals prize money with the team? *Kenny Alty (via Facebook)*

No. I didn't have to share the money, I chose to. I was gutted that I didn't say to them let's put it to charity, with all the problems I had with the taxman later. That's the only thing I would be gutted about, that I didn't suggest we give it to charity.

Was Gordon (Lee) a moron? *Dave Kelly, Bootle.*

Certainly not, no. He's an intelligent man; he's a bright man. He's just football daft; he's a football man. But a moron? No, far from it.

Should Everton have hired Brian Clough or Bobby Robson after Billy Bingham left? *James Donovan, Liverpool.*

If it was possible, yes, they probably should have. In terms of if they wanted a big name coach or manager, and if they'd had aspirations, yes. For me Cloughy would have been the ideal man. But as I mentioned in the book, I don't think Everton would have taken too kindly to Cloughy and his methods. But Cloughy, with hindsight – hindsight is great – Cloughy would have been the man. He should have been England manager after they got rid of Alf. I think The FA were a bit premature getting rid of Alf. But Cloughy was the person, he could have done something with England back in the 70s; really could have done, because there was enough talent there.

What was the biggest mistake of your career? *Ray Jones, Liverpool.*

Not having an agent!

What was the biggest regret of your career? *Michael Murphy, Dublin.*

Not having an agent!!!

Who was the best goalkeeper you faced in your career? *Paul Keatings, Birmingham.*

Probably Shilts. He just edges it over Ray Clements, although Pat Jennings would run them close, to be honest.

Did you ever have a goalkeeper who you just couldn't score past, who would have a purple patch every time he played you? *Mary Healy, Birmingham.*

I don't think so. I suppose you could say Arsenal were a bogey side, because I never really scored against them. Bob Wilson, Jimmy Rimmer, Pat Jennings – I always seemed to struggle to find the net against them. Most other goalkeepers I never seemed to have a problem scoring against. Even Ray Clements (CLEMENCE?) when I was with Birmingham I didn't have any problems, or with Swansea. It was just with Everton I had problems with him. Shilts, I didn't have a problem scoring against.

Were you ever tempted to follow your England team mates, Trevor Francis and Kevin Keegan and play abroad at the height of your career? *Paul MacAnthony, Birmingham.*

I could have gone to Germany at around the same period Kevin Keegan joined Hamburg. Schalke 04 were interested in me at a time when I was in dispute with Everton over a contract. There was some interest in '77, '78 from an Arab club as well. I was contacted through an agent, who told me there was a representative from some Arab club and they were interested in buying me. If it had come off it would have been huge money and I probably would have been very tempted. It never happened of course.

What was the best part of your trip to Brisbane, as a guest player at the Brisbane Lions before going to Swansea? *Damian Templeton, Brisbane.*

Apart from playing for them. It was really just having the family there and seeing part of the country. We lived for about three, four weeks down on the south of Brisbane, on the Gold Coast, then we went up north of Brisbane for a couple of weeks. We saw a whole swathe of Queensland and things that we're never likely to see again. I like Australia, I like the way they live. I could easily live there. I could have easily, like Lyonsy, gone and lived in Australia. It's a good way of life.

Who was the hardest player that you ever came up against? *Peter Turley, Liverpool.*

Charlie Hurley, an Irish lad, who used to play for Sunderland. I met him when he was at Bolton, right at the end of his career – thank goodness. You talk about hard players, he was so physically hard he was intimidating, Charlie. Not in a bad way, he was just so imposing. He could play a bit as well. I think he was Sunderland's all-time player of the century. He was an Irish International. But in terms of being hard, just physically hard – not dirty, but tough and intimidating, he'd take some beating. I would not have liked to have played against him in his prime.

Who had the best perm in the Everton dressing room? *Darren Rowan, Liverpool.*

I think there was me; Kingy; Mick Lyons and Greame Sharp. Kingy would probably say, if he was still with us, God bless him, his, so I'll go with that. Gary Stanley had the best hair: he didn't need a perm, he had the film star looks naturally.

Given that you could walk on water, when and where did you use this particular skill, and how far could you go? *Justin Hengler (via Facebook)*

Dear me! If I had that sort of skill and ability I'd be making an absolute fortune for myself; or would have made a fortune for myself with that particular ability. But as I say to people, I knew of one man who could do that and he lived about 2000 years ago.

Do you wish that you'd played under Howard Kendall? *Nicky Jones, West Derby.*

Hindsight is a wonderful thing. I could have stayed there for a season and played under Howard, but there was no guarantee I would have been there during those years when they were most successful. That's the point. I really could have stayed because he wanted me to stay, but I'd already made up my mind to go. With hindsight it would have been a lovely end to my career just staying there and seeing it all through to 1986 or 1987, but it wasn't to be.

If you could play under any Premier League manager, who would it have been, and why? *Gary Jones, Liverpool*

It's a close call between Jose Mourinho and Alex Ferguson because of the passion they show. I think I've said before, I connect with people with passion about the game, and they're full of that, especially Alex. With Alex he's a little bit more old school passion; Mourinho is different – thoughtful, technically very good. But both of them I think are so passionate that it would have been easy to have played under either one.

Since retiring, who's been the best forward you've seen in an Everton shirt? *David Jones, Manchester*

It would have to be the man who succeeded me, Graeme Sharp, who was a terrific player for a decade and scored lots of goals. For a club that has a reputation for great number nines, there's not really been that many in the past 35 years. Duncan Ferguson is a hero to many but, for me, an enigma. He was somebody who had everything about him, that would make one of the great centre forwards, but for inexplicable reasons – and only he knows why – he probably fell short of what he could have achieved. He could have been one of the greats, a really great centre forward.

BOB LATCHFORD

ACKNOWLEDGEMENTS

THE PROCESS OF WRITING A BOOK INVOLVES MANY PEOPLE, MOST of whom remain hidden to the reader, but whose assistance makes the book that you read what it is today. Some of these people had a hands on role in this book's production, others offered their support and friendship through the process of writing it; all, in little ways and large, added something tangible to A Different Road. I'd like to thank: Izzy, Richard and their families; my brothers John, David, Peter and their families; on Merseyside: my UK agent Dave Cockram, Paul Cronin, Andy Nicholls, Derek and Julia Mountfield, Martin and Melanie O'Boyle, Simon and Hayley Paul. Billy Smith, Rob Sawyer, Allen Mohr, Peter Mills, Ian Allen, Leslie Priestley, Steve Welsh, Sabahat Muhammad, Kate Highfield, Simon Hughes and Thomas Regan all played important roles in the editorial, design and production processes. None of my journeys in this part of my life would be complete without the daily love and support of my family in Germany: Andrea, Sam and Sina. To them, my deepest thanks.

While in the latter stages of working on this book, I lost two of my former teammates. Andy King was an effervescent and bubbly member of Gordon Lee's Everton squads; he was also a terrific footballer and a good friend. I was deeply saddened when he unexpectedly passed away in May 2015. I was shocked too, to learn from my brother, Peter, that Denis Thwaites, who was part of the Birmingham team I supported as a boy and later played alongside, was killed with his

192

wife Elaine in the Tunisian terrorist attack in the resort of Sousse in June 2015. English football is all the poorer for losing these two great characters.

INDEX

T

V

W